E

Dr. Bahkou has produced a unique and remarkable book, and I trust that it will be of great benefit to many beyond the Lutheran Christian community. As someone who has studied Islam and Christian approaches to Muslims for many years within the African context, as well as in Europe and the United States, I can say without any hesitation that Dr. Bahkou has done justice to the subject matter and has accurately and substantively examined the historical context, introducing us to earlier Christians who engaged both Muslims and the Muslim text as well as their attitudes. He has also made the proper distinction between Muslim scripture and Christian Scripture and highlighted the reverence Muslims and Christians have for their own scriptures—and their skepticism toward the holy books of the other. Dr. Bahkou discusses what many people have written about Islam over the centuries, including our own benefactor, Martin Luther.

Utilizing his Middle Eastern background and familiarity with the culture and languages there, Dr. Bakhou goes through the biblical Christian narrative, including the ministry of Jesus, the Word of God, as well as His Spirit, His death, and His resurrection while covering the key topics of salvation, creation, and redemption with unique insight. We should congratulate and admire his perspective. He has made a significant contribution to the field while also providing Christian leaders with a pragmatic way to engage their Muslim friends and neighbors.

Finally, I was interested in the topic of the proclamation of the Gospel to Muslims because that is an area I work on in my own ministry. I am grateful for benefiting from the insight I have gained through the work of Dr. Bahkou. It is my joy and privilege to have spent time reviewing and engaging and experiencing Dr. Bahkou's enlightening work. I highly recommend this book for readers not only in America but far beyond, even in Europe and Africa.

Rev. Dr. John Loum, director of the Ethnic Immigrant Institute of Theology, Concordia Seminary, St. Louis

SHINING the GOSPEL LIGHT on the QURAN

SHINING the GOSPEL LIGHT on the QURAN

UNDERSTANDING AND ENGAGING MUSLIMS

ABJAR BAHKOU

CONCORDIA PUBLISHING HOUSE · SAINT LOUIS

Published by Concordia Publishing House
3558 S. Jefferson Avenue, St. Louis, MO 63118-3968
1-800-325-3040 • cph.org

Copyright © 2021 Abjar Bahkou

All rights reserved. No part of this publication may be reproduced, stored in a retrieval system, or transmitted, in any form or by any means, electronic, mechanical, photocopying, recording, or otherwise, without the prior written permission of Concordia Publishing House.

Unless otherwise noted, Scripture quotations are from the ESV® Bible (The Holy Bible, English Standard Version®), copyright © 2001 by Crossway, a publishing ministry of Good News Publishers. Used by permission. All rights reserved.

Unless otherwise indicated, the edition of the Quran referenced is Nasr, Seyyed Hossein (Editor-in-chief), *The Study Quran: A New Translation and Commentary*, New York: HarperOne, 2015.

Catechism quotations are taken from *Luther's Small Catechism with Explanation*, copyright © 1986, 1991 Concordia Publishing House. All rights reserved.

Manufactured in the United States of America

Library of Congress Cataloging-in-Publication Data
Names: Bahkou, Abjar, author.
Title: Shining the gospel light on the Quran : understanding and engaging Muslims / Abjar Bahkou.
Description: Saint Louis, MO : Concordia Publishing House, [2021] Includes bibliographical references. | Summary: "Dr. Bakhou wrote this book to help Christians better understand Muslims and thus reach out to them in more effective ways. The book examines the Christian-Muslim encounter as a journey at three distinct and interrelated levels: first, we meet as human beings; second, as monotheistic believers; and third, as witnessing believers. Dr. Bakhou follows in Jesus' steps as He spoke with the Samaritan woman at the well and the two disciples walking to Emmaus. He also discusses lessons learned by Christian leaders in the Eastern Church when their lands came under Muslim rule. The book will include both a Leader Guide and a Study Guide for small groups"-- Provided by publisher.
Identifiers: LCCN 2021020631 (print) | LCCN 2021020632 (ebook) | ISBN 9780758670489 (paperback) | ISBN 9780758670496 (ebook)
Subjects: LCSH: Islam--Relations--Christianity. | Christianity--Relations--Islam. | Qur'an--Christian interpretations. | Bible New Testament--Islamic interpretations.
Classification: LCC BP172 .B2525 2021 (print) | LCC BP172 (ebook) | DDC 297.2/83--dc23
LC record available at https://lccn.loc.gov/2021020631
LC ebook record available at https://lccn.loc.gov/2021020632

1 2 3 4 5 6 7 8 9 10   30 29 28 27 26 25 24 23 22 21

In loving memory of my
dear friend and brother,
Bishop Saliba Toma.
1969–2004

CONTENTS

Foreword	10
Rev. Dr. Douglas Rutt	
Introduction	14
Part 1: Islam and Muslims	23
Chapter 1: The Islamic Challenges	25
Chapter 2: Muslims and Sharia Law	41
Part 2: The Quran and the Gospel	63
Chapter 3: The Revelation of the Quran and the Bible	65
Chapter 4: The Quran's Perspective on Interfaith Dialogue	89
Part 3: God and His Creation	113
Chapter 5: Creation and Its Redemption	115
Chapter 6: Salvation in Muslim-Christian Perspectives	127
Chapter 7: God in Islam	139
Chapter 8: God in Muslim-Christian Perspectives	151
Chapter 9: The Triune God in the Quran and in the Gospel	167
Part 4: Jesus the Messiah	177
Chapter 10: The Nativity of Jesus	179
Chapter 11: The Ministry of Jesus	191
Chapter 12: Jesus, the Word of God, and His Spirit	205
Chapter 13: The Death and Resurrection of Christ	215
Part 5: Perspectives on the Encounter	229
Chapter 14: Proclaiming the Gospel to Muslims	231
Chapter 15: Proclaiming the Cross to Muslims	245
Chapter 16: Following the Steps of Jesus	259
Conclusion: Encounter and Mission	275
Answer Key	291
Bibliography	318

Foreword

Having taught missions and evangelism for over twenty-five years, both at Missouri Synod seminaries and in various countries around the world, I have tried to help students understand that very few people will give your Christian witness much of a hearing if your starting point is to humiliate them or show how preposterous their religious beliefs are. This approach seems to be especially prevalent in studies devoted to reaching the followers of Islam. I have found that all too many Christian approaches to engaging with our Muslim neighbors are polemic in nature and implementation, often leading with historical, theological, and cultural arguments. They attempt to demonstrate that Islam's foundational claims are illogical, filled with factual errors, and will lead to a society that is abusive of women and intolerant of "infidels."

Not only is this true in recent years, of course, but it has also been the case for hundreds of years. John of Damascus (eighth century), Peter of Cluny (twelfth century), and Andrea da Barberino (fourteenth century) are just a few examples of an apologetic approach that endeavored to paint Islam as a fraudulent, illegitimate religion, begun by a misguided, immoral, and ignorant tyrant. Arguments were developed along many lines to debunk the teachings of Islam in ways that resorted to insult and caricature. One must admit that it is anachronistic to judge earlier polemic defenders of the faith based on modern sensibilities. Much of the offensive and deprecating material was written to help Christians in conquered lands resist conversion to Islam and survive in their faith, rather than for the purpose of presenting a winsome testimony of the joy and beauty of the Gospel so that Muslims might be persuaded and become followers of Jesus.

Martin Luther was in some ways an expert on Islam for his time and place. After all, the threat of an Islamic invasion was very real during his lifetime. The preface to the Augsburg Confession of 1530 states that the first item of business for the meeting called by Emperor Charles V, which occasioned the production of this confession, was "to consider taking action against the Turk" (AC Preface 1).

While the threat was real, and Luther in no way considered Islam legitimate, he desired greatly to get to the know the beliefs and customs of Islam firsthand. For many years, he wanted to get his hands on a copy of the Quran so he could read and study it himself, but he didn't obtain a copy until 1542. He was then instrumental in promoting the production of a Latin version so that others also could read it for themselves. Although Luther's approach to Islam could not be considered friendly, it could, in some ways, be considered respectful, in the sense that he sought understanding before judgment. He lauded the external righteousness of Muslims and their orderly way of life. Nevertheless, when it came to the doctrine of how humankind obtains righteousness before God, he made the distinctions between Islam and Christianity clear in no uncertain terms. It should be noted that as far as we know, during his entire lifetime, Luther never actually interacted with a Muslim.

While many approaches to Islam today continue to follow the arguments of previous polemicists, this book is different. Written by my colleague Dr. Abjar Bahkou, a Syrian Christian and Lutheran theologian, *Shining the Gospel Light on the Quran: Understanding and Engaging Muslims* is guided by an approach more consistent with the counsel of the apostle Peter:

> But in your hearts honor Christ the Lord as holy, always being prepared to make a defense to anyone who asks you for a reason for the hope that is in you; *yet do it with gentleness and respect.*
> (1 Peter 3:15, emphasis added)

Today's globalized and multicultural world affords us opportunities that people such as Martin Luther never had. It is no longer difficult for anyone living in most parts of the world, particularly the Western world, to interact and even become friends with people of other, vastly differing religious commitments, including Muslims. It is a different milieu than much of the Middle Ages. Living side by side with people from different worldviews, cultures, and religious belief systems is the norm, especially in Europe and North America.

In the contemporary world, then, understanding others and engaging them in discussions of important matters of ultimate truth, life, and death requires respect. It demands seeing Muslim neighbors as intelligent fellow human beings, worthy of establishing true friendships, so that you can know them well enough to discern not only what they think but also how they think. Dr. Bahkou invites the reader to enter into the world of Islam, to try to understand it in its own terms.

Any truthful and trustworthy treatment surely is a critical analysis of Islam, its teachings and expressions of faith. Bahkou does not minimize serious divergences between Christianity and Islam, and yet he invites the reader to allow him- or herself to examine Islam from what anthropology in the service of missionary outreach calls an *emic* perspective. It is a way to seek understanding based on what has meaning and value for people of a particular group, how they explain things and their cognitive thought processes, from within. The complementary, *etic* approach is of value also, because these things can be evaluated based on our understandings, and especially based on the Word of God. Nevertheless, an important initial step is to seek understanding before rushing to judgment.

Of most importance, Dr. Bahkou advocates in this book that our perspective should be one in which we are more concerned about Muslim people than with Islam. When talking with students about being friends with people of different backgrounds and the need to carefully try to understand their thinking and way of being, to try to avoid intentionally, and even unintentionally, causing offense, on more than one occasion a student has asked, "But isn't the Gospel offensive? Isn't that what Peter says when he calls Jesus 'a stone of stumbling, and a rock of offence' [1 Peter 2:8]?" My reaction is that yes, the Gospel is offensive—it's offensive enough on its own! But let us make sure it is the offense of the Gospel that comes through and that it is not your offense that causes someone to stumble.

The approach to Islam of this book may challenge you and some of your notions about Islam and Muslims, but through its study, I am sure you will be enriched and enabled to give faithful witness to the joy you have in you as a follower of Christ when you encounter your Muslim neighbor. And thus I am thrilled that Concordia Publishing House is making it available to the public.

Douglas Rutt, provost, professor of practical theology
Concordia Seminary
The Festival of St. Timothy, 2021
St. Louis, Missouri

Introduction

I was born in a small town in Northeast Syria called Dereek. It is a border town between Syria, Turkey, and Iraq. In 1986, I left my hometown and traveled five hundred miles to enroll at St. Ephraim Theological Seminary in Damascus. The seminary was across the street from the house of Ananias, where Paul was baptized. We read in Acts 9:11, "The Lord said to [Ananias], 'Rise and go to the street called Straight, and at the house of Judas look for a man of Tarsus named Saul.'" The "street called Straight" is the area where I spent my childhood and teenage years.

Although Christians are a minority in Syria, making up less than 10 percent of the population, the Christian community there is diverse. I grew up around Bab Tuma, a neighborhood in Damascus, which is the seat of three patriarchates: the Syrian Orthodox, the Greek Orthodox, and the Greek Catholic churches. In addition to these global centers, the Maronite Church, the Armenian Church, the Syrian Catholic Church, and the Presbyterian and Evangelical Churches all have local centers there.

Neighboring these churches are many mosques. One of them is the well-known Umayyad Mosque, also known as the Great Mosque of Damascus. For over thirteen centuries, this historical Islamic center has stood amongst these ancient churches. Every morning and evening, the bells of the churches ring, calling people to gather for prayer, and five times a day the minarets of the mosques call the same people not only to pray but also to meet and dialogue with Muslims.

Growing up in such a diverse multiethnic and multireligious context, spontaneous encounters with Muslims occurred daily. Since I was a child, I always knew that I held different beliefs; however, it was not enough simply to feel different. I gradually realized the challenges of building bridges, and trying to walk over them, to reach our Muslim friends and neighbors. A river cuts between Islam and Christianity: in certain places, the banks are close together and the river is narrow, while in other areas, the expanse of rushing water is too broad and deep to ford. Our purpose here is to find those parts of the river where we can cross, so that we can lead our Muslim friends and neighbors to the banks of the Gospel, where Christ stands and calls to them.

For the last fifteen years, I have been studying and teaching about Islam, both in academic contexts as well as in missionary activity among Muslims here in America. Therefore, this book is a combination of my academic research and ministry experience among Muslims. The contents of this book were developed through many years of teaching about Muslim-Christian encounters locally, in the United States, and globally, in Europe and Africa. In addition, I have been teaching this course within the master of divinity and doctoral programs at Concordia Seminary in St. Louis, Missouri. In this journey, as I studied and personally lived these challenges, I was always encouraged to face them by learning about God, who in the incarnation breaks in and builds bridges with humans. He did that by becoming one of us: He built the bridge to us in the person of Jesus Christ so that we could become His children.

This book divides the task of sharing the Gospel with Muslims into five parts. In parts 1 and 2, we will discuss how to engage with Islam and its teachings critically and respectfully, examining the primary sources of Islam and its implications on the life of ordinary Muslims. In part 3, we will consider the teachings of Islam from a Christian perspective, explaining the radical differences between Islam and Christianity. In part 4, we will answer, in a respectful way, Islam's challenging questions to Christian doctrine about Jesus. Finally, in part 5, we will explore practical steps to minister and share a contextualized Gospel message with Muslims.

The apostle Peter encourages Christians to revere Christ in their hearts, "always being prepared to make a defense to anyone who asks you for a reason for the hope that is in you; yet do it with gentleness and respect" (1 Peter 3:15). If someone asked you in what or in whom do you hope, what would you answer? Is it learning the story of Jesus? memorizing some verses from the Bible? living a morally good life? While these things are good, they are not the ultimate source of our hope. Christian hope is instead found in Jesus Christ Himself, the incarnate God, who suffered, was crucified, died, and rose on the third day to conquer sin, death, and the devil. Our hope is in the cross of Christ, where God meets us, His straying, rebellious, human creatures. On the cross, God reveals who He is and who humans are. This is the most challenging difference between Islam and Christianity. The message of the cross is foolishness to Islam, while for us it is the power of God (1 Corinthians 1:18). This book offers practical suggestions on how to share Christ and His saving work, the reason for our hope, with gentleness and respect.

Islam and Muslims

Another important distinction is that our challenges as Christians are not with Muslims; our challenges are with the teachings of Islam and its implications on the life of ordinary Muslims. While the teachings of Islam are, of course, completely at odds with Christianity, Muslims are people whom God loves and for whom Christ died, as He did for you and me. This book will examine how to engage with Muslims in a genuine friendship relation, as well as how Muslims see life and what moves their emotions. Our approach in studying Islam insists that the study of religion is the study of human persons who are not merely representatives of a system. This approach requires building friendships with Muslims, understanding their worldview, and connecting with them as neighbors. Studying Islam means to enter the minds, hearts, and souls of Muslims.[1]

Understanding the Primary Texts of Islam

To study the formative period of Islam, we need to examine the primary sources of the Muslim faith. Rather than having one scripture, like Christians do with the Bible, Muslims have three texts: the Quran, the hadith, and the biography of Muhammad, known as *al-Sīra al-Nābāwīa*. These three sources make in Islam what is called the *sunna*.

In 1977, John Wansbrough (1928–2002), professor of semitic studies at London's School of Oriental and African Studies, published a book entitled *Quranic Studies: Sources and Methods of Scriptural Interpretation*. A year later, Wansbrough published *The Sectarian Milieu: Content and Composition of Islamic Salvation History*.[2] His theory was that in order to understand the formative period of Islam, we need to understand it in the context into which it was born. Islam was born in the seventh century, in a sectarian Arabian environment professing Christianity, Judaism, and other monotheistic faiths; however, the Islamic texts developed progressively and did not find their final form until the ninth century.

Wansbrough suggested a new interpretation, different from Muslim orthodoxy and most Western scholars. He analyzed early Islamic historiography as a late manifestation of Old Testament salvation history. Wansbrough argued that the traditional biographies of Muhammad are best understood not as historical documents that relate what really hap-

---

[1] For more on this approach, see Wilfred Smith, "Comparative Religion: Whither and Why?" in Mircea Eliade and Joseph Kitagawa, eds., *The History of Religion: Essays in Methodology* (Chicago: University of Chicago Press, 1959), 34–66; Roland Miller, *Muslim Friends: Their Faith and Feeling* (St. Louis: Concordia Publishing House, 1995), 15.

[2] John Wansbrough, *Quranic Studies: Sources and Methods of Scriptural Interpretation* (Oxford: Oxford University Press, 1977); Wansbrough, *The Sectarian Milieu: Content and Composition of Islamic Salvation History* (Oxford: Oxford University Press, 1978); Carlos A. Segovia, Basil Lourié, eds., *The Coming of the Comforter: When, Where, and to Whom? Studies on the Rise of Islam and Various Other Topics in Memory of John Wansbrough* (Piscataway, NJ: Gorgias Press, 2012).

pened, but as literary texts written more than one hundred years after the fact, heavily influenced by Jewish and (to a lesser extent) Christian and interconfessional polemics. He suggested that Islamic history was mostly literary reconstruction, which evolved in an environment of competing Jewish and Christian sects. Wansbrough suggested that it is difficult to find the small amount of historical truth in works that were written chiefly to serve later religious situations. He proposed that the most efficient way to analyze such texts was literary analysis.

In 2004, Andrew Rippin republished Wansbrough's *Quranic Studies*,[3] enhanced with a foreword, new annotations, and a glossary in order to counter some of the ideological and nonscholarly ways in which the book has been used during the first twenty-five years of its existence. About the same time that *Quranic Studies* was first published (1977), Patricia Crone and Michael Cook published a book entitled *Hagarism: The Making of the Islamic World*,[4] in which they argued that Muslim literary sources are untrustworthy, and that we ought to turn instead to independent non-Muslim tradition. This school of thought moved the nascent Islam from the Arabic Peninsula to greater Syria and Iraq. After the publication of these books, many scholars began researching the Eastern Churches and their development in the pre-Islamic and early Islamic period.

This school of thought relies heavily on the literary genre of the Quran. When we read the Quran in Arabic, we see poetic dialogues and monologues. This style was common in the ancient Mesopotamian genre of the dispute poem, in which two speakers conduct an argument in alternating short stanzas. A prime example of this style is the poetry of Ephrem the Syrian (AD 303–373). Ephrem pairs biblical characters, such as Cain and Abel, Joseph and Potiphar's wife, Mary and the angel Gabriel, Mary and Joseph, the two thieves on the cross, and many others, even Death and Satan during the descent of Christ

---

3   John Wansbrough, *Quranic Studies*, with foreword, translations, and expanded notes by Andrew Rippin (Amherst, NY: Prometheus, 2004).

4   Patricia Crone and Michael Cook, *Hagarism: The Making of the Islamic World* (Cambridge: Cambridge University Press, 1977).

into hell.⁵ Günter Lüling argued that the Quran contains remnants of ancient Christian hymnals, which were Islamized during and after Muhammad's life.⁶ Likewise, Gabriel Said Reynolds⁷ and Sidney Griffith,⁸ who wrote extensively on this topic, suggested that the Quran is always in conversation with biblical and nonbiblical literatures.

It is not the scope of this book to examine all the research done in this field. My analysis will follow this method: I will analyze the biography of Muhammad and the Quran in its religious, theological, and cultural context. Then I will look at the biblical and nonbiblical parallel stories, see what the differences are between them, and examine how we might use them as a bridge to build with our Muslims friends.

READING THE QURAN CHRONOLOGICALLY

Unlike the Bible, the Quran was not written in a chronological order. In the nineteenth century, scholars of Eastern culture began to study the Quran using the historical-critical method, which was also being applied to the Bible. One of the most prominent scholars in this field was the German scholar Theodor Nöldeke, author of *The History of the Qur'an*. He and other scholars of Eastern culture attempted to reconstruct the text in chronological order. According to R. Caspar⁹ and J. M. Gaudeul,¹⁰ who followed the steps of other scholars such as

---

5   For the influence of Syriac Christianity on the Quran, see Christoph Luxenberg, *The Syro-Aramaic Reading of the Koran* (Berlin: Hans Schiler, 2007).

6   Günter Lüling, *A Challenge to Islam for Reformation: The Rediscovery and Reliable Reconstruction of a Comprehensive Pre-Islamic Christian Hymnal Hidden in the Koran under Earliest Islamic Reinterpretations* (Delhi: Motilal Banarsidass, 2003).

7   For more on this subject, see Gabriel Said Reynolds, *The Qur'an and Its Biblical Subtexts* (London and New York: Routledge, 2010); Reynolds, *The Qur'an and the Bible: Text and Commentary* (New Haven: Yale University Press, 2018); Reynolds, ed., *The Qur'an in Its Historical Context* (London and New York: Routledge, 2008); Reynolds, ed. *New Perspectives on the Qur'an: The Qur'an in Its Historical Context 2* (London and New York: Routledge, 2011).

8   Sidney Griffith, *The Bible in Arabic: The Scriptures of the "People of the Book" in the Language of Islam* (Princeton: Princeton University Press, 2013); Griffith, "The Bible in the Qur'an," in David Thomas, ed., *Routledge Handbook on Christian-Muslim Relations* (London and New York: Routledge, 2018), 42–49; Griffith, "The Gospel, the Qur'an, and the Presentation of Jesus in al-Ya'qubi's Ta'rikh," in John C. Reeves, ed., *Bible and Qur'an: Essays in Scriptural Intertextuality* (Boston: Brill, 2003).

9   For more on this approach, see Robert Caspar, *Islamic Theology: Doctrines*, vol. 2, Studi Arabo-Islamici del PISAI, no. 17 (Rome: Pontificio Istituto di Studi Arabi e d'Islamistica, 2007), 23–44; Caspar, *A Historical Introduction to Islamic Theology: Muhammad and the Classical Period*, Studi Arabo-Islamici del PISAI, no. 11 (Rome: Pontificio Istituto di Studi Arabi e d'Islamistica, 1998), 26–28.

10 Jean-Marie Gaudeul, *Encounters and Clashes: Islam and Christianity in History*, vol. 1, Studi Ara-

Theodor Nöldeke[11] and Richard Bell,[12] this reading helps us understand the formative period of Islam in a chronological order. This method, which I also adapt in this book, was avoided by scholars such as Gabriel Said Reynolds, who suggested that rather than asking when and where certain passages of the Quran were originally proclaimed, we ought to consider the entire unified text as it currently exists. Reynolds called this method *narrative criticism*, which was adapted from the Pakistani Islamic scholar Fazlur Rahman (1919–1988).[13]

THE STRUCTURE OF THIS BOOK

This book is divided into five parts, with sixteen chapters and a conclusion. Part 1 considers Islam's theological challenges as well as the challenges Muslims are facing in the contemporary world, along with the difficulty of defining and responding to Islam and Sharia law. Part 2 compares the concept of divine revelation in Christianity and Islam, Islam's claim that the Quran is the product of divine revelation, and the Quran's perspective on interfaith dialogue. Part 3 examines God, His creation, and the fall, from both Muslim and Christian perspectives. Part 4 examines Jesus in the Quran and the Bible, covering His birth, ministry, death, and resurrection. Part 5 presents ways to proclaim the Gospel to Muslims. The Islamic worldview is based on shame and honor paradigms, which present a unique challenge to contextualizing the proclamation of the Gospel in this culture. We will also examine encounters with people who are very different than us, endeavoring to share the love of Christ by considering the journey of Jesus with the disciples of Emmaus (Luke 24:13–35) and the conversation between Jesus and the Samaritan woman (John 4:1–30) as models for outreach to Muslims.

---

bo-Islamici del PISAI, no. 15 (Rome: Pontificio Istituto di Studi Arabi e d'Islamistica, 2000), 12–13.
11   Theodor Nöldeke, *The History of the Qur'an* (Leiden and Boston: Brill, 2013).
12   Richard Bell, *A Commentary on the Qur'an*, ed. Clifford E. Bosworth and M. E. J. Richardson (Manchester: University of Manchester, 1991); Richard Bell, *The Origin of Islam in Its Christian Environment* (London: MacMillan, 1926).
13   See Gabriel Said Reynolds, *Allah: God in the Qur'an* (New Haven and London: Yale University Press, 2020), 9.

Introduction

This book is entitled *Shining the Gospel Light on the Quran: Understanding and Engaging Muslims*. It is a stimulating title, and the reader might have many questions in mind before reading this book. Am I reading this book to be armed to defeat Islam? Am I reading it to get information to respond to Islamic objections to Christianity? Am I reading it to learn how to convert Muslims to Christ? Whatever you hope to gain from reading this book, my hope and prayer is that you will be challenged and gain a new perspective on the tenets of Islam, the life of everyday Muslims, and the love of Jesus for our Muslim brothers and sisters.

PART 1:
ISLAM AND MUSLIMS

Chapter 1: The Islamic Challenges
Chapter 2: Muslims and Sharia Law

CHAPTER 1

THE ISLAMIC CHALLENGES

೭ುಲ

In March of AD 632, which is the year 10 on the Islamic calendar, Muhammad made his first and last pilgrimage to Medina, known as the Farewell Pilgrimage, in which he communicated to the Muslim community the last received verse of the Quran:

> This day I have perfected for you your religion and completed my Blessing upon you, and have approved for you as religion, Submission (*Islam*) (Quran 5:3)

What does it mean to choose Islam as one's faith? How can we define Islam? Many books have been written about Islam and have asked the question, "What is Islam?" The ordinary citizen is lost and puzzled by the labyrinth of definitions spreading all over the world through social media and television. After the terrorist attack on the World Trade Center on September 11, 2001, two questions have resurfaced time and again: Is Islam a religion of peace, or does it incite violence? What is the connection between Islamic terrorist groups and Islam?

We witness conferences on interfaith dialogue, and frequently Christian and Muslim leaders alike condemn the violence and the killing of the innocent. In May 2017, for the first time in history, the world witnessed an American-Islamic conference, attended by then-president Donald Trump and the Saudi Arabian king, Salman bin Abdulaziz Al

Saud. Heads of state and representatives of more than fifty-five countries met in the Saudi capital city of Riyadh to condemn terrorism. On April 2, 2019, a historic meeting took place in the United Arab Emirates between Pope Francis and the Grand Imam of al-Azhar, Ahmed el-Tayeb. The two leaders strongly condemned terrorism and violence: "God . . . does not want His name to be used to terrorize people."[14]

Muslim leaders are adamant that terrorist groups do not represent Islam. Yet ISIS and al-Qaeda leaders often quote the Quran and Islamic traditions. President Barack Obama refused to call these groups Islamic, while President Donald Trump called them "the Islamic terrorist organization," connecting the name of Islam with terrorism.

Many voices are calling for an "Islamic Martin Luther." Many hope that a reform movement can put an end to the strife Muslims face within the Islamic faith and in encounters with non-Muslims. But is that possible? In fact, many scholars believe that this is impossible. In this chapter, we will attempt to define Islam and then turn to consider the differences between Islam and Christianity, as well as the challenges Christians and Muslims face because of these differences.

The Challenging Task of Definition

The Islamic scholar Daniel Brown showed the challenge of defining Islam in his book *A New Introduction to Islam*. Brown argues that there is no single Islam because there are many forms of Islam, or islams, and each one must be examined as a separate phenomenon. To illustrate his argument, Brown takes the analogy of the Arabic language. Arabic has a formal written and spoken language; however, there are various spoken colloquial Arabic dialects, such as Levantine, Egyptian, and Moroccan. All of them originate from the Arabic language, and all of them are called Arabic. However, they are completely different in their grammatical structure.[15]

---

14 Andrea Tornielli, "Pope and the Grand Imam: Historic Declaration of Peace, Freedom, Women's Rights," *Vatican News*, February 4, 2019, https://www.vaticannews.va/en/pope/news/2019-02/pope-francis-uae-grand-imam-declaration-of-peace.html.

15 See Daniel Brown, *A New Introduction to Islam* (Hoboken, NJ: Wiley, 2004), 3–5.

In his book *The Call of the Minaret*, the late Bishop Kenneth Cragg agreed with Brown's answer to the question, "What is Islam?" With the wide diversity within the Islamic world today, the word *Muslim* entails a wide variety of attitudes. For example, Pakistani modernist scholar and philosopher Fazlur Rahman was requested by the president of Pakistan to direct the Central Institute of Islamic Research. His purpose was to implement Islam into the nation's daily dealings. However, orthodox Islamic scholars opposed his modernist interpretations. After a press conference, they called him an infidel and sought his death. In September 1968, he resigned his post and came to live in the United States. Cragg also cited Ahmadiyya, a Muslim sect that called itself "the true Islam." In 1975, Pakistan declared it a non-Islamic sect.

What Is Islam?

In his book *The House of Islam*, Ed Husain defined Islam as having three parts: believing in one god (Allah), holding the message of the prophet Muhammad, and following the path of salvation in the coming life. Whoever holds these three beliefs is a Muslim.[16]

The term *Islam* means "submission" or "peace." Both of these words derive from the Arabic root *Salama*. Thus, Islam is living in submission to Allah's sovereign will who already predestined the universe and made humankind in order to worship him (Q 51:56).

Islam as the Final Divine Revelation

According to the Quran, Allah sent prophets to all people to lead humanity out of ignorance (Q 4:163–65). The first one was Adam, followed by Noah, Abraham, Ishmael, Isaac, Jacob, Job, Moses, and Jesus. These prophets were all Muslims because they practiced submission to Allah, even if they were born before Muhammad. All who follow the prophets and submit to Allah are also considered Muslims. Islam teaches that Allah dictated his revelation to the prophets according to

---

16   Ed Husain, *The House of Islam: A Global History* (New York: Bloomsbury Publishing, 2018), 17–24, 31–42.

the needs of the people they served. In Moses' time, the people needed a revolutionary leader, because they needed motivation to revolt against Pharaoh. Thus, Allah dictated the law that states, "Eye for eye and tooth for tooth." When Allah sent Jesus, the people needed a peaceful prophet, and so Allah dictated his law that commanded them to turn the other cheek.

Moses, Jesus, and other prophets received divine scripture from Allah. In each case, the Quran teaches that angels dictated Allah's revelation to the prophets. That revelation was written down as the Torah, the Gospel, and other books. But the people failed to follow the prophets Allah sent them. Yet in mercy, Allah sent Muhammad and gave him the Quran. Thus, Allah gave humankind Islam, the final perfect religion (Q 5:3).

Islam teaches that Judaism, Christianity, and all other world religions were in line with Islamic teaching when they began. Since Islam is the culmination of these revelations, all people who are still following these religions are either misled or rebellious. Only Islam will be accepted on the day of judgment, not other religions (Q 3:18–85). The Quran emphasizes that on that day, all people will be judged for their sins (Q 6:146; 17:15; 35:18; 39:7; 53:38).

Islam is grounded in the Quran, the life and teachings of Muhammad. The Quran reveals Islam, and Muhammad defines it. Muslims are to follow Muhammad as the perfect example. His life and teachings are recorded in the vast body of literature called *hadith*, which is considered the source of authority to Muslims. In his book *The House of Islam,* Ed Husain explains how every detail in a Muslim's life is guided by the Quran and Muhammad. Love for Allah leads Muslims to imitate Muhammad's life and makes all Islamic rituals a joy instead of a burden.

THE CHALLENGES BETWEEN THE QURAN AND THE GOSPEL

When we read the Quran, we notice it is always in a challenging dialogue with Christians, Jews, and polytheist groups in Arabia. Islam continues to challenge Christianity today. What are the challenges that the Quran presents to Christians? The theological challenges raised by Islam can be summarized in three points:

First, Islam is the only major world religion that has arisen since the birth of Christianity. According to the Quran, Islam is the final divine word to humanity before the judgment. Although Islam recognizes Judaism and Christianity as having been revealed by Allah through his prophets, it teaches that the ultimate message Allah revealed was in the Quran through his messenger Muhammad:

> You are the best community brought forth unto mankind, enjoining right, forbidding wrong, and believing in God [Allah]. And were the People of the Book [Christian and Jewish] to believe, that would be better for them. Among them are believers, but most of them are iniquitous. (Q 3:110)

According to Islamic commentators, this verse states that the Muslim community is destined to be the best religious community and therefore should live up to this destiny. It describes the Muslim community as a dominant and protecting community with regard to other people. Thus, just as the Quran is described as dominant, or protector,[17] or guardian (*muhaymin*)[18] over other scriptures (Q 5:48), the Muslim community plays a similar role.[19]

Second, Islam is the only major world religion that claims to reform Christianity. Christian communities have experienced many reformations; however, these reformers have come from *within* Christianity and have accepted basic Christian doctrines, such as the Nicene Creed. Islam, however, aims at reforming Christianity from *without* and rejects the central teaching of the faith.

---

[17] This reading is according to the translation by various authors, Seyyed Hossein Nasr (editor-in-chief), *The Study Quran: A New Translation and Commentary* (New York: HarperOne, 2015).

[18] Translated by Ali Quli Qarai, in Reynolds, *The Qur'an and the Bible*.

[19] This is a summary of al-Razi, al-Tabari, and Ibn Kathir; see *The Study Quran*, 161.

If we were to ask "What is the clearest way for anyone to become Christian?", the answer, in its purest form, is found in Romans: "If you confess with your mouth that Jesus is Lord and believe in your heart that God raised Him from the dead, you will be saved" (Romans 10:9). In these verses, we find the entire Gospel message formulated in three statements: Jesus died for our sins, He rose from the dead, and He is the Lord and the incarnate God.

Islam rejects these three statements. The Quran explicitly denies that Jesus ever claimed to be God (Q 5:116). It claims that He did not die by crucifixion (Q 4:157) and, by implication, denies that He rose from the dead. Islam totally rejects the idea that Jesus died for forgiveness of sin. Thus, Islam explicitly rejects the central claims of the Gospel.

Islamic doctrine is the antithesis to the core message of Christianity, and yet it is the only other major world religion that uses many Christian symbols, stories, thoughts, and concepts that are found in the Bible. The Quran, however, interprets them differently. It is no wonder that John of Damascus, one of the first Church Fathers who studied and debated Islamic teachings, called Islam an "Ishmaelite heresy." We will look at Islam's use of Christian concepts in the course of this book.

Third, Islam, like Christianity, is the only major religion motivated by a significant missionary zeal. In Christianity, Jesus commanded all believers, "Go therefore and make disciples of all nations, baptizing them in the name of the Father and of the Son and of the Holy Spirit, teaching them to observe all that I have commanded you" (Matthew 28:19–20). The term Christians use is *evangelism*, which means "sharing the Good News of the Gospel with the world."

The Islamic term used for evangelization is *al-Dawa*, which means "the call." *Dawa* is "the one who invites or calls people to Islam."[20] This term is used more than a dozen times in the Quran. For example: "Call unto the way of thy Lord with wisdom and good exhortation.

---

20 For a complete and comprehensive study about the Islamic missionary effort, see Patrick Sookhdeo, *Dawa: The Islamic Strategy for Reshaping the Modern World* (McLean, VA: Isaac Publishing, 2014).

And dispute with them in the most virtuous manner" (Q 16:125). The Quran also encourages not only individuals but also the whole community to call people to Islam. Witnessing is the prime reason for the creation of the Islamic community, called *umma* in Arabic. The Quran says, "Thus did We make you a middle community, that you may be witnesses for mankind and that the Messenger may be a witness for you" (Q 2:143).

The Quran explains that the goal of *Dawa* is not only preaching but also establishing the rule of Islam and its law, Sharia, thus changing the whole society: "Let there be among you a communing calling to the good, enjoining right, and forbidding wrong. It is they who shall prosper" (Q 3:104). The "right" in this verse means "Islam." Based on this verse, Islam established the well-known principle of "commanding right and forbidding wrong." This principle commands the community to call all people to live according to Sharia, which can be done either in a gentle way, such as by preaching, or by force. The Quran, the life of Muhammad, and hadith literature all command Muslims to engage in outreach and invite non-Muslims to Islam.[21] However, becoming Muslim is a call to reverse, not convert. In Islamic teaching, every human being was a Muslim at birth, after which some went astray and followed other religions. We will examine the Muslim concept of predestination in chapter 7.

According to Patrick Sookhdeo, there are two challenging differences between the Islamic *Dawa* and the Christian missionary call to repent and believe in Christ. First, Christians have no problem living alongside other religious groups, especially in the West, where freedom of speech is the norm. In Islam, especially in most Islamic countries, all Christian missionary activity is forbidden and considered deceitful and evil. Second, the aim of *Dawa* is not only preaching and calling people to Islam but also to convert an entire society and its structures and create an Islamic state, or at least areas ruled by Islam.[22]

---

21 Sookhdeo, *Dawa*, 7–13.
22 Sookhdeo, *Dawa*, 2. See also Muhammad Aboukhir Badawi, *Islam in Britain: A Public Lecture 1981* (London: Ta-Ha Publishers, 1981), 25–49.

The Challenges of Demographic Changes

In 1945, Islam claimed 250 million adherents, slightly smaller than the population of the United States today. Current data estimates that there are approximately 1.8 billion Muslims worldwide, a sevenfold increase in the last seventy years. The cause of the growth is both biological (high birth rate) and missiological (missionary activities). Islam is the second-largest religion, second only to Christianity. On April 2, 2015, the Washington Post published an article titled "There Will Be Almost as Many Muslims as Christians in the World by 2050,"[23] based on research conducted by the Pew Research Center.[24]

The Pew Research Center reported that Islam is the world's fastest growing religion. Looking over the next four decades, it projected the populations of the world's major religions. If current data is accurate and these projections hold true, the global population of Muslims will nearly match that of the world's Christians by 2050.

Pew considered many complex factors in making this projection. Some of these factors included fertility rates, the size of youth populations, the effects of migration, and rates of religious switching. An example of religious switching is when members of religious communities became "unaffiliated," as the study labeled it.

Of the world's religious communities, the Muslim community was one of the few that was projected to increase at a rate faster than the world population. Pew predicts that after 2070, it is likely that there will be more self-identifying Muslims than Christians. And even though India is still expected to be a country in which Muslims are a minority, it will likely also be the nation that holds the largest number of Muslims by 2050.[25]

---

23   Ishan Tharoor, "Chart: There Will Be Almost as Many Muslims as Christians in the World by 2050," *The Washington Post*, April 2, 2015, https://www.washingtonpost.com/news/worldviews/wp/2015/04/02/chart-there-will-be-almost-as-many-muslims-as-christians-in-the-world-by-2050/.

24   Michael Lipka and Conrad Hackett, "Why Muslims Are the World's Fastest-Growing Religious Group," *Pew Research Center*, April 6, 2017, https://www.pewresearch.org/fact-tank/2017/04/06/why-muslims-are-the-worlds-fastest-growing-religious-group/.

25   See David Goldman, *How Civilizations Die (And Why Islam Is Dying Too)* (Washington DC: Regnery, 2011), 9–23.

Many Muslim political and religious leaders brag about the prediction that there will be almost as many Muslims as there are Christians by 2050.[26] Some claim that Islam will eventually dominate Europe and the continent will become an Islamic land. However, other scholars have criticized the Pew demographic projection. In his book *How Civilizations Die (And Why Islam Is Dying Too)*, David Goldman criticized the Pew demographic projection. He argues that a decline in the fertility rate in the Islamic world is beginning to happen even more quickly than that of the Western world because Muslims are being exposed more rapidly to Western culture, with its education, technology, and freedom.[27]

The second point we need to consider is that in the Islamic countries, conversion is not allowed. Many Muslims who converted to Christianity or became either atheists or non-affiliated with any religions are officially documented as practicing Muslims.

The Challenges of Geographic Changes

Islam began in the Arabian Peninsula in two cities, Mecca and Medina, and later expanded into North Africa, Western Asia, Egypt, Central Asia, India, and Indonesia. Travelers to the Middle East witness this expansion embodied in the ruins of ancient sanctuaries, some of which are named in Scripture and Early Church history. The ghost of vanished churches and forgotten Church history lingers in these places.

Greater Syria, also known as the Levant, home of Jesus and the disciples, birthplace of the Early Church, and former site of a vibrant, historic Christian community, is now a Muslim country. Egypt was home to the Alexandrian fathers, such as Clement, Origen, and Athanasius; now, however, it is the center of the largest Islamic University, al-Azhar, in Cairo. North Africa was home to the Latin Fathers and was the spiritual birthplace of Western Christianity. But now it is virtually

---

26   "The Future of World Religions: Population Growth Projections, 2010–2050," Pew Research Center, April 2, 2015, https://www.pewforum.org/2015/04/02/religious-projections-2010-2050/.
27   See Goldman, *How Civilizations Die*, 9–23.

devoid of Christians. Anatolia, or Asia Minor, was the home of the seven churches that received letters in Revelation. It saw the three ecumenical creeds, the seven ecumenical councils, and numerous Syriac and Greek fathers. But now it is Muslim land. Jerusalem, Antioch, Alexandria, Constantinople, and Rome are known as Christendom's historical centers. Except Rome, all these centers are now major Islamic cities.

Islam constitutes one of the largest invisible religious empires. The House of Islam, or *Dar al-Islam*, encompasses forty-nine nations and 1.8 billion Muslims; approximately one in four people alive today are Muslim. The first is the Arab-speaking world, which stretches from Iraq to Mauritania and is home to approximately 400 million Muslims. Approximately 100 million Muslims live in the area that was formerly Persia, which now consists of modern-day Iran, Afghanistan, and Tajikistan. Some 250 million Muslims live in sub-Saharan Africa, and the Indian subcontinent, which includes Pakistan, India, Bangladesh, Burma, Nepal, and Sri Lanka, has approximately 400 million Muslims. There are around 170 million Turkish-speaking Muslims, which include Azeri, Chechens, Chinese Uyghur, Uzbek, Kyrgyz, and Turkmen Muslims. The Malay area of Southeast Asia, consisting of Indonesia, Malaysia, Brunei, Thailand, and the Philippines, has more than 200 million Muslims. There are around 60 million Muslims currently living in the West.[28]

Due to global migration, Turkish people are settling in Germany, Algerians in France, Pakistanis in Britain, and Moroccans and Indonesians in the Netherlands. Muslims in England outnumber Methodists, and in France the second-largest religion is Islam. Berlin has one of the largest Islamic populations in Europe.

The Christian Church faces many mission fields in the twenty-first century. First is China, which has 1.5 billion people (and by God's grace, the Christian Church is growing there). India is second, with over one billion people. The third and most challenging is Islam. It urgently

---

[28] See Marilyn R. Waldman and Malika Zeghal, "Islamic World," in *Encyclopedia Britannica*, August 21, 2019, https://www.britannica.com/topic/Islamic-world.

challenges Christians to invest time, prayer, and personnel to extend the kingdom of God among them.

Based on this data, two challenges require our attention: a local challenge and a missiological challenge. These statistics tell us that Muslims are here among us: our neighbors, our friends, and our co-workers. The Arab American Institute reported that between 2000 and 2010, the Arabic-speaking population in America grew by more than 72 percent.[29] These statistics were conducted before the Arab Spring, the uprisings and revolutions that took place across the Arab-speaking world in the early 2010s; if the Institute conducted another census, they would almost certainly see an even higher rate of growth. This means that Muslims are not geographically distant from us; as Christians, we are invited and challenged to interact with them daily and build relational bridges to them.

Second, we consider the missiological challenge. Islam is a religion motivated by missionary zeal. Muslim theologians[30] and missionaries[31] believe that Europe and North America are ripe for conversion. Islam strongly desires to convert the West. One way to accomplish this is the Islamization of societies. Islamization is a process by which a whole society is shifted toward Islam, when not only individuals but also groups, societies, and cultures become more and more Islamic.[32]

THE CHALLENGES OF FUSING RELIGION AND POLITICS

According to Islamic history, Islam took its final form in Medina in the seventh century (AD 622–37). Muhammad presented a message that was not only spiritual and theological but also a blended political, social, and theological one. In the spiritual and theological message, the substance of the Quran, as it was revealed and interpreted in the life of

---

29 "Demographics," Arab American Stories, https://www.arabamericanstories.org/arab-americans/demographics/.
30 The Islamic term used for *theologian* is the Arabic term *Faqeeh*.
31 The Islamic term used for *missionary* is the Arabic term *Da'eah*.
32 Sookhdeo, *Dawa*, 69–99.

Muhammad, consecrated the political and social message. In Medina, Islam became a comprehensive system that encompassed the religion, society, and politics of the state. For the last thirteen centuries, this intimate and interwoven relationship between religion and politics has remained in Muslim areas. It is not the purpose of this chapter to examine the historical and political development of Islam; however, we will briefly look at this development since 1945 to see its effects, not only on the Muslim community but also across the globe.

In 1945, most of the Muslim world was under Christian dominance. Between the Western powers and the Soviet Union, nearly all the Islamic lands were possessed: the French had established themselves in North Africa and Syria; the Italians in Libya, Eritrea, and Somalia; the British were controlling East Africa, India, and Malaya; the Dutch had Indonesia; and the Soviets ruled most of Central Asia.

However, after World War II, the Muslim world was swept by independence movements. In Iran, the Pahlavi dynasty first asserted itself, and then in 1979, the Ayatollah came to power. When British imperialism ended, a number of Muslim states arose, including Pakistan and Bangladesh, which rose out of the ruins of the British Raj. Despite being prolonged, the French mandate ended in Algeria, freeing the Arab West, or Maghreb, from foreign rule. Italy forfeited its empire and had to abandon its Dutch colonies after World War II. When the Soviet Union collapsed in 1991, six new Muslim states emerged in Central Asia. By 2000, there were forty-four member states of the World Muslim Congress, twenty-two of them Arabic.

In 1882, when Charles Montagu Doughty wrote the chronicle of his epic journey in *Travels in Arabia Deserta,* he described the Saudi capital city Riyadh as a "dead land."[33] However, with the discovery of oil at the beginning of the twentieth century, the dead land was revived, and the dramatic and negative depiction of the Arabian desert has completely changed. Much of the region rose from poverty to

---

33   Charles Montagu Doughty, *Travels in Arabia Deserta*, vol. 1 (Cambridge: Cambridge University Press, 1888), 56.

plenty, abruptly converting from shortage to affluence. The Saudi capital, Riyadh, is now the home of the richest monarchy on earth. Consumer goods are available in abundance. The region became the focus of global attention due to the international business interest and political turmoil; the Persian Gulf War over Kuwait in the early 1990s indicated the significance of the region to the industrialized world.

With this newfound independence and economic affluence, the Muslim world moved from decadence to renaissance, from a sense of inferiority to the West to a sense of moral superiority over it. This sense of liberation released a surge of self-confidence and hope. Islamic ideology could now both speak on and react to issues that had been discussed by Europeans for many decades, such as peace, justice, equality, economic welfare, family, capitalism, communism, and banking.

To interact with broader contemporary society, many Muslims returned to the history of Islam. Turning back to old religious practices and convictions produced extremism. Extremist Muslim groups look at the life of Muhammad, especially in Medina, and the first four Caliphs, called the Rightly Guided Caliphs,[34] as a divinely inspired model of life. These groups copy the practices of faith that were developed in the Arabian Peninsula between the seventh and ninth centuries.[35]

Muslims today look at Islam as the way forward and the only solution to the political corruption, lack of freedom, and economic stagnation many face. When the Gallup World Poll surveyed Islamic countries, the majority of them credited the progress of Muslim societies to their "attachment to their moral and spiritual values."[36]

Muslim apologists argue that Islam alone can save Europe and North America from impending doom. This kind of assertiveness was illustrated in 1979, when the Mullahs of Iran overthrew the Shah, a

---

34 The "Rightly Guided Caliphs" is a term used by Sunni Muslims to refer to the first four successors of Muhammad; they are also called the Righteous Caliphs. They were Abu Bakr (AD 632–34), Umar ibn al-Khattab (Umar I, AD 634–44), Uthman ibn Affan (AD 644–56), and Ali ibn Abi Talib (656–61).

35 Patrick Sookhdeo, *Unmasking Islamic State: Revealing Their Motivation, Theology and End Time Predictions* (McLean, VA: Isaac Publishing, 2015), 17–61.

36 See John Esposito and Dalia Mogahed, *Who Speaks for Islam? What a Billion Muslims Really Think* (New York: Gallup Press, 2007), 25–26.

dictator backed by the American government, in the name of Allah and Shiite Islam. Despite predictions that the Mullahs would fail, the Iranian Revolution was successful and set off a bloody reaction from the Sunni majority nations. This revolution was a powerful reminder that Islam has the vitality and ability to release enormous power.

Islam is different from any other religion in that from its beginnings, Islam created a fusion of religion and politics. Religious doctrine sanctified political power, and political power confirmed and sustained religion.

Islamist and Islamism

Contemporary Muslims who place a major emphasis on the political aspects of Islam are called *Islamists*, and their ideology is called *Islamism*. They uphold that faithfulness to Allah's message and mission has produced a vast empire and civilization, starting with the Islamic community in the seventh century, and spanning much of the world until the dawn of European colonialism in the eighteenth century. Therefore, only the return to the pure form of Islam as expressed in the life of Muhammad and the first Islamic community would guarantee an Islamic empire under the leadership of the prince of believers, the Caliph.

Islamism is a political ideology that sees Islam as a total system of life, not separating sacred from secular. Based on classical Islam and early Islamic sources, it sees Islamic states ruled by Islamic law (also known as Sharia law) as the most desirable method of governance. It seeks political dominance for Islam across the whole globe, sees the states as the best tool for implementing Sharia, and believes peace is only possible under Islamic rule. Islamists are not content with a society containing or composed of Muslim people; instead, they require society to be Islamic in its basic structure.[37]

---

37 For more on the ideology of Islamism, see Ed Husain, *The House of Islam*, 117–32. See also Anna Bekele, Patrick Sookhdeo, eds., *Meeting the Ideological Challenge of Islamism* (McLean, VA: Isaac Publishing, 2015).

In 1956, the late Bishop Kenneth Cragg argued in his book *The Call of the Minaret* that politicized Islam, or Islamism, is the most important development in this current period of Islamic history.

Islamists are increasing the influence of Islam across the globe by fusing politics and religion and by using the twin concepts of *Dawa* and *Jihad*. This influence is accompanied by a growing Islamization of Muslim majority states and a drive to destabilize secular non-Muslim states in order to Islamize them. These movements have become more complex as they merge and splinter. A few have become household names, such as the Taliban, al-Qaeda, and the Islamic State (often abbreviated as IS, ISIL, ISIS, or in Arabic *Daesh*). Many other Islamist groups are notorious in their own part of the world, such as Boko Haram in West Africa, Al-Shabaab in Somalia, Seleka in the Central African Republic, and the Allied Democratic Forces in Uganda and the Democratic Republic of the Congo.

In the next chapter, we will examine the challenges Muslims face when practicing Sharia law. Chapter 3 will examine the Quran's view of Christians and Jews. These two chapters will clarify points made in this chapter.

QUESTIONS FOR DISCUSSION
CHAPTER 1

SEE ANSWER KEY ON PAGE 291.

QUESTION 1

We define Islam in terms of submission and peace. In their daily lives, Muslims practice absolute submission to the will of Allah, believing that by living this life of submission, they obtain peace with Allah. How would you define Christianity?

QUESTION 2

The three tenets of Islam—the existence of Allah, the Quran, and Muhammad—are proclaimed in what is called the "Islamic confession of faith" (the *Shahada*). It states, "I bear witness that there is no god but Allah and Muhammad is his prophet." Any person who converts to Islam must publicly recite the *Shahada* three times. If you are asked to summarize the Christian confession of faith in three tenets, what would you say, and how would you share it with your Muslim friend?

QUESTION 3

We talked about two major local and missiological challenges in responding to Islam; however, these challenges are also opportunities. How can we face these challenges?

CHAPTER 2

Muslims and Sharia Law

In the first three centuries of Islam (AD 622–922), Muslim scholars developed a system of religious and civil law called Sharia law. This law expresses the Islamic way of life and is the key to understanding Islam. Sharia directs all aspects of life, including both the religious and secular spheres. Its rituals and rules provide the framework within which a Muslim leads his or her life. Likewise, the behavior and worldview of most Muslims is guided by Sharia. As a result, most Muslims believe that Sharia is like a fence or roadblock that protects them from sin. It also clearly distinguishes Muslims from non-Muslims.

Sharia is an Arabic term that means "path" or "law." In the English language, it has been interpreted as "the Islamic Law." According to Islam, humanity's basic problem is ignorance. We need to be guided if we are to live a good life. Learning and practicing the doctrine leads Muslims to the knowledge of Allah. Sharia is founded on three sources: the Quran, the life of Muhammad, and hadith literature. These three sources are called *sunna*. According to Islamic teachings, the answer to humankind's ignorance is Sharia, which was drawn from the Quran and lived out in Muhammad's life and hadith literature, as it is taught by the *imams*.

THE APPLICATION OF SHARIA

With the wide range of teachings in the Quran and the diverse teachings of the hadith, discerning Sharia requires learning. Those who study and teach Sharia are called *imams*, and the faithful turn to them to ask questions about behavior in all areas of their daily lives. The Arabic term is *faqeeh*, which reminds us of the doctors of the Law in the Old Testament.

These scholars may or may not agree on certain religious or civil matters; therefore, they use a methodological principle to make any legal decision. These principles are *ijma*, which means "consensus," and *qiyas*, which means "human or logical reasoning." These two principles form the third and fourth component of Sharia when there is no clear precedent in the Quran and hadith.

The application of *qiyas* is applied, for example, to the Quran's prohibition of drinking wine, expanding it to forbid the use of cocaine and other drugs. The application of *ijma* is chiefly found in how and when Muslims are to pray.

The Muslim jurist Imam Abu Hanifa (d. 767) introduced the element of *qiyas* (human reasoning) into Islamic legal thinking. He based it on the instructions that Muhammad gave to Muadh, who was the leader of a delegation sent to Yemen to call people to worship Allah.

Before the delegation departed, Muadh asked how they were to settle disputes if there were differences between the groups or with the people they would meet in Yemen. Muhammad told him to refer to the Quran. If the answer was not in the Quran, he was to consult Muhammad's way in Medina. If none of the *sunna* had a precedent for settling the disputes, he was to use his own reason and judgment.

The *sunna*, *ijma*, and *qiyas* are the sources of Sharia and are all agreed upon by the vast majority of Sunni Muslims. The jurists must study the vast traditions and the legal precedents before reaching a legal judgement, called a *fatwa*.

However, not all Islamic schools of thought agree upon these principles. For some, the *sunna* is enough for Sharia. They consider *qiyas* to be heavily influenced by Greek logical thinking. The school of thought that puts the strongest emphasis on *qiyas* are traditionally known as the *Mu'tazila*. They were rejected by the school of Imam Malik (d. 795), who preferred to follow the practice of the people of Medina.

Because of these differences, there are four main juridical schools in Islam, also called "rites."[38] The Maliki rite was founded by Malik ibn Anas, who came from Medina and died there in 795. This school gives priority to the hadith and the practice of the first Muslim community in Medina. Only these two sources are considered the foundations of Sharia. Today, they make up the majority in North Africa and Upper Egypt.

The Hanafi rite was founded by Abu Hanifa of Kufa (d. 767), which is found in modern-day Iraq. He was originally from Persia but lived and helped build Baghdad, where he died. His school is known for allowing a higher degree of juristic flexibility than other schools, through the application of personal judgment (*ra'y*) and juristic references (*istihsan*). This branch is predominant in Central Asia, Turkey, Cairo and the Nile Delta in Egypt, and the Indian subcontinent.

The Shafiite rite was founded by al-Shafi'i, who came from Gaza and died in Cairo (d. 820). This school gives priority to *ijma*. Al-Shafi'i taught that jurisprudence (*fiqh*) is not an individual but collective enterprise, so a ruling carries weight only to the extent that it is affirmed by other scholars and adopted by the community. This school is very popular in Malaysia, Indonesia, Southern Arabia, East Africa, and part of Upper Egypt.

Finally, the Hanbali rite was founded by Ahmad ibn Hanbal (d. 855) in Baghdad. It is the most strictly literalist, based on the Quran and the hadith to the exclusion of all reasoning. Throughout history

---

[38] For a study of the schools of thought, see Ignaz Goldziher, *Introduction to Islamic Theology and Law* (Princeton: Princeton University Press, 1981), chapters 2 and 6; Ameer Ali, *The Spirit of Islam* (Delhi: Islamic Book Trust, 1981), chapter 8; Michael Nazir-Ali, *Islam: A Christian Perspective* (Exeter: Paternoster Press, 1983), 43–53; Patrick Sookhdeo, *Understanding Islamic Theology* (McLean, VA: Isaac Publishing, 2013), 59–76.

and down to our day, all fundamentalist groups of Islam have followed this school (Wahabism, Muslim Brotherhood, Salafiyya, al-Qaeda, ISIS, Boko Haram, and others).

The Christian Perspective on Sharia

It is difficult to make a comparison between the Islamic and Christian worldviews. However, by looking at the definition and the goal of Sharia, we can see three important differences between Islam and Christianity.

The first difference is that in Islam, things must be done in one particular way. Muslims must pray by performing certain rites, such as prostrating oneself, in a way that is formally perfect. These prayers last from five to ten minutes and are performed five times a day, but they must be performed perfectly. If they make an error—for example, if they accidentally pray without observing the purification rituals beforehand—it is as though they had not prayed. During a woman's menstrual period, she is considered impure and is not able to accomplish the ritual prayer. As a result, she must make up the prayer time on another day. The same is true for fasting days during Ramadan; women who are menstruating are considered impure and cannot fast correctly, so they must make up for days they lost in Ramadan during the rest of the year. Prayer and fasting are law-driven rituals that must be accomplished in certain ways or they will not be accepted.

This is not the case in Christianity! Jesus did not teach us to do any rituals before prayer. When He was asked by the disciples how to pray, He did not teach them rules and regulations; rather, He simply told them:

> When you pray, you must not be like the hypocrites. For they love to stand and pray in the synagogues and at the street corners, that they may be seen by others. Truly, I say to you, they have received their reward. But when you pray, go into your room and shut the door and pray to your Father who is in secret. And your Father

who sees in secret will reward you. And when you pray, do not heap up empty phrases as the Gentiles do, for they think that they will be heard for their many words. Do not be like them, for your Father knows what you need before you ask Him. (Matthew 6:5–8)

The second difference is in the way Islam and Christianity look at spiritual growth. In Christianity, the inner, spiritual life of the individual believer is a major concern, while in Islam, the emphasis is on outward behavior and legalism. In this way, it is very similar to the laws found in Judaism. That is why the main scholarly discipline in Islam is jurisprudence, the study of how to live out Sharia law, rather than theology, the study of who God is and what He has done for us, as in the Christian tradition. Legalism is central to Islam in the same way legalism was in the time of Christ. Consider Jesus' debate with the Pharisees, the recognized specialists on the Torah, against whom Christ preached:

Do you not see that whatever goes into the mouth passes into the stomach and is expelled? But what comes out of the mouth proceeds from the heart, and this defiles a person. (Matthew 15:17–18)

This same Pharisaic interpretation of the Old Testament can be seen in Islam. Prayers are only acceptable to Allah when accompanied with the proper ablution. A woman having her menstrual period is impure, and a man is forbidden to touch her at that time; if he does so, he becomes impure as well.

All the rules in Islam are framed within the Arabic culture of the seventh century. Therefore, that culture must be kept in mind if anyone wants to understand Muhammad's Muslim religion. That context also explains why Islam contains a holistic design for a social, political, cultural, and religious community.

For many Islamic believers, to be Muslim means to pray and dress in a certain way, to eat some food and refuse other (pork, for example), and to behave in a specifically prescribed way, both externally and internally.

This practice is radically different from Christianity, which does not offer a way for humans to attempt to please God through ethical actions and ceremonial rites. Christianity is the revelation of God, who answered a human longing by making Himself present to humanity. He did this by becoming a man and dying to save us, because we were unable to save ourselves. We will look at this point in chapter 3.

According to Islam, the way to enter paradise is by observing a code of law. In Christianity, the way to eternal life is Jesus, who said, "I am the way, and the truth, and the life. No one comes to the Father except through Me" (John 14:6). In Islam, Sharia is the way, while in Christianity, Jesus is the way. Salvation in Islam is achieved by obeying the law, while in Christianity salvation is freely given to the person who believes in Jesus as his or her Savior.

Third, the Christian serves and worships God out of love, not out of obligation. The Christian counterpart to Sharia is based on reflecting the love of God toward our neighbor:

> You shall love the Lord your God with all your heart and with all your soul and with all your mind. This is the great and first commandment. And a second is like it: You shall love your neighbor as yourself. On these two commandments depend all the Law and the Prophets. (Matthew 22:37–40)

In Christianity, God is one, but He consists of three persons: Father, Son, and Holy Spirit, who share that one divine essence. The essence of the Trinity is love between each person. In love, God created humankind in His image, so that He might love humankind and humankind might love Him. To give this love value, it has to be voluntary. That is why God gave Adam the choice to love or reject Him. When Adam rejected the love of God, he rejected the source of life and love. This rejection brought death to humankind. We will examine this point further in chapters 5 and 8.

BUILDING BRIDGES

Since the first encounter between Muslims and Christians, the subject of the divine law has been a point of debate. In what follows, I present a testimony of Gerasimus, an Arab Christian theologian who lived in the twelfth century in Syria. Gerasimus responded to the main objections made against Christianity. In his apology or defense, he gave a summary of Christian law.[39]

Gerasimus said that Christian law is love; it is a spiritual law. It is light and guidance, it raises us up from earth to heaven, from slavery to filiations, from defect to perfection. His comments are based on Matthew 7:12; Luke 6:31 ("And as you wish that others would do to you, do so to them"); and John 13:34 ("A new commandment I give to you, that you love one another: just as I have loved you").

Gerasimus then presents four meanings of love:

- First, the love of parents for their children is natural love. But since human and animals both display it, this is not genuine love.
- Second is carnal love, which is the desire of the body, the love of man and woman. This is not a permanent, true love either, because when the beauty of a woman changes, the cause and the love of carnal pleasure also ceases.
- Third is worldly and human love. It has many diverse causes, but it is temporary. Typical causes are praise that the lover gives to his beloved, a gift given to the lover, or rescue by the lover, saving the loved one from certain distress. If the cause ceases, the love also ceases, showing that this love is not lasting and true.
- Fourth, the true love is spiritual love, which our Lord initiated and commanded us to practice. Our Lord taught us,

---

[39] See Abjar Bahkou, *Defending Christian Faith: The Fifth Part of the Christian Apology of Gerasimus* (Boston: De Gruyter, 2014).

> "Greater love has no one than this, that someone lay down his life for his friends" (John 15:13).

Gerasimus offers more Scripture verses on love, rephrasing John 3:16 and making direct quotes from Luke 6:32–35:

> If you love those who love you, what benefit is that to you? For even sinners love those who love them. And if you do good to those who do good to you, what benefit is that to you? For even sinners do the same. And if you lend to those from whom you expect to receive, what credit is that to you? Even sinners lend to sinners, to get back the same amount. But love your enemies, and do good, and lend, expecting nothing in return, and your reward will be great, and you will be sons of the Most High, for He is kind to the ungrateful and the evil.

More verses follow from Matthew 5:

> For I tell you, unless your righteousness exceeds that of the scribes and Pharisees, you will never enter the kingdom of heaven. (v. 20)

> But I say to you, Do not resist the one who is evil. But if anyone slaps you on the right cheek, turn to him the other also. And if anyone would sue you and take your tunic, let him have your cloak as well. And if anyone forces you to go one mile, go with him two miles. (vv. 39–41)

> But I say to you, Love your enemies and pray for those who persecute you, so that you may be sons of your Father who is in heaven. For He makes His sun rise on the evil and on the good, and sends rain on the just and on the unjust. (vv. 44–45)

> You therefore must be perfect, as your heavenly Father is perfect. (v. 48)

He concludes by stating, "This is the Divine Law and these are its commandments and its lawfulness and unlawfulness. These are the very same laws of Christians."

In conclusion, from a Christian point of view, we can say that for Islam, ignorance is the problem of humankind; to overcome ignorance, humankind needs a pathway, which is Sharia law. However, even when a person performs them perfectly, he or she is not sure of his or her salvation. We will examine this point in chapter 6.

In Christianity, sin is the problem. Sin against God is basically the rejection of His love. Sin separates us from God's presence and all the resulting benefits. Anyone who wants to enjoy the love of God and the life He offers must first admit that there is such a thing as sin and that we all share its devastating effects. In this book we will elaborate more on these points.

Lastly, we come to the appeal of the rituals in Sharia. These ceremonies are collective actions. Our individualistic society has taught us to worship in an individualistic way, with or without a body of fellow believers. However, the Bible teaches us that worship is a collective act, a *leitourgia*, a Greek word meaning "the work of the people." In Islam, the word describing the place of worship and the day of worship come from the same root: *jama'ah*, which means "gather together." The mosque is called *jame'*, which means "a place of gathering," and Friday is called *Jumuah*, which means "the day of gathering."

Islam has adapted these terms and practices from Eastern Christian churches. In Arabic, Aramaic, and Hebrew, the term *church* is derived from the verb *kanash*, which means "gathering together." At the mosque, worshipers all gather at the same time, perform the same gestures, and speak the same prayers. The same things happen when millions of Muslims make their pilgrimage to Mecca. This collective synchronism unites and immensely strengthens Muslims. Something similar happens at Ramadan. All Muslims fast during the day; after sunset, they rush to drink water. This social event is very important and often involves non-Muslim citizens as well.

This is the power of Islam and the religious vision Muhammad sought, and this is one of the major aspects that attract Westerners to Islam, especially women.[40]

In the fall of 2010, I took a group of college seniors to the Islamic Center in Richardson, Texas, one of the largest Islamic centers in north Texas. The person who gave us a tour of the mosque was a white American, a former agnostic who converted to Islam. He explained to us the different postures of prayer. He said that one of the important aspects of prayer was praying with his fellow Muslims and lying prostrate with them, which gave him a sense of power, security, and unity with his fellow believers.

However, this element of corporate, communal worship is something that Christianity also has, and it can form a touchstone in our relations with our Muslim neighbors. The Christian is a person who shares the divine life with other believers. Between them exists an unbreakable bond, binding all together into Christ's body. This connects us to the doctrine of the Holy Trinity. Being created in the image of a triune God means that we are given a share in who God is and what God does.

In our individualistic society, it is important for us to recover that sense of getting together as one body and caring for one another, both as a confession of our faith and as a witness to Muslims and all those outside the faith.

The Two Versions of Islam

Studying the history of Islam, we see that there are two faces of Islam and two messages that Muhammad preached. Broadly speaking, Muhammad set forth two versions of Islam, one in Mecca (AD 610–22) and the second in Medina (AD 622–32).

In Mecca, Muhammad's message was clear, simple, and religious:

---

40 For more information about the reasons Western women convert to Islam, see Rosemary Sookhdeo, *Stepping into the Shadows: Why Women Convert to Islam* (McLean, VA: Isaac Publishing, 2005).

- Believe in Allah and believe in the day of judgment, when everyone will be judged according to his deeds.
- Implore from Allah pardon for your sins.
- Twice each day, pray the prescribed prayer.
- Flee adultery.
- Show mercy and justice toward widows, the orphans, and the poor by detaching yourself from riches.

This message was similar to the message of Amos in the Old Testament.

In Mecca, Muhammad avoided any mention of violence, presenting Islam as a peaceful and loving religion. Muhammad declared that Allah had chosen him to be the prophet to communicate his divine revelation to humanity, and Allah transmitted it to him though the archangel Gabriel. There was much preaching and little legislating.

At Medina, the majority of people accepted the message and along with that success came the problems of organizing the new believers. This meant legislating and administration.

From Muhammad's arrival in Medina onward, the Muslim community became a separated group, the center and head of which was the Islamic prophet. He alone had divinely-given authority over the community's spiritual and temporal concerns. Gradually, necessity demanded a state with its own laws, justices, taxes, and military commanders. The Quran's revelation intervened on all of these points, and thus it ceased to be a simple religious message and became the organizing principle of the temporal state. Religion thus became religion and state, and temporal affairs were, in a sense, sacralized by the revelation of the Quran.

According to Islamic tradition, this Medina period is considered the golden age of Islam. In Medina, the Islamic community, originating from diverse tribes and diverse social classes, formed a new society, united in a bond no longer racial or tribal but religious. Muhammad and the four Rightly Guided Caliphs are considered a model to imitate for people and states that wish to be truly Muslim. They are the divine model of virtue for all people and all time.

The preaching at Mecca was essentially religious and against the grain of the surrounding society. At Medina, a new society came into being as a result of the preaching of Muhammad and the teachings of the Quran, and a large part of the Medina surahs[41] are devoted to the social and judicial organization of this new community. Islam was no longer a mere religion; it had now become a religion and a state and, subsequently, the state religion (*Din al-Daūla*). We can say that the period at Medina witnessed how profound Islamic sentiment often brings about an intense interest in administrating and legislating social concerns.[42]

Reconciling the Two Versions

Whether Muhammad was in Mecca or Medina, Muslims hold that Muhammad was steadily and consistently guided by Allah throughout his prophetic career in all that he said and did. Thus, for Muslims there is no meaningful change in Muhammad's calling over time; the change seen between Mecca and Medina is simply in style and context.

No matter how Muslims justify it, we cannot ignore the fact that there were clearly two different versions of Islam. This evolution is still the basis of debates among Muslims. Which version of Islam should be considered the true one: the first period in Mecca, with its peaceful and spiritual aspect, or the second period in Medina, with its strong social and political nature? How can Muslim scholars reconcile between the two versions of Islam, and which version should Muslims adapt?

The Islamic teachings contain a method called *Asbab al-Nuzul*, "the reasons of the revelation." It is used in three ways: first, to determine a chronological order of surahs; second, to explain the reason of the revelation; and third, to identify the last verse revealed on any determined subject.

---

41 *Surah* is the Arabic word for "chapter." Each chapter in the Quran is called a *surah*.
42 See Robert Caspar, *Islamic Theology: Doctrines*, vol. 2, Studi Arabo-Islamici del PISAI, no. 17 (Rome: Pontificio Istituto di Studi Arabi e d'Islamistica, 2007), 55–56.

This method is connected to another system called *al-Nasekh was al-Mansūsk*, "the abrogating and abrogated." The Quran explains this system: "No sign do We abrogate or cause to be forgotten, but that We bring that which is better than it or like unto it" (Q 2:106; see also 16:101; 13:39). After determining the chronological order of the revelation, the last verse revealed on any subject abrogates or annuls the earlier verses.

Based on this system, the religious and peaceful verses of Mecca were revealed earlier; therefore, the latter verses in Medina abrogated or annulled the Mecca ones. For example, the verses about the sword in Medina alone abrogated 124 earlier verses calling for peace and tolerance.

Challenges Faced by Muslims

Based on the two versions of Islam and the different schools of thought, we can distinguish three kinds of Muslims: cultural, Quranic, and militant.[43]

- Cultural Muslims are those who are born Muslim and adhere to the social norms rather than to theology. They are like many cultural Christians who are born into a Christian family and baptized into the Church, but who don't go to church regularly and are not part of any Christian discipleship.

- Quranic Muslims are those who embrace Islam and adhere to the explicit teaching of the Quran. They follow Islam closely and seek to apply the teachings of the Quran in their daily lives.

- Militant Muslims are those actively engaged in defending Islam by means of armed conflict and other strategic efforts aimed at the destruction or subjugation of non-Muslims,

---

43   For a detailed study of these doctrines, see Nabeel Jabbour, *The Crescent through the Eyes of the Cross* (Colorado Springs: NavPress, 2008), 82–86, 100–104; Jabbour, *The Rumbling Volcano: Islamic Fundamentalism in Egypt* (Pasadena, CA: Mandate Press, 1993). Jabbour based his idea on John Clark Mead, *The New World War* (Maitland, FL: Xulon Press, 2002).

whom they believe constitute a threat to Islamic civilization in general.

The Quranic and militant Muslims can also be divided between fundamentalists and fanatics. The fundamentalists are the committed Muslims who are going back to the literal fundamentals of Islam. They are deeply committed and willing to pay any cost to follow Allah. A biblical illustration of a fundamentalist can be seen in Paul's past as Saul, the Jewish militant fundamentalist, as described in Philippians 3. Fanatics are not driven by theology but by an attitude of hate and self-righteousness. They demonize whoever does not agree with them, and they tend to be legalistic and hypocritical. They are very similar to the Pharisees at the time of Jesus.

Based on these different responses, three doctrines in Islam are treated differently depending upon whether a Muslim is cultural, Quranic, or militant: jihad, separation, and following the model of the prophet.

JIHAD

Jihad is an Arabic word that means "to strive or struggle." Muslims scholars give three main interpretations for this doctrine:

- Cultural Muslims believe that to practice jihad is to strive to live a life of righteousness by avoiding sin.
- Quranic Muslims go a step further by teaching that it is not enough to strive to live a life of righteousness. There should be a social compulsion to that righteousness. We examined this in chapter 1, when we talked about the social implication of *Dawa* and the establishment of the well-known principle of "promoting virtue and preventing vice" (*al-amr bi al-ma'ruf wa al-nahi an al munkar*). This principle commands the community to call all humans to live according to Sharia, which can be done either by preaching or by force.

- Militant Muslims go further, justifying the use of militancy to create the right environment so that Muslims can practice Islam properly. If someone is killed in the process, it is considered collateral damage.

Separation

Cultural Muslims and some Quranic Muslims believe that to be separated from the world means to be in the world and yet not of the world. This interpretation is similar to the way many Christian follow what Jesus said: "They are not of the world, just as I am not of the world" (John 17:16).

Some Quranic Muslims take this doctrine further by interpreting separation as having fellowship only with other like-minded committed Muslims. For example, a committed Muslim living in Cairo would be motivated by duty and commitment to drive or walk five miles from his home to do his shopping at a supermarket owned by a committed Muslim like himself. He should not be lazy by doing his shopping at the nearby supermarket owned by a cultural Muslim, Christian, or Jew.

Another group of Quranic Muslims go a step further by advocating that separation does not occur unless committed people live together in communion, like the Amish community in America. This doctrine is shared by some fundamentalist groups, such as the Taliban in Afghanistan.

The third group, militant Muslims, divide the world in two conflicting parts: the house of Islam (*Dar al-Islam*), the believers who are practicing the pure form of Islam, and the house of war (*Dar al-Harb*), the rest of the world that does not share Islamic values. Based on this view of separation, they teach their followers that trusted and committed Muslims who belong to the house of Islam can be sent to the house of war, meaning the enemy land, to live there as a sleeper. Their duty is to appear to be fully assimilated so that they can fulfill the mission for which they were sent. Some Muslim sleepers in the West might force themselves to sin and drink alcohol a few days before the mission begins in order to deceive whoever is watching them. This is a challenging point for geopolitical security, and political terms such as "sleeper cells" or "lone wolves" developed out of this doctrine and have become a part of the conversation about the challenges of militant Islam.

Following the Prophet

The two versions of Islam presented above (Mecca and Medina) leave Muslims with a challenging doctrinal question: What does it mean to follow the footsteps of Muhammad in their daily lives? There are three different answers to this question.

First, some cultural, Quranic, and fundamentalist Muslims will try to imitate the life of Muhammad and the first Muslim community in Medina to the point of regressing to a seventh-century mentality. We discussed this point in chapter 1.

Second, following the steps of Muhammad can also mean to identify evil and have the courage to confront it. Muhammad risked his life to confront the evil of idol worship. The inhabitants of Mecca worshiped many gods and dedicated four months of the year to pilgrimage. Pilgrims came to the city, and the businesses thrived during those months. Muhammad's message centered on the teaching that there is only one god and his name is Allah. Muhammad focused on the oneness of Allah; his claim that all gods are idols was a blunt confrontation to the idol worship that flourished in Mecca. Muslims who adhere to this spiritual interpretation believe that they should identify the evil of their day and have the courage to confront it.

Third, following the steps of Muhammad means imitating the stages of his life and ministry. Muhammad went through three main stages: underground, consolidation, and discipleship.

When the fundamentalist is imprisoned, he sees himself like Muhammad in his underground stage, when he was persecuted in Mecca. Once he is out of prison, he identifies with Muhammad, as he moved his followers to Medina. This was considered a consolidation and discipleship stage. Muhammad consolidated his followers in Medina and, for the first time, Muslims were able to worship Allah in freedom. This second stage led to the stage of expansion within their cities and other cities, tribes, and countries. This book will not examine the life of Muhammad; however, we need to briefly describe the way Muhammad consolidated and expanded his mission.

In Medina, Muhammad established himself as a military and religious leader. As a religious leader, he was able to convert the Jews and Christians to Islam. As a military leader, he provided for his followers by resorting to raids (*ghazwat*). From AD 622 until his death in 632, Muhammad was responsible for nineteen raids. At the time of his death, most of Arabia was subdued under the banner of Islam and formed a unified nation (*Ummah*).

In the last two years of his life (AD 630–32), Muhammad established control over the influential cities on the west coast of Arabia, which would become the launching pad for the momentous conquests to come. Upon his death in 632, Muhammad's successors, the caliphs, faced a brief struggle for control over the Arabian Peninsula. These successors, known as the Rightly Guided Caliphs, quelled the rebellion and promptly turned their attention northward.

In August of AD 636, at the Battle of the Yarmuk, the Muslim armies solidified power over the Levant. A few months later, in November of that same year, they gained control of the Persian Empire at the Battle of al-Qadisiyyah. Just four years after Muhammad's death, the Muslim caliphs had conquered all the major kingdoms to the north of them; from there, it was on to Egypt. Alexandria surrendered in AD 641, after a long siege. The entirety of the present-day Middle East, not including Turkey, came under Muslim control within the span of a century.

These military victories were regarded by Islamic sources as a gift from Allah, who rewarded Muslims for their faithfulness to his message dictated to Muhammad in the Quran: "And fight them until there is no strife, and religion is wholly for God [Allah]" (Q 8:39; see also 2:193). It was also a reward to faithfulness to his messenger Muhammad, who said:

> I have been commanded to fight against people till they testify that there is no god but Allah, that Muhammad is the messenger of Allah, and they establish prayer and pay Zakat.[44]

These successful military expansions are also regarded as a fulfillment of the Quran prophecy: "He it is Who sent His Messenger with guidance and the Religion of Truth to make it prevail over all religion" (Q 9:33). Followers of Muhammad and many Islamic militant groups see these events as consolidations and discipleship after the period of persecution in Mecca. They also model this kind of militarism and violent expansion, and they likewise believe they are obeying the will of Allah in doing so.

CONCLUSION

In her book *Heretic: Why Islam Needs a Reformation Now*, Ayaan Hirsi Ali looks at the two versions of Islam and proposes that even today, we can divide the Islamic community into Meccan Muslims (those who favor only peaceful preaching) and Medinan Muslims (those who would like to see Islam dominate politically). She then suggests that if Meccan Muslims were to prevail, the problems of human rights violations and jihadism would disappear from the Islamic world.[45]

Many Muslim leaders and theologians have tried to advocate this line of thought, but they have been rejected, imprisoned, and even killed. One of them is the prominent Sudanese reformer Mahmoud Taha, who was imprisoned and hanged in 1985 because of his theology. In "The

---

[44] "Sahih Muslim," compiled by Imam Muslim ibn al-Hajjaj al-Naysabury, book 1, hadith 36, Sunnah. com, https://sunnah.com/muslim/1.

[45] See Ayaan Hirsi Ali, *Heretic: Why Islam Needs a Reformation Now* (New York: Harper Collins, 2015); Ali, "Why Islam Needs a Reformation," *Wall Street Journal*, March 20, 2015, https://www.wsj.com/articles/a-reformation-for-islam-1426859526.

Second Message of Islam," Taha argues that in Mecca, Muhammad was given a supreme revelation, which is equivalent to the way we look at the Sermon on the Mount (Matthew 5–7). In Medina, the message was diluted. Taha and his followers believed that Mecca surahs—and thus, the more peaceful, spiritual approach—should be seen as superior to the message that was given to Muhammad in Medina (the more warlike and politicized approach).[46]

Against this spiritual and religious view of Islam, fundamentalists see the Medina version of Islam as the only way for Islam to dominate. The prime example of a proponent of this view is Osama bin Laden, who constantly quoted the Medinan verses in his writings.[47]

The Medinan version of Islam is a challenging point for Muslims, especially those living in the West. Islam in the West is looked at as simply another religion, and thus Muslims have the right to worship. Though this is true, Islam is not only a religion. If we look at Christianity, for example, we see a system of faith and morality that can exist within any national or state system. But that is not the case with Islam, which has its own political-judicial system expressed in Sharia law. This system governs every Muslim. For this reason, Islamic fundamentalists living within a secular political system, even in a moderate Islamic state, will attempt to overthrow this system. To them, only Sharia law sufficiently embodies the principle of Islam being both religion and state. These are the motives and the theological bases for all the fundamentalist groups, such as Wahhabism, Salafism, and the Muslim Brotherhood.

In the last part of this book, we will look at how Christians can engage with Muslims despite these great differences.

---

46 See Mahmoud Mohamed Taha, "The Second Message of Islam," in Charles Kurzman, ed., *Liberal Islam: A Sourcebook* (Oxford: Oxford University Press, 1998), 270–83.
47 See Martin Accad, *Sacred Misinterpretation: Reaching across the Christian-Muslim Divide* (Grand Rapids, MI: Wm. B. Eerdmans Publishing, 2019), 326.

SHARING THE GOOD NEWS

In this chapter, we studied three rites followed by Muslims and their approaches to three doctrines. This will help you get to know your Muslim friends. Remember, do not ask Muslims which school of thought they belong to or what kind of Muslim they are! The author presented them for the reader to break the stereotypes about Muslims, but most Muslims do not know which rite they belong to.

QUESTIONS FOR DISCUSSION
CHAPTER 2

SEE ANSWER KEY ON PAGE 291.

QUESTION 1
What is Sharia law? What would be the consequences of Sharia law being implemented in your country?

QUESTION 2
What are the sources of Sharia law?

QUESTION 3
What are the four main juridical schools that interpret Sharia? What are the differences between them?

QUESTION 4

Which of the four schools that interpret Sharia would work with our current system of government? Which are not compatible?

QUESTION 5

What are the three important differences between Islam and Christianity with regard to the Law?

QUESTION 6

How should we talk to Muslims about how we view the Law as Christians?

PART 2:
THE QURAN AND THE GOSPEL

Chapter 3: The Revelation of the Quran and the Bible

Chapter 4: The Quran's Perspective on Interfaith Dialogue

CHAPTER 3

The Revelation of the Quran and the Bible

Dictation or Inspiration?

In the biography of Muhammad, we read that when Muhammad was in his twenties, he worked for a rich widow named Khadija. She also worked in trade, sending caravans with goods from Arabia to trade them in the Levant region. Khadija was also a powerful woman and a member of the Quraysh.[48] During his service with Khadija, Muhammad was known to be an honest and trustworthy businessman; this reputation gave him the nickname of *al-Ameen*, which means "the faithful one" or "the reliable and trustworthy person." His reputation and success attracted the attention of Khadija, who was fifteen years his senior. She proposed a marriage, and the couple were wed around AD 595.

After his marriage, two important developments took place in Muhammad's life: first, he became a leader in his tribe and clan, and second, he joined an independent monotheistic religious organization called *Hanafi*. This group had a strong presence in Arabia, especially in Mecca. The Quran calls them the "Nation of Abraham" (see Q 16:120; 6:161; 10:105; 22:31; 30:30). The group became troubled with the polytheistic worship in Mecca and around the Kaaba; in

---
48 Ibn Ishaq, *Sirat Rasul Allah* (Arabic), ed. by Ismael Bin Ummar (Beirut: Dar Al-Ma'rifah, 1960), 82.

response, they preached a strict monotheistic message and practiced asceticism. According to Ibn Ishaq:

> Every year during that month [of Ramadan] the apostle would pray in seclusion and give food to the poor that came to him. And when he completed the month and returned from his seclusion, first of all before entering his house, he would go to the Kaaba and walked around it seven times, or as often as it pleased God [Allah]; then he would go back to his house.[49]

Aisha, Muhammad's favorite wife, recounted his ascetic practices: "He used to go in seclusion in the cave of Hira where he used to worship (Allah alone) continuously for many days and nights, till suddenly the truth descended upon him."[50]

In around AD 610, when Muhammad was in his yearly seclusion in a cave near Mecca, Gabriel appeared to him in a dream. In that dream, he handed Muhammad a piece of richly woven fabric with writing on it and said, "*Iqra*"[51] (which means "read" or "recite"). But the prophet said, "What shall I read?" The angel pressed him forcefully with it and again said, "Read." Muhammad again said, "What shall I read?" Then the angel pressed him a third time, to the point that Muhammad thought he was dying, and said, "Read." The prophet said, "What then shall I read?" Muhammad explained, "I said this only to deliver myself from him, lest he should do the same to me again." Then the angel said:

> Recite in the Name of thy Lord Who created, created man from a blood clot. Recite! Thy Lord is most noble, Who taught us by the Pen, taught man that which he knew not. (Q 96:1–5)[52]

Muhammad woke up from his dream; "It was as though the words

---

49 Ibn Ishaq, *Sirat Rasul Allah*, 105.
50 *Sahih Bukhari*, vol. 1., book 1, no. 3, https://www.sahih-bukhari.com.
51 See Theodor Nöldeke, *The History of the Qur'an*, Arabic edition, 29–32; Arthur Jeffery, *The Foreign Vocabulary of the Qur'an* (Baroda, India: Oriental Institute, 1938), 233–34.
52 According to the Islamic tradition, this is the first verse revealed to Muhammad.

were written on my heart."⁵³ But afraid he might be a poet inspired or possessed by *jinni*, he fled the cave, saying, "I will go to the top of the mountain and throw myself down that I may kill myself and gain rest."⁵⁴

> But as he climbed the mountain, a voice above him said, "O Muhammad, thou art the messenger of God [Allah], and I am Gabriel." He lifted his eyes and saw his visitor. It was the same creature, but now clearly an angel. Gabriel filled the whole horizon, and said, "O Muhammad, thou art the messenger of God [Allah], and I am Gabriel." After gazing at the angel; Muhammad turned to look elsewhere. But wherever he looked, whether to the north, south, east or west, he saw the angel. Finally, Gabriel left him, and Muhammad left the mountain and entered his house.⁵⁵

Muslims call this night the Night of Destiny, or power, *Laylat al-Qadr*. It is a significant night in the life of Muslims. All over the world, Muslims gather on the twenty-seventh day of Ramadan to celebrate it as the night Allah revealed the Quran to Muhammad. The Quran says of this night:

> The Night of Power is better than a thousand months. The angels and the Spirit descend therein, by the leave of their Lord, with every command. Peace it is until the break of dawn. (Q 97:3–5)

In the Islamic traditions, this is how the revelation of the Quran began. We have examined the first stage. Islam teaches that the second stage occurred between AD 610 and 623 (see Q 17:106; 25:32).

What Is the Quran?

The Quran is a collection of all the revelations given to Muhammad between the years AD 610 and 632. It contains 114 chapters, known as

---

53 Ibn Ishaq, *Sirat Rasul Allah*, 105.
54 Ibn Ishaq, *Sirat Rasul Allah*, 106.
55 Ibn Ishaq, *Sirat Rasul Allah*, 106.

surahs. Apart from the first surah, called *al-Fatiha*, "the opening surah," or *exordium*, all other surahs follow from longest to shortest.

Muslims believe the Quran had been kept in heaven, written on guarded tablets. But that night Allah sent it down to Muhammad, who later in various circumstances spoke it to his followers.

Muhammad died in AD 632 and did not leave any written scripture. Muslims believe the Quran was written in the hearts of the believers. Islamic tradition teaches that the various passages of the Quran were spoken to Muhammad by the angel Gabriel over twenty-three years from AD 610 to 632 (Q 25:32; 17:106). After hearing them, the prophet taught the words to his followers. Muhammad's believers memorized these passages as he taught them, using them in their private meditation and for public worship. This was especially true of the Meccan surahs, which were shorter. Other traditions state that Muhammad's scribes recorded the revelations on various materials, such as palm leaves, shoulder blades, ribs, stones, pieces of paper, and bits of leather.

THE COMPILATION OF THE QURAN

Muhammad spoke his revelations aloud; he did not write them. While he was still alive, he was Allah's mouthpiece to the community, and there was no urgent need to gather all the revelations he had received into one collection. But when he died, his followers believed Allah's revelation to humanity was completed (Q 5:4). They quickly gathered all the scattered passages into one book for the community.

Within a year of Muhammad's death, many Muslims who had memorized the Quran were killed in battles. Under the leadership of Umar, who became Caliph of Islam (AD 634–44), some of Muhammad's companions collected the Quran before the knowledge of it could fade away. Zayd ibn Thabit, one of Muhammad's most trusted secretaries, was charged with this task. Zayd claimed that during the prophet's lifetime, all of the Quran had been written down but not gathered in one place or arranged in order. Zayd expressed his feelings when he was asked to undertake such a project:

> By Allah! If they had ordered me to shift one of the mountains, it would not have been heavier for me than this ordering me to collect Quran. . . . So, I started looking for the Quran and collecting it from what was written on palm-leaf stalks, thin white stones, and from the men who knew it by heart.[56]

The above account comes from the most trusted traditionalist in Islam, Imam al-Bukhari (d. 870). But despite this trusted account, orthodox Muslims teach the arrangement of the Quran by Zayd exactly matched its arrangement under the direct supervision of Muhammad and Gabriel.

Later, when Uthman, the third Muslim Caliph (AD 644–56) was ruling, Muslims faced another problem surrounding the Quran. Uthman learned different versions of the Quran were being used by different Muslim communities. Uthman feared this would create disunity and instability among the Muslim community; subsequently, it would lead to a greater doctrinal and religious confusion and would create military and political rifts between Muslims.

In order to unite the community under one message, Uthman called Zayd to oversee a new official revised version of the Quran. After its production using the Quraysh dialect, Caliph Uthman ordered this new, authoritative Quran to be sent to each major Islamic center and for all the other copies of the Quran to be recalled and burned. All scholars of the Quran agree that Uthman's version has remained practically intact since.

But the debate did not cease. The seventh-century Uthmanic version was written in an imperfect form of Arabic script. This allowed for a variety of possible readings, which caused a series of discussions on exactly how that script should be read. This debate ended in 1924, when a committee was appointed by the Egyptian Ministry of Education to

---

56   *Sahih al-Bukhari*, vol. 6, book 61, no. 509, https://www.sahih-bukhari.com.

establish a definitive and completed edition of the Quran. The variant versions were removed and thrown into the Nile River. This edition became the standard text by the virtue of the famous Al-Azhar University of Cairo.[57]

The Arrangement and Literary Style of the Quran

The Quran itself is slightly shorter than the New Testament. It consists of 114 chapters, called surahs. After the first surah, all the rest are arranged from longest to shortest. Of these surahs, eighty-six were revealed during the Meccan period (AD 610–22) and twenty-eight at Medina (AD 622–32). The chapters are divided into verses. The longest chapter is the second surah, at 286 verses long. The last three surahs are the shortest and each consist of three verses (Q 103; 108; 110). With only one exception, each surah begins "In the name of God [Allah], the Compassionate, the Merciful." A title is provided for each surah. It often comes from a word or phrase within the chapter, such as "The Cow," "Jonah," or "The Fig." Interestingly, most often, these titles do not reflect the chapter's main theme.

In addition to being an Arabic edition of Jewish Scripture (specifically, the Torah, the Psalms, and the Gospel), the Quran was revealed to confirm the former scripture (Q 35:31; 46:30). At the end of each recitation, Muslims end with a proclamation in Arabic, *Sadaqa Allahu Al-Azeem*, which means, "Allah the great has stated to be true [or confirmed] the authenticity of what has been recited." Muslims believe that the Quran was given to settle the differences between the People of the Book (Q 16:64) and to explain all things (Q 16:89).

The Meccan period could be considered the high point of the Quran in religious terms. Muslims consider the Quran to be in line with the earlier messages, which are the Torah and the Gospel; it even includes the great prophets of those messages. However, the Quran was

---

57   Reynolds, ed., *The Qur'an in Its Historical Context*, 1–26. See also from the same author, *Allah: God in the Qur'an*, 23–24.

revealed to explain to the children of Israel those things about which they disagreed with Muslims (Q 27:76), and it reduces Jesus to only a servant (Q 19:34–35; 43:57–63).

The composition of the surah often follows a triple rhythm: first, introduction on the truth of revelation; second, narratives of the prophets; and third, apologetic conclusions. The composition makes use of all oratory resources, which include parables, metaphors, poetic description, and multiple arguments. Above all, it gives the example of people being punished for having rejected the prophet sent to them by Allah.

In his newly published book *Allah: God in the Qur'an*, the Islamic scholar of the Quran Gabriel Said Reynolds compares the composition of the Quran to the process of writing a homily, in which the preacher is actively involved in the interpretation of the Bible and the biblical traditions. A major difference between the Quran and the homily is that unlike a Christian preacher, the Quran claims to be speaking with the authority of Allah.[58]

The Prophetic Narrative in the Quran

The many narratives concerning earlier prophets reflect the biblical tradition, canonical or apocryphal. Several passages indicate a sympathy and attraction for those who would later be named "the People of the Book." It would seem that the prophet considered himself in continuity with them, and some passages reflect the authority of the People of the Book in the matter of revelation and in the case of any dispute (see Q 21:7; 26:197).[59]

Narratives concerning the prophets that preceded Muhammad constitute the main part of the surahs of this period. Briefly, they can be divided into two categories. The first category contains the biblical prophets from Adam to Jesus; they are the only ones called *Nabi*, which means "prophet." The second category contains names like *Hud*, *Salih*, and *Shuʿayb*; these names came from Arabic and nonbiblical sources,

---

58   See Reynolds, *Allah: God in the Qur'an*, 26–28.
59   See Robert Caspar, *Islamic Theology: Doctrines*, Studi Arabo-Islamici del PISAI, no. 17 (Rome: Pontificio Istituto di Studi Arabi e d'Islamistica, 2007), 34.

and they are called *Rasul*, which means "messenger" or "envoy." The sources of the Quran about the two categories are interpolated between canonical, biblical, Jewish, Christian, and Arabic apocryphal traditions. We will see this when we examine the story of Jesus in the Quran.

The narratives of the prophet almost all fall into the same pattern: Allah chooses a man from the midst of impious polytheistic people and sends him to remind them there is only one god; the people refuse to listen to the prophet, persecute him, and try to kill him; Allah saves his prophet and punishes the faithless and wicked people. It is possible to recognize the outline of Muhammad's personal experience as a part of the narratives.

The prophetic narratives have three aims: First, the story of the prophets gives a warning to the people of Mecca, who rejected Muhammad's message: "If you continue to reject the message of the Quran, the same punishment will befall you." Second, the story has an apologetic significance: the narratives of the prophets root the message of the Quran in human religious history and answer the objections of the Meccans, who reproached Muhammad for abandoning the religious traditions of the ancients. The Quran replies that monotheism is the true tradition, recalled in the same terms by the prophets through the ages. Polytheism is a corruption of this tradition, and the preaching of the Quran aims only at recalling the true traditions of Mecca. Third, these narratives have indirect moral goals; they present outstanding examples of faithfulness (Abraham, Mary) and transgression (Pharaoh, Lot's wife). The aim is avoiding transgression and imitating faithfulness.

Robert Caspar believes that these aims are the reason behind the differences between the biblical and the Quranic narratives of the prophets. The writer of the Quran presented the stories to parallel the immediate situation of Muhammad. We may also note that the Quran adds extra nonbiblical figures and misses other prominent biblical prophets, such as Isaiah, Jeremiah, and Ezekiel. Of the twelve Minor Prophets, only Jonah is mentioned in the Quran. The Quran therefore focuses on the patriarchs of the faith and not the prophets.[60]

The three great prophets in the Quran are Abraham, Moses, and Jesus; they are seen as models of the true prophet and are used as prestigious reference points to Muhammad's own mission. Later in this book, we will examine the story of Jesus with some references to Abraham and Moses.

Few prophetic narratives cover the prophets. Two important items appear: first, the pact (*mithaq*) that Allah made in preeternity with every human being, even before birth, consists of a promise of fidelity to monotheism to be able to obtain divine assistance (Q 7:172–73). Thus, the monotheism preached by the Quran is not only humanity's primordial tradition but also rooted in preeternity. Every human being is already a monotheist, even before birth. The traditions and the theologians claim that every person is born a natural Muslim. Infidelity is thus a fabrication.

The second item is the link the text of the Quran makes between Abraham and Mecca. According to the Islamic teachings, Abraham prayed in Mecca and established his progeny there (Q 14:35–37).[61]

Why does the Quran try to establish this connection between Abraham and Mecca? After the emigration, or *Hijrah*, of the first Muslim community from Mecca to Medina (AD 622), Muhammad tried to reach an alliance with the Jews to serve his cause and interests against his enemies, the Meccans; however, the attempt failed. Twice in 624, Muhammad tried to secure the religious independence of Islam and open an entrance to particular political orientations for the Islamic community.

In the first attempt, Muhammad assigned his religion directly to Abraham, the father of believers; in this way, he attempted to overtake the claims of Christians and Jews to be the only inheritors of Abraham. The Quran affirms that the religion of Abraham was before Judaism and

---

60 Caspar, *Islamic Theology: Doctrines*, 36.
61 For a study on Abraham in the Quran, see Michael Lodahl, "Disputing Over Abraham Disputing with God: An Exercise in Intertextual Reasoning," in *Christian Scholar's Review*, vol. 34, no. 4 (Summer 2005): 488–98. Also see his book, *Claiming Abraham: Reading the Bible and the Qur'an Side by Side* (Grand Rapids, MI: Brazos Press, 2010), 9–24.

Christianity. In this way, the Quran asserts Islam's independence from Judaism and Christianity (Q 3:67).

In the second attempt, which was both political and religious, Muhammad endeavored to assert that all Muslims belong to Abraham. The Quran pronounces the *Kaaba* as the sacred shrine in the Arabic Peninsula. Abraham is said to have built it with his son Ishmael. It was not a pagan temple but a holy place built for the worship of the one god (Q 2:142–50). Therefore, Muhammad commanded his followers to change the direction they faced when praying. Instead of praying toward Jerusalem, Muslims began to pray toward the *Kaaba*.

Islam used these attempts to confirm its autonomy while relating its foundations to the biblical tradition of Abraham. Furthermore, the *Kaaba* became a symbol of political and religious unity to all the Arabic tribes.

Based on these new convictions, Muslims believe they have priority over Jews and Christians. The Quran affirms that "Truly the people worthiest of Abraham are those who followed him, and this prophet and those who believe" (Q 3:68). The Quran continues to affirm that when Abraham and Ishmael built the *Kaaba*, they asked Allah to send to their descendants a messenger, and this messenger is no one but Muhammad (Q 2:127–29).

The Islamic traditions regarding Abraham and the practice around him is extended in a parallel way with the Jewish and Christian traditions. Two important preliminary observations merit our attention. First, Muhammad understood his message to possess a potentially unifying power among Jews, Christians, and his new Muslim community. Second, Muhammad understood himself to be offering a message that had potential to heal the rift between Jews, Christians, and the growing Muslim community of his own day.

In Islamic and Quranic traditions, Abraham has the honorary title of "the friend of Allah" (*Khalil Allah*, see Q 4:125). Allah bestowed on him a special grace. He was a servant who walked all the way with

Allah, despite all the obstacles he had to face. Abraham is a model of faithfulness and commitment to Allah for all Muslims (Q 60:4, 6). Thus, he is "an imam for mankind" (Q 2:124).

Islam saw Abraham as a model believer who was completely open to the call of Allah because he was given a "sound heart" (Q 37:84). Allah guided him to faith with a special understanding, while his father did not receive that privilege (Quran 19:43). He was able to isolate himself from the sins of his forefather and direct himself to Allah: "Truly as a *hanif*, I have turned my face toward Him who created the heavens and the earth, and I am not of the idolaters" (Q 6:79); "And he said, 'Truly I am going unto my Lord. He will guide me!'" (Q 37:99).

The Quran asserts that Allah guided Abraham and delivered revelation and prophecy to him (Q 2:136; 4:163). Not only that, but Allah also bestowed on him a holy book entitled "the Books of Abraham" (*Suhuf Ebrahim.*)[62] It is mentioned with the Books of Moses (Q 53:36–37; 87:19).

The Quran calls Abraham the first Muslim, a model believer who submitted his life wholeheartedly to Allah. His commitment to Allah directed him to do good works, establish regular prayers, and practice charity (Q 21:73). He completed the pilgrimage, *al-Haj*, including the ablution, *al-Woudu'* (Q 22:26–29). Finally, Abraham received a promise of blessed descendants: Isaac, Jacob, and the long line of descendants that extended to Jesus Christ. Allah himself guided these privileged descendants to the right path (Q 6:84; 19:49; 21:72; 29:27: 37:112). Allah gave the family of Abraham "the Book and Wisdom" and bestowed on them a "mighty sovereignty" (Q 4:54).

Based on these blessings, Abraham became a father for the supporters of the right religion. The Quran commanded Muhammad, saying, "So follow the creed of Abraham, a *hanif* [the sane in faith], and he was

---

62 Many books that are assigned to Abraham are mentioned in the apocryphal books, including *The Revelation of Abraham*, which is a Jewish book from the first century AD, and *The Covenant of Abraham*, by a Jewish writer, unknown date. Christian literature mentions an unknown document entitled *The Ascertainments of Abraham*. See Adel Theodor Khoury, "Abraham: A Blessing for all Nations" (in Arabic), in *Al-Massarah*, vol. 90, no. 87 (2004): 394–508.

not of the idolaters" (Q 3:95); also, "Follow the creed of Abraham, a *hanif* [the true in faith], and he was not among the idolaters" (Q 16:123).[63]

THE QURAN AS THE WORD OF ALLAH

The Quran is the speech of Allah, who mostly speaks in the first-person plural *We*; even when Muhammad speaks to his fellow citizens, his words are introduced by a divine order, "Say." This means that Muhammad is only conveying what Allah dictates to him. Allah in the Quran reminds believers that the Quran is not a human product; it is the speech of Allah, dictated by the angel Gabriel, to Muhammad:

> Praise be to God [Allah], who sent down the Book unto His servant, and placed no crookedness therein. (Q 18:1)

> The revelation of the Book from God [Allah], the Mighty, the Wise. Indeed, We have sent down unto thee the Book in truth. (Q 39:1–2)

> The Compassionate taught the Quran; created man; taught him speech. (Q 55:1–3)

(See also Q 2:2–4; 3:7; 6:19; 12:1–2; 20:113; 25:6; 39:41; 41:2–3; 43:43–44.)

Additionally, the Quran is not simply a revelation from Allah but a book that finds its origin in a preserved heavenly tablet, called "the mother of the book" (Q 85:21–22).

> Truly We have made it an Arabic Quran, that haply you may understand, and truly it is with Us in the Mother of the Book, sublime indeed, wise. (Q 43:3–4; see also 13:39)

From Islam's very beginning, all Muslims considered the Quran to be the word of Allah. Many Islamic traditions demonstrate the absolute

---

[63] See George Bristow, "Abraham in the Qur'an," in Gordon D. Nickel, *The Quran with Christian Commentary* (Grand Rapids: Zondervan, 2020), 90–92.

admiration Muhammad and his companions had for this book. After Muhammad's death, this reverence for the Quran continued to grow, reaching a point that the Caliph al-Moutawakel (d. AD 850), decreed the death penalty for anyone who taught that the Quran is created. The Gospel of John states, "In the beginning was the Word. . . . And the Word became flesh" (John 1:1, 14). In contrast, the Quran states, essentially, "In the beginning was the Word, and the Word became a Book!" The Quran as a dedicated word of Allah is compared to Jesus, the incarnate Word of God.[64]

The Quran as a Divine Guide to Humankind

On many occasions, the Quran refers to itself as a "clear argument" (*al-Burhan*), or light (*al-Nur*), or "the explanation" (*al-Bayan*). In fact, the second surah starts with the verse, "This is the Book in which there is no doubt, a guidance for the reverent, who believe in the Unseen [Allah]" (Q 2:2-3).

In Christianity, Christ is the climax and finality of God's revelation to humankind; in Islam, the Quran holds a similar role. The fundamental difference is that in Christianity, God revealed Himself in His Son, Jesus Christ, while in Islam, the Quran's emphasis is not revealing Allah, as such, but more important, disclosing Allah's commands. Based on this emphasis, Muslims view the Quran as the ultimate divine guidance for humankind.[65]

The Quran as a Divine Miracle

Muslims consider the Quran not only to be the ultimate divine revelation but also the ultimate divine miracle. Its miraculous quality is the

---

64 For further study on comparing Jesus as the Word of God with the Quran, see Charis Waddy, *The Muslim Mind* (London: Pearson Longman, 1976), 14; Norman L. Geisler and Abdul Saleeb, *Answering Islam: The Crescent in the Light of the Cross* (Grand Rapids, MI: Baker Publishing, 1993), 98; Seyyed Hossein Nasr, *Ideals and Realities of Islam* (London: George Allen & Unwin, 1975), 43–44.

65 See Adeleke Ajijola, *The Essence of Faith in Islam* (Lahore, Pakistan: Islamic Publications, Ltd., 1978), 104.

most fundamental and popular doctrine for Muslims, even exceeding the doctrine of the eternality of the Quran. From the start of his ministry, when people asked Muhammad to perform miracles like Moses and Jesus, he responded that the Quran was his only miracle.

In surah 2:23, Allah commands the prophet to say, "If you are in doubt concerning what We have sent down unto Our servant, then bring a *surah* like it; and call your witnesses apart from God [Allah] if you are truthful" (see 10:38).

Surah 17:88 answers another bold challenge from the unbelievers to the prophet: "Surely if mankind and Jinn banded together to bring the like of this Quran, they would not bring the like thereof."

To this day, Muslims have this absolute confidence in the miracle of the Quran, and it remains unshaken. Muslims consider this the foundation of Islam and the most convincing evidence for Muhammad's prophethood.

The Quran's View of the Bible

The Quran perspective on the Jewish and Christian Scriptures can be summarized in the following points:

1. The whole Bible is judged by the Quran, which is regarded as the model for all scriptures. The Quran, as revealed word by word to Muhammad, is the standard truth by which all scriptures must be tested; therefore, the Bible can only be regarded as the Word of God as long as it agrees with the teachings of the Quran. The one who possesses the Quran does not need to read any other scripture.

2. There is only one eternal scripture, the mother of scripture, which is with Allah (see Q 3:7; 13:39; 43:4). It is the very word of Allah, written and preserved in the well-guarded Tablet (Q 85:22). This primal scripture has been revealed gradually in the course of time to various great prophets: to Moses, in the form of the Torah; to David, in the form of the Psalms (called *Zabbūr* in the Quran); to Jesus, in the form of the Gospel (called *Injeel* in the Quran). Finally, Allah sent the last revelation to Muhammad, in the form of a plain Arabic Quran. All these scriptures were dictated by Allah to the prophets, whose task was simply to transmit them, faithfully, to their people.

3. Though each of these scriptures corresponds to a new stage in the progress of humanity, they are only successive editions of the same eternal scripture, and they all carry the same message: a command to worship the one and only true god, Allah. Therefore, they must be in agreement with the Quran. Consequently, if disagreements arose, it is because their guardians, the Jews and Christians, have falsified their scriptures. The genuine edition of the Gospel was originally in agreement with the Quran.

Based on these teachings, Islam challenges the Christian Scriptures by asking these critical questions:

- Why are there four gospels, and not just one? Which one is the real one? Furthermore, these gospels are full of discrepancies and contradictions. This is the proof that the Gospel in Christian narrative has been falsified.

- The authentic gospel was in agreement with the Quran and announced the coming of the prophet. (We will examine this point in chapter 4.) Christians have lost this gospel, or changed its text, or have failed to understand it properly.

- The gospels, like the Bible, cannot be the word of Allah, since they bear names of their authors, Matthew, Mark, Luke, and John, who at best can only be the transmitters. Even these transmitters do not represent a continuous chain of witness, for some of them, like Luke, had never met Christ.

THE CHRISTIAN PERSPECTIVE

In Christian revelation, the writers of Holy Scripture are considered coauthors with God, each word being produced under the influence and inspiration of the Holy Spirit. The term *inspiration* refers to the way God led people by His Spirit to write down His Word, taking into account their historic context and the context of those to whom their writings were intended. In his second letter, Peter explains this truth:

> Knowing this first of all, that no prophecy of Scripture comes from someone's own interpretation. For no prophecy was ever produced by the will of man, but men spoke from God as they were carried along by the Holy Spirit. (2 Peter 1:20–21)

Based on this perspective, the Bible is the product of divine inspiration. When Christians open the Gospel, they read the Gospel of Jesus Christ according to Matthew, Mark, Luke, or John. This "according to" is essential, and the style of one or another evangelist is clearly recognizable.

Following a period of oral transmission, the message was progressively committed to written text, under the guidance of the Holy Spirit, and the result is the actual text of the Christian Scripture, witnessing to God in a very special way. Christ and the apostles are continually referring to Scripture (the Old Testament and what the Jewish culture of the first century acknowledged as inspired Scripture). Therefore, we need to pass through Scripture to discover the Word of God.

The Gospel is not primarily a book. The Greek word *euangelion* means "the good news [of salvation]," which is the message of Jesus. This message was delivered orally by Jesus, then transmitted, also orally, by the disciples, who lived with Him and became witnesses of His life, death, and resurrection.

What we call the four Gospels represent four traditions. Each of them can be traced back to the apostles who knew Jesus. Luke says that he took information from eyewitnesses before beginning to compile his Gospel (Luke 1:1–4), and Mark was the disciple of Peter. These four Gospels are therefore connected with the person and life of Jesus; however, they represent four different ways to tell the facts of Jesus' life and the message He taught, according to the need of Gospel writers' audiences. The early Christians came from various different backgrounds: some converted from Judaism, while others came from a Greek background. For example, Matthew wrote to the Jewish community; therefore, he presented Jesus as the Son of David, and so the genealogy of Jesus is different from the one in Mark, who presented Jesus as the Son of God. This explains why there are differences and divergences between the Gospels: they are facets of the same prism.

The text of the Gospels has remained the same since they were edited in the first century, apart from minor variations. We possess papyrus manuscripts of the Gospels dating from the beginning of the second century, less than fifty years after the redaction of the last Gospel. Critical editions of the Gospels have been published that take into account the slightest textual variations.

Contrary to the Quran, the Gospel is not a book that God dictated to Jesus. The traditions contained in the four Gospels represent the Christian interpretation of the life of Jesus Christ. They have been drawn up in the light of faith in the risen Christ, and they require the same faith if the reader wished to meet Christ as the object of that faith. The Gospel according to John explains this truth:

> Now there are also many other things that Jesus did. Were every one of them to be written, I suppose that the world itself could not

contain the books that would be written. (John 21:25)

Now Jesus did many other signs in the presence of the disciples, which are not written in this book; but these are written so that you may believe that Jesus is the Christ, the Son of God, and that by believing you may have life in His name. (John 20:30–31)

Revelation in Christian Teachings

In the Christian perspective, revelation is a self-disclosure of God. In this disclosure, not only does God reveal Himself, but He also expresses His desire to enter into a relationship with humankind. At its highest expression of love, speech unveils a person's inner thoughts and dispositions and his or her longing to share them; it shares all that is most inward and personal in the life of a speaker, and it invites a similar gift in return. This genuine expression of self leads to a communion in love and a real sharing of life.[66]

A similar experience arises when God speaks His Word to us. God reveals His inner life to us; He discloses to us the secret of His being. It thereby becomes possible for us to share God's inmost being, in which God's loving action invades a person's whole personality and takes him or her into fellowship of life, raising him or her to a new creature.

This is why theology speaks of sanctifying grace, which enters the soul through justifying faith, or the supernatural life to which God raises humanity through Christ. John refers to this life when he says that eternal life consists in the knowledge of God and Jesus Christ (John 17:3).[67]

Kenneth Cragg describes the differences between Islam and Christianity in the way God bridges the gulf between His divine glory and humankind. He argues that the gulf is bridged or there would not be either revelation or religion. In Islam, Allah bridges it through intermediaries, archangels, angels, prophets, and teachers to whom he sent

---

[66] See René Latourelle, *Theology of Revelation* (Staten Island, NY: Alba House, 1966), 319.
[67] Latourelle, *Theology of Revelation*, 320–24.

down his revelation. For Muslims, Allah sends instead of comes, he gives rather than brings. For Muslims, the thought of God coming in Christ is unworthy because Allah is and always remains transcendent over his creation. To imply that God becomes man implies something about the divine being that they consider unthinkable. To safeguard this concept of Allah's divine majesty, Muslims have resisted the Christian teaching of Christ being true God and true man.[68]

REVELATION IN HISTORY

For Christians, the Word of God is not primarily the written word of Scripture, but instead that to which the Scripture bears witness: God's action in human history. Revelation has a historical character that can be summarized in three points:

First, it is revelation that has revealed movement, growth, and direction within history. It rescued humanity from a meaningless cycle of the same pattern of events endlessly repeating themselves. It does this by promising a future fulfillment, first through the coming of the Messiah, and then through His return in glory at the consummation of all things.

Second, revelation is a sacred history of God developing and achieving His saving plan through a series of events linked together. That is the reason that the exodus, the Sinai covenant, and other events of Old Testament history still have great significance for us today.

Unless we have some idea of their meaning, we cannot really grasp who God has made us and what He is doing for us in His Church. For instance, if we isolate the Sacrament of Baptism from the long series of preceding events, beginning with the exodus, by which God saved His people, our faith is greatly impoverished. These Old Testament events were recapitulated, fulfilled, and perfected in Jesus' life, death, resurrection, and glorification. And now, in the regenerating water of Baptism, they come to fruition for the individual.

---

[68] Kenneth Cragg, *The Call of the Minaret*, third edition (London: Oneworld, 2000), 263.

Third, revelation took place in and through human history. God revealed Himself in the historical facts and events that make up human life; He reveals Himself in men, women, and children's relationships, in their accomplishments and failures, in their sins and their virtues, in their deeds both good and evil, in their lives and in their deaths. God speaks, acts, and reveals Himself to people, carries out His plan, and accomplishes His grand design for humans through His Son.

THE FULLNESS OF REVELATION

Although revelation is a continuing process, at a certain point it reached fulfillment. At a specific moment in history, God fully revealed and gave Himself to humankind. Jesus' incarnation ushered in that moment. The human form of God's eternal, substantial Word appeared on earth. In Jesus Christ, God established the perfect exchange between Himself and humanity, and from Christ His fellowship spreads out to take hold of the entire world.

God's desire for perfect fellowship with the human race has now become a reality. In Christ, God discloses Himself and gives Himself fully to our human race. The perfect expression of this supreme love was manifested in the death, crucifixion, and resurrection of Christ.

In the risen Christ, God's revelation is present in all its fullness. Since God's whole saving plan has been accomplished, all that remains is that through faith created and sustained by the Spirit through Word and the Sacraments, humankind should share in the knowledge and love of Christ. Only in and through the risen Christ is it possible for a person to respond to God's advances. This is why Christ instituted the Church and entrusted it with His Word and Sacraments, through which His Spirit comes to dwell in our hearts.

CONCLUSION

In the Bible, God reveals Himself in a personal way. This is radically different from the Islamic understanding. Islam is much closer to the understanding of Allah as taught by the philosophers of ancient Greece. At their best, they saw their god as the first cause, unmoved mover, or supreme, self-existent good. Through these abstract categories, their god remained remote and transcendent.

Revelation is the self-disclosure of God, so it is a communication of a personal message. By God speaking to us and offering us a relationship through faith, God revealed something about Himself to us. This offer of personal communion clearly shows that God is a loving God.

This idea is absent in the Islamic teachings about revelation. In Islam, Allah has always spoken in a book, which was given to many prophets. When Allah finally gives his ultimate revelation, he also gives a book, and Muhammad is canonized as the last messenger, who carried the last revelation to humans. Thus, in Islam, Allah simply gave humankind a book, in which humankind could read about him. Imparting knowledge in this way is indirect, impersonal, and abstract. In Islam, Allah does not reveal himself; he only reveals guidance.[69]

In Islam, the message is about what Allah is and what his laws are, and how humankind can follow his rules and regulations. It does not unveil anything about who Allah is. The loving and covenantal relation that God is offering when revealing Himself is absent from the Islamic teaching. We will talk more about this point in chapters 5 and 8.

What is the attitude of the Quran toward other religions? We will discuss this in the next chapter.

---

69 See Arthur Arberry, *Revelation and Reason in Islam* (London: George Allen & Unwin, 1958), 11–15.

QUESTIONS FOR DISCUSSION
CHAPTER 3

SEE ANSWER KEY ON PAGE 291.

QUESTION 1

In Islamic teaching, the Quran is "the word of Allah," "the divine guide to humankind," and a "divine miracle." How is this different from what Christianity says about the Bible?

QUESTION 2

What is the Quran's perspective on the Bible?

QUESTION 3

What are the critical questions with which the Quran challenges Christians?

QUESTION 4

How do you respond to these challenges?

QUESTION 5

What do we mean when we say that revelation has a historical character?

QUESTION 6

When did God give us His final revelation?

QUESTION 7

How do we read the Bible to Muslims?

are washed by the blood of the Lamb, as John announces in Revelation: "Blessed are those who wash their robes, so that they *may have the right to the tree of life* and that they may enter the city by the gates" (Revelation 22:14, emphasis added).

The liturgy of Good Friday according to the Syrian Antiochian tradition describes how the death of Jesus on the cross reversed the condemnation brought by Adam. At midday, Adam ate the forbidden fruit of the tree and plunged humanity into sin; at midday, Christ bore the sins of the world on the tree of the cross. Even as the world plunged into darkness at His death, He brought life and salvation, the new fruit, this time not of condemnation but of redemption; by His death, He restored life. While Adam's hands outstretched to take the fruit brought us death, Christ—the new Adam—with His hands outstretched to take the wrath of God, brought us life.

Many Early Church Fathers stress the connection between creation and the cross in the Sacrament of Baptism. According to Ephrem the Syrian (306–73), Christian Baptism is a reentry into paradise. Biblical and symbolic expressions such as *new creation, born again*, and the *spiritual womb* of the baptismal waters point back to the state of Adam in paradise before the fall. After Baptism, the newly born Christian puts on the robe of glory and praise, with which Adam and Eve were clothed before falling into sin. Jacob of Serugh (451–521) says, "The robe of glory, that was stolen [by Satan] among the trees of paradise, I put on in the water of baptism." Ephrem stresses this topic, "Instead of fig leaves, God clothed man with glory in the baptismal water." The baptized person receives communion, which symbolizes the fruit Adam was no longer allowed to eat. When given communion, some Christian traditions chant, "The fruit that Adam was not allowed to eat in paradise, [this fruit] today is put into your mouth with joy."

Is Adam the First Sinner or the First Prophet?

The fifth difference between Islam and Christianity on the topic of creation is the view of Adam. In the Bible, Adam is the first sinner; in Islam, Adam is the first prophet, or the first one who submitted to Allah's will, and thus, the first Muslim. According to the Quran, Adam received the first prophetic revelation from Allah: humanity must perform good works in order to earn salvation (Q 2:37–38). Thus, not only does Adam's sin have no consequences for the rest of humanity, but there is also no need for Christ's sacrificial death and atonement on the cross. This is the sixth and final difference between the Islamic and Christian understandings of creation, and it is very significant. In Islamic theology, humanity was not born with a sinful nature. Even though the Quran uses words such as *ignorant, weak willed, arrogant, easily led astray,* and *ungrateful* to describe human nature, Islam does not consider humanity to be essentially fallen or sinful. That is one of the fundamental differences between Islam and Christianity. The bad news that we are all born sinners in need of salvation is an alien concept to Muslims. Instead, Muslims believe that humans can retain the state of sinlessness if we follow Allah's commandments and strive to live a righteous life. If someone falls into sin, he or she only needs to sincerely repent and seek God's forgiveness. Sin is only what a person does, not a part of human identity after the fall.

In Christian theology, however, sin is an evil resident in human hearts (Jeremiah 17:9). God created humanity in His image and without sin. Adam's fall into sin separated us all from God (Habakkuk 1:13; Isaiah 59:2). God banished Adam and Eve from the Garden of Eden (Genesis 3:23); the prophet Isaiah announces, "All we like sheep have gone astray; we have turned—every one—to his own way" (Isaiah 53:6); Paul declares, "None is righteous" before God (Romans 3:10). But God is our loving Father and seeks communion with His prodigal children despite their sinful past (Luke 15:11–32). Yet before an individual can be restored, sin must be dealt with and forgiven by the Father. This idea has no parallel in Islam, in which sin does not affect the relationship between Allah and humanity.

In Christianity, God is holy, and in His holiness, He cannot tolerate any unrighteous thing in His presence. Therefore, sin results in the separation of God and humankind, ultimately culminating in death and hell, the ultimate, irreversible separation of humankind from God (see Genesis 2:17; Deuteronomy 24:16; James 1:15). In Christianity, sin turns people into slaves and binds them under its power (Proverbs 5:22; John 8:34). Sin cannot be removed by human efforts or acts of righteousness. Individuals are incapable in themselves of adequately dealing with the problem of sin. Thus, God came in Christ to deliver us from the moral and spiritual consequences of sin. For this reason, Paul declares, "For the wages of sin is death, but the free gift of God is eternal life in Christ Jesus our Lord" (Romans 6:23). Our understanding of the fall, sinful human nature, and death are vital to our proclamation of the Gospel (which we will discuss in greater detail in the next chapter), especially to Muslims, since their version of the creation account leaves out these vital truths.

QUESTIONS FOR DISCUSSION
CHAPTER 5

SEE ANSWER KEY ON PAGE 291.

QUESTION 1

What are the main differences between the versions of the story of creation in the Quran and in the Bible?

QUESTION 2

How might you explain the concept of the image of God to a Muslim?

CHAPTER 6

SALVATION IN MUSLIM-CHRISTIAN PERSPECTIVES

In Islam, salvation begins with Adam, who was made from the earth. When he was placed on earth, the battle between good and evil began. Salvation is won when this battle is finally concluded with the divine victory of the good. The evil hypocrites and polytheists will fall into the bottomless pit, while believers will enjoy paradise (Quran 49:5–6). Paradise is a heavenly garden cultivated by Allah; however, Allah does not dwell in it, because the god of Islam does not commune with humanity. He is not a god who enters into covenantal fellowship. Any sense of intimacy is viewed in the perspective of submitting to his will.

In Christianity, God initiates and maintains a covenant with humanity. This covenant is fulfilled in Christ, the mediator between God and humanity (Acts 4:12; 10:43; 1 Timothy 2:5). Salvation in Christianity comes from the life and death of Christ. Christians believe Christ is fully God and fully man; His death on the cross paid for our sins, and His resurrection from the dead bore witness to His divinity.

Islam views salvation in terms of Allah's provision for the devout to avoid destruction on the day of judgment. Muslims look for deliverance from the punishment of hell, and they believe that they can earn deliverance from eternal death by following the law given by Allah. The

Quran uses the image of a scale to explain judgment day, when all of a person's works will be weighed; those who have done enough good works will attain salvation, but those who have not done enough good works will go to hell (Q 23:102–3). Salvation is what men and women do through repentance, expiation, prayers, fasting, and giving alms to the poor.

THE MEANS OF SALVATION

Within Islam, the means of salvation are achieved through believing in the five basic elements, or pillars, of the faith as they are recorded in the Quran:

> It is not piety to turn your faces toward the east and west. Rather, piety is he who believes in God [Allah], the Last Day, the angels, the Book, and the prophets; and who gives wealth, despite loving it, to kinsfolk, orphans, the indigent, the traveler, beggars, and for [the ransom of] slaves; and performs the prayer and gives the alms; and those who fulfill their oaths when they pledge them, and those who are patient in misfortune, hardship, and moments of peril. It is they who are the sincere, and it is they who are the reverent. (Quran 2:177)

The five elements in this verse are summarized in the Five Pillars of Islam. They are as follows:

1. Profession of faith in Allah and his prophet Muhammad (*Shahada*)
2. Ritual prayer five times a day (*salat*)
3. Fasting in the month of Ramadan (*sawm*)
4. Offering ritual charity that is, almsgiving (*zakat*)

5. The pilgrimage to Mecca (*hajj*) to be accomplished at least once in a lifetime for those who have the financial means

Additionally, some consider *jihad* to be the sixth pillar.

One of the most important pillars is the reciting of the *Shahada*. A Muslim is one who proclaims, "There is no god but Allah, and Muhammad is the messenger of Allah." This acknowledgment of and commitment to Allah and his prophet is the first step in becoming a Muslim. It also affirms Islam's absolute monotheism, its unshakable and uncompromising faith in Allah's oneness, or unity (*tawhid*). On judgment day, when a person's deeds are weighed, if he or she recited the *Shahada* even once, Allah will forgive all his or her transgressions. In Christianity, Christ saves humanity through faith; in Islam, Allah redeems those who say the *Shahada*. Therefore, salvation is earned in Islam and is not a free gift as it is in Christianity.

The Absolute Will of God in Salvation

In Islamic dogma, humankind can be saved by faith and works of righteousness. At the same time, the Quran states that Allah has the right to punish and forgive whomever he pleases. Surah 5 of the Quran says, "To those who believe and perform righteous deeds, God [Allah] has promised forgiveness and a great reward" (Q 5:9). This involves believing and obeying the command of Allah as defined in the Quran. Further, the Quran makes it clear that those who refuse to act righteously will be condemned for their sins: "We shall say to those who do wrong, "Taste the punishment of the Fire that you used to deny!" (Q 34:42; see also 39:24).

However, there is no actual assurance of salvation; Allah saves or condemns as he wishes: "Your Lord knows you best. If He wills, He has mercy upon you, and if He wills, He punishes you" (Q 17:54).[95] For many Islamic groups, the only guaranteed path to salvation is

---

95   See A. Christian Van Gorder, *No God but God: A Path to Muslim-Christian Dialogue on God's Nature* (Maryknoll, NY: Orbis Books, 2003), 126.

martyrdom: the person who dies as a martyr, fighting for the cause of Allah, is guaranteed salvation. The Arabic word for "martyr," *shahid*, comes from the root word *Shahada*, which means "to witness." This assurance is based on the following verse from the Quran:

> And indeed if you are slain or die in the way of God [Allah], truly forgiveness and mercy from God [Allah] are better than what they amass. And indeed if you are slain or die, truly unto God [Allah] shall you be gathered. (Q 3:157–158)

This lack of assurance of salvation has led many Muslims to question the teachings of Islam and consequently come to saving faith in Christ. Fuller Theological Seminary surveyed six hundred former Muslims who had converted to Christianity. The two most common theological factors that drew former Muslims to Christianity was the Christian emphasis on the loving relationship believers have with God as their heavenly Father and the assurance Christians have of their salvation.[96]

Salvation by Intercession

Additionally, Islam puts forward the concept of salvation by intercession, which is considered by some to be the only truly legitimate type of Islamic redemption.[97] The Quran sends mixed signals of salvation by intercession. A number of passages from the Quran insist that no soul can bear the burden of another (Q 2:286; 4:111; 6:164; 17:13–15; 29:12; 35:18; 39:7; 53:38–42; 82:19). However, other passages allude to the possibility of intercession with the permission of Allah. Any intercession must be a divine gift. The Quran tells us, "Who is there who may intercede with Him save by His Leave?" (Q 2:255). The Quran relates that certain groups do intercede for humans, including angels

---

[96] J. Dudley Woodberry, Russell G. Shubin, and G. Marks, "Why Muslims Follow Jesus: The Results of a Recent Survey of Converts from Islam," *Christianity Today*, vol. 51, no. 10 (October 2007), http://www.christianitytoday.com/ct/2007/october/42.80.html?start=3.

[97] For more on this topic, see Mahmoud Mustafa Ayoub, "The Idea of Redemption in Christianity and Islam," in Spencer J. Palmer, ed., *Mormons and Muslims: Spiritual Foundations and Modern Manifestations* (Provo, UT: Religious Studies Center, Brigham Young University, 2002), 157–69.

(Q 53:26), "witnesses" (Q 43:86), and those who have made a covenant with Allah (Q 19:87). This mixed message has produced conflicting theological conclusions on the subject of intercession. Some theologians argue that Muslims receive help from the prophet in the form of intercession by Muhammad or others, while other theologians hold that humans will be judged strictly on the basis of their individual actions. A number of passages in the hadith indicate that Muhammad will intercede on behalf of the entire world. According to one tradition, on judgment day, all of humanity will be forced to stand awaiting judgment for seventy years. First, they will weep tears. Then, when their tears run out, they will weep blood until it stops their mouths. But still they will not be judged until Muhammad goes and prostrates himself before Allah, interceding for all people. He will not intercede for them to be saved but for Allah to relent and judge them. Only then does the final judgment begin. If this is the image of their god, it is no wonder that many Muslims convert to Christianity in search of comfort and assurance of salvation!

According to the Quran, pious Muslims can also intercede on behalf of others. A very interesting verse in surah 2 seems to indicate that the only thing stopping Allah from destroying the world is the presence of devout Muslims, which most take to mean that there must always have been (and must always be) praying Muslims, or else the earth would have been destroyed (see Q 2:251). The hadith confirms this idea by saying that Allah gives blessings through prayerful servants of Allah, blessing not only the Muslim and his family but also his neighbors and his neighbor's neighbors, to the seventh neighbor. Islamic mysticism most eloquently expresses this notion of the earth being preserved, made whole, and redeemed from evil through piety and prayers. Sufism speaks about the perfect man, called *qutb*. It says every age must have a *qutb*; otherwise, the earth could not remain in its place. Through the grace of these perfect men, the universe goes on running. Thus, humanity can achieve wholeness, redemption, salvation, and restoration through their personal expiation and intercession.

Perspective on Muslim-Christian Encounters

In 2010, a meeting took place between a group of Muslim and Christian theologians on the topic of salvation, and a central issue in the discussion was the role of works.[98] In the meeting, Muslims stated that their objection against Christianity was that Christians believe works are not required for salvation; thus, they believed Christians taught they were given *carte blanche* for sin, even after conversion. The Muslim and Christian presenters eventually agreed on the following formulation for the role of works.

> Islam: Faith + works + Allah's mercy = salvation
>
> Christianity: Faith + grace = salvation + works

In Islam, a combination of three things results in salvation: the faith of the believer, the works or deeds of the believer, and Allah's mercy at the point of judgment. In Christianity, the role of works is on the other side of the equation. For the Muslim, works result in salvation; for the Christian, however, works result from salvation, as a response to the grace one has received from God.

The Christian presenters explained that justification is by faith, "apart from works of the law" (Romans 3:28). They also argued that works were demonstrated in the life of the believer as a normal consequence of regeneration (see James 2:17, 26); furthermore, someone who claims to be saved but does not demonstrate a changed life has a dead faith (James 2:22, 24). Works are the evidence of authentic conversion, and they accompany conversion, even though works play no role in earning our justification in any way. Thus, works appear alongside salvation as an outward sign that the faith and grace on the other side of the equation are genuine. Works can also be understood as acts of obedience that are done as a result of a genuine faith and are evidence of our submission to the will of God. (This, of course, needs to be

---

98   Paul Martindale, "A Muslim-Christian Dialogue on Salvation: The Role of Works," Missio Nexus, January 1, 2010, https://missionexus.org/a-muslim-christian-dialogue-on-salvation-the-role-of-works.

distinguished carefully from empty, legalistic works that are done out of self-righteousness, not genuine faith.)

THE RESULTS

As a result of these discussions, Muslims were able to see that Christians take works seriously, since works are an outcome and the evidence of salvation and submission to God. Additionally, they were also able to see that the Christian does not have permission to sin, as this would call into question the veracity of the person's salvation and submission to God. For the Christian, works, a sign of an authentic conversion, leads to assurance of salvation, which is absent in Islam except for martyrs who die in battle defending Islam. Islam teaches that a Muslim will not know whether he has been saved until the moment of Allah's judgment. Therefore, a biblical theology of works as the evidence and assurance of salvation in the believer's life may be very attractive to a Muslim who is seeking to understand and compare his or her faith to our own. Additionally, much of the Muslim's misunderstanding on works may be the result of contact with nominal Christians and the Western style of extremely informal, lifestyle-type faith.

SUGGESTIONS

A Muslim interested in becoming Christian would likely be more attracted to a more formal, ritualized practice of Christianity than what they see as the loose and careless informal Christian practice of most Westerners. Viewing us through their Islamic framework, Muslims often equate this informality and laxity with a lack of commitment and dedication on our part, and they may call into question the authenticity of Christianity, reinforcing their view that Islam was revealed to replace and update a corrupted Christianity.

It is certainly appropriate that we keep the biblical emphasis on faith and grace in salvation. However, it is also important that we recognize the proper place of works in the sanctified life of the believer, both in our theology and our own lives. The role of works is a central issue for Muslims, and they need to see that Christianity affirms the importance of works. Muslims will be less hostile to Christianity if they are able to observe a large degree of similarity between what they already believe and what they perceive as our beliefs and practices; there are enough legitimate, important differences between Islam and Christianity that it is important to avoid introducing unnecessary or even inaccurate differences and controversies. Therefore, it is essential that we understand the role of works clearly and are able to communicate this well with Muslims in a way that helps them take Christianity seriously.

Conclusion

Concluding these two chapters about redemption and salvation, we can see that the Islamic view of salvation differs radically from the Christian view. These differences stem from the fact that Islam and Christianity disagree on the doctrine of sin. Muslims do not view sin as a radical problem: sin is simply an action performed by people in ignorance; repentance and good deeds can ransom the sinful action. In Islam, Allah does not judge sin harshly: "And were God [Allah] to take mankind to task for their wrongdoing, He would not leave a single creature upon [the earth]" (Q 16:61). Allah is compassionate because he knows that humans are in inherently weak (Q 4:28). Since Islam does not regard sin as a radical problem, it follows that salvation is also not as radical of a solution as it is in Christianity. Islam teaches that humans are born good. Allah has given humankind the moral ability to perform good deeds of righteousness and to obey him. Humankind can (hopefully) earn salvation by obeying Allah and fulfilling his commands.

Christians and Muslims both claim to depend entirely on God's mercy for salvation. Islam views sin strictly in legal and social terms, while Christianity views it as an offense against God. Both agree that the chaos of disobedience is the common denominator in every life, including all the prophets, except for Jesus. Both the Bible and the

Quran state that Jesus is pure and without sin (see Quran 19:19; 1 Peter 2:22; 2 Corinthians 5:21; 1 John 3:5).

To build a bridge, Christians can ask Muslims why the Quran calls Jesus pure and faultless, when not even Muhammad himself was described as such. Christians can answer that only Christ's purity dwelling in our hearts can purify us from our sins (see 1 John 1:6–7). We have also seen that Muslims believe that the intercession of Muhammad and other Muslims is an important part of their salvation. This may be because Muslims also sense their need for one who can stand between their transgressions and the Almighty.

For Christians, Jesus alone is the mediator between humans and God. He alone can restore our relationship with God, because He is divine and equal with God; thus, He can bridge the gap between humanity and God. At His crucifixion, Matthew records that the veil of the temple was ripped in two (Matthew 27:51). This means that Christ's work made it possible for humanity to enter God's presence (Hebrews 9:1–4). On the road to Emmaus, Jesus revealed that He is the culmination of the covenant plan that began with Moses and the prophets (Luke 24:25–27), because God's holiness required a holy mediator, just as Paul summarized it:

> God our Savior . . . desires all people to be saved and to come to the knowledge of the truth. For there is one God, and there is one mediator between God and men, the man Christ Jesus. (1 Timothy 2:3–5)

QUESTIONS FOR DISCUSSION
CHAPTER 6

SEE ANSWER KEY ON PAGE 291.

QUESTION 1
According to Islam, how is a person saved?

QUESTION 2
Explain the idea of salvation by intercession in Islam.

QUESTION 3
Explain the two formulas for salvation:

Islam: Faith + works + Allah's mercy = salvation

Christianity: Faith + grace = salvation + works

QUESTION 4

Why do Islam and Christianity differ so greatly on the topic of salvation?

QUESTION 5

How can you build a bridge to explain salvation to Muslims?

CHAPTER 7

God in Islam

Students frequently ask me, "Is it appropriate to refer to God as 'Allah' in our conversation with Muslims? Are we not referring to the god of Islam when using the name *Allah*?" My answer is always that *Allah* is a universal name for God, just like our own word *god*, which is used by Christians and non-Christians alike. *Allah* does not refer to an Islamic god. The name has Aramaic and Hebrew origins, related to the words *Allaha* and *Elohim*. Arab Christians and Muslims alike use the word *Allah* in their daily conversations and liturgical texts. That being said, the god of the Quran is not the same as the God of the Bible, the true, triune God. This chapter will examine how the Quran describes Allah and his relation to the world, and how in turn humans relate to Allah in Islam.

God Is One

Allah is one and has no associate or child. Surah 112 summarizes this point: "He, God [Allah], is One, God [Allah], the Eternally Sufficient unto Himself. He begets not; nor was He begotten. And none is like unto Him" (Quran 112:4). Allah punishes those who associate him with another god, which is the unforgivable sin (see Q 4:48, 116). The unity of Allah, or *tawhid,* is a foundational doctrine in Islam. It is expressed in the first part of the *Shahada,* or declaration of faith: "There is no god but

[Allah]." According to Roland E. Miller[99], the word *but* (in Arabic *illa*) is significant and conveys two powerful statements about Allah. First, "There is no god *except* Allah," and second, "There is no god *like* Allah." The statement means two things: first, Allah is the only god, and second, he is an incomparable god. While Muslims confess the unity of Allah, they also celebrate the power of Allah. One method is by the repetition of familiar phrases that praise almighty Allah: "Allah is great" (*Allahū Akbar*), "Glory be to Allah" (*Sūbhana Allah*), and "Praise Allah" (*al-hamdū li-allah*). The first phrase holds a special place in Muslim devotion as the most appropriate term for expressing Allah's greatness and power. The second is a liturgical praise that is used in every prayer. The third is an everyday expression that Muslims and Christians alike use. Muslims also use it as a reply to a greeting, "How are you?" Muslims and Arab Christians reply, "*Al-hamdū li-Allah*," that is, "Praise God [or Allah]."

CONNECTION WITH THE BIBLE

The unity of Allah expressed in the first part of the confession, "There is no god but Allah," is based on the Quran: "There is no god but God [Allah]" (Q 37:35). In "He, God [Allah], is One" (Q 112:1–2), the word used for *one* is *ahad*. Connecting this to the Bible, we can see a clear connection with the *Shema* in Deuteronomy: "Hear, O Israel: The LORD our God, the LORD is one" (Deuteronomy 6:4). Similar to the Arabic of the Quran, the Hebrew text in the Bible emphasizes that the Lord is one, which is also *ahad* in Hebrew.

Jews use the *Shema* and Muslims use the *Shahada* to begin formal worship, much in the same way that many Christians begin their formal prayers with the trinitarian invocation: "In the name of the Father and of the Son and of the Holy Spirit." Arab Christians add, "One true God, amen." They intentionally added this sentence to send a message to Muslims that Christians believe in the unity of God. For all three of these religions, this confession is what separated them from the

---

99   Roland E. Miller, *Muslim Friends: Their Faith and Feeling, An Introduction to Islam*, Concordia Publishing House, St. Louis, 1995, p. 43.

polytheists that surrounded them.

There is also a link between the unity of God and humanity's obligations to Him. The longer version of the *Shema* is found in Numbers 15:37–41. The last sentence affirms the unity of God: "I am the LORD your God, who brought you out of the land of Egypt to be your God: I am the LORD your God." (Numbers 15:41). This verse forms the basis of the first commandment, "You shall have no other gods before Me" (Exodus 20:3). In the *Shahada*, the profession of faith is directly connected to the believer and his or her obligations before Allah. We see this clearly in the Quran, as Allah declares: "Truly I am God [Allah], there is no god but I. So worship Me, and perform the prayer for the remembrance of Me" (Q 20:14). This is also seen in the New Testament, when Jesus gives the most important command: "Hear, O Israel: The Lord our God, the Lord is one. And you shall love the Lord your God with all your heart and with all your soul and with all your mind and with all your strength" (Mark 12:29–30). Both the *Shahada* and the *Shema* require that believers not only recite them by mouth but also live them out in their daily lives. In the *Shahada*, the believer first states, "I witness"; in the *Shema*, we read first, "Hear, O Israel." This introductory call requires faith that must be translated in action and bear fruits. It is more than a confession only of the mouth.

GOD IS TRANSCENDENT AND MERCIFUL

The Quran speaks about Allah's majesty and transcendence. He is mighty and holy (Q 74:2–3). Everything is transient, except the majesty and generous face of Allah (Q 55:26–27). He is provident and generous (Q 85:14), merciful (Q 52:28), the one who pardons (Q 53:32; 85:14), the almighty lord who decrees and predestines, and all must submit to his will (Q 18:23–24, 29, 69; 37:102). He takes special care of his prophets; he chooses them, equips them, sends them forth, protects them, tests them, and saves them. In other words, he is a god who intervenes in human history.

The Quran frequently refers to Allah as merciful and compassionate, *al-Rahman* or *al-Rahim*. Muslims use these names in an invocation before reading the Quran, praying, preaching, and even secular public speaking. The invocation means, "In the name of Allah, the compassionate and merciful." It is similar to the Christian invocation discussed above, "In the name of the Father and of the Son and of the Holy Spirit, one true God. Amen." These names share a root word with the Arabic words for "womb," *rahm*, and "family relations," *arḥām*. These names evoke sympathy, kindness, gentleness, and compassion. Examples of Allah's mercy as seen in his creation include a mother's love for her child, the eyes Allah has given us with which we see, the food the earth provides to us, and the generosity and kindness we show to others.

The Bible speaks of God in similar terms. The Book of Isaiah describes God as the mother who loves her children: "Can a mother forget her nursing child, that she should have no compassion on the son of her womb? Even these may forget, yet I will not forget you" (Isaiah 49:15). God's compassion and mercy will never fail: "'For the mountains may depart and the hills be removed, but My steadfast love shall not depart from you, and My covenant of peace shall not be removed,' says the Lord, who has compassion on you" (Isaiah 54:10). This parallel language offers a potential bridge to speaking with Muslims about the God of the Bible and His mercy expressed through the sacrifice of Christ Jesus, His Son.

God Is the Creator and Ruler of Life

A famous verse in the second surah of the Quran describes the incomparability and power of Allah. It is known as the Throne Verse, and it is frequently displayed in Islamic calligraphy and art. It says:

> God [Allah], there is no god but He, the Living, the Self-Subsisting. Neither slumber overtakes Him nor sleep. Unto Him belongs whatsoever is in the heavens and whatsoever is on the earth. Who is there who may intercede with Him save by His Leave? He knows that which is before

them and that which is behind them. And they encompass nothing of His Knowledge, save what He wills. His Pedestal embraces the heavens and the earth. Protecting them tires Him not, and He is the Exalted, the Magnificent. (Q 2:255)

These verses remind us of Daniel 6:26, when the Persian king identified the God of Israel as "the living God, enduring forever." The phrase, "Neither drowsiness befalls him nor sleep," reminds us of Psalm 121:4, "Behold, He who keeps Israel will neither slumber nor sleep." The mention of Allah's seat and throne can be compared to Psalm 103:19: "The Lord has established His throne in the heavens, and His kingdom rules over all." As discussed previously, this similarity is likely because the Quran drew from Christian texts and hymnody.

In addition, the god of Islam is invisible (Q 2:55); he is the light that enlightens human beings. He is most generous in his gifts and near to those who pray (Q 2:186). He loves the believers, and the believers love him (Q 2:195; 3:74). He is the witness and the supreme arbitrator in discussions (Q 4:59; 5:48; 60:10). He pardons the believers and punishes the rebels. Allah predestines the embryo in its mother's womb (3:6; 22:6) and decides the day of its death (3:154, 156–158). Good and evil come from Allah (Q 9:51).

The Protector and Defender

The Quran also presents Allah as a warrior god who sends his angels to defend believers and help them in battles (Q 22:38; 2:250, 286; 48:4, 7). He organizes the battle (Q 8:42) and fights alongside believers (Q 4:108; 9:36–40). He strengthens their hearts and their footsteps (Q 2:250; 3:147; 8:11–12, 26). He is the one who gives victory (Q 8:62; 48:3). If the soldiers are fewer than their enemies, he strengthens them and makes them see their enemies as less numerous than they are in reality. He sends terror into the hearts of their enemies (Q 8:12, 26, 43). It is he who kills them, whether by the hand of believers or by himself firing arrows at the enemies of Allah (Q 9:14, 52; 8:17). All these descriptions are similar to the images and descriptions of the God of Sabaoth (hosts or angel armies), as presented in the Old Testament.

THE ABSOLUTE WILL OF GOD

The Quran treats the issue of predestination in an inconsistent way. It says that Allah is the omnipotent creator who created all things (Q 6:101; 24:2; 39:62), including humankind (Q 37:96). Allah creates faith or unbelief in the hearts of humankind. From before their birth he foreordained human destiny (Q 3:6). However, the Quran also strongly affirms that human beings are free and responsible for their actions: "So whosoever will, let him believe, and whosoever will, let him disbelieve" (Q 18:29; 73:19; 76:29), and "Whatever good befalls thee, it is from God [Allah], and whatever evil befalls thee, it is from thyself" (Q 4:79).

While the Quran neither confirms nor denies human responsibility and free will, Muslim theology and tradition affirm the doctrine of predestination. In about AD 702, orthodox Islam condemned the idea of free will or humankind's independence from Allah as the worst heresy. They condemned those who upheld the doctrine of free will. They asserted that if humankind initiated their own actions and determined their own destiny, they would be in the status of a co-creator with Allah.[100] Several statements in the hadith affirm predetermination. Allah declares, "I am destiny." All is written by the heavenly pen, in the eternal book, before anything takes place. Every action of a human being is written by the angels when the embryo is still in the mother's womb: a person's sex, the material and spiritual provision he or she will have during his or her whole life, the length and the ending of his or her life, the good and evil deeds he or she will carry out, and his or her eternal destiny to paradise or hell.[101] This explains why for most Muslims, every decision in life proceeds conditionally with the caution of

---

[100] See Caesar Farah, *Islam: Beliefs and Observances*, seventh edition (Hauppauge, NY: Barron's Educational Series, 2003), 2078.

[101] Morris Seale, *Muslim Theology: A Study of Origins with Reference to the Church Fathers*, vol. 1 (London: Luzac & Co., 1964), 23–26.

"Allah willing" or *Inshallah*. The Islamic worldview is colored with the indisputable certainty of the divine will.

THE EXISTENCE OF GOD

The Quran does not spend much time demonstrating the existence of Allah, who at that time was hardly ever questioned. At most, it refers to unbelievers who contend that destiny is all that governs their existence. The Quran condemns them and states, "They say, 'There is naught but our life in this world. We die and we live, and none destroys us save time.' But they have no knowledge thereof. They do naught but conjecture" (Q 45:24). This fatalist thinking belonged to the wealthy, who wrongly made use of it to justify their oppression of the poor. The Quran condemns this moral attitude and considers it the result of such fatalism (Q 36:47).

The Quran speaks frequently and at length of the marvels of creation, which are signs of Allah. All creation and the phenomena of heaven and earth proclaim the existence of Allah. The Quran gives three indicators as proof of Allah's existence. First, the sufficiency of the Quran, which contains enough signs and indications to prove its validity. The Quran argues that rational proofs of the existence of Allah are merely an unfortunate convention originating with the philosophers and are hardly persuasive. Second, the created world proves the existence of Allah. It is a hymn to the existence of Allah, who shines forth throughout the whole universe. Finally, the world is fleeting, and Allah is the sole being truly and eternally existent. All creatures are perishing except Allah: "All that is upon it passes away. And there remains the Face of thy Lord, Possessed of Majesty and Bounty" (Q 55:26–27). Here we see one of the central themes of the Quran and the starting point of the mystical path within Islam. The early theologians and even some authors of the present day find in this central theme of the Quran the sole proof of the existence of Allah, which can be summarized, "The world needs Allah to exist."[102]

---

102   See Caspar, *Islamic Theology*, 51–79.

The Names of God

Muslims believe that one of the most effective ways to strengthen one's status with Allah is by studying the names and attributes of Allah found in the Quran. Each name and attribute nourishes humility and piety. Additionally, according to the hadith, Muhammad said, "Allah has ninety-nine names, [that is], one-hundred minus one, and whoever knows them will go to Paradise."[103] Elsewhere, Muhammad says, "There are ninety-nine names of Allah; he who commits them to memory would get into paradise."[104] The hundredth name is considered the mystery of Allah.

When Muslims call upon Allah, they are to use the most appropriate names that relate to what they are asking. For example, if they seek forgiveness from Allah for a sin they have committed, they should call upon him by the name *al-Ghaffer*, meaning "the ever-forgiving." If asking for peace and tranquility during a period of tension in their life, they would call on the name *al-Salam*, meaning "the ultimate source of peace."

The Attributes of God

Islamic tradition makes distinctions between the divine names and the divine attributes. The names are what in European languages would be called adjectives or participles, such as *knowing, wishing, able,* or *powerful*. The attributes are what we call substantive nouns, indicating a quality such as knowledge, ability, or power. The names generally take precedence over the attributes, since they occur more frequently in the Quran, and one must first name Allah as he names himself. The Quran contains numerous divine names, which often form the end of verses in rich, deep rhymes. Muslims recite these names using a prayer rope that contains ninety-nine beads, representing the ninety-nine names of Allah. As a Muslim fingers a bead, he or she calls to mind one of the names of Allah and meditates on it.

---

103 *Sahih Bukhari*, 50:894.
104 "Sahih Muslim," book 48, hadith 5, Sunnah.com, https://sunnah.com/muslim/48.

Based on these names, Muslim scholars derive thirteen divine attributes of Allah: he is eternal and exists without any beginning; he takes priority and is before anything else; he is eternal, unique, self-subsistent, and exists in unity, meaning there is only one god; he is omnipotent, he controls all things, he is omniscient, he is the source of life, he hears all things, he sees all things, and he communicates his will.

GOD IN THE ORDINARY LIFE OF MUSLIMS

Muslims prefer to see Allah in the way he is expressed in their ordinary lives. If Allah is real, he therefore must be worshiped and glorified, and all must surrender to him. Muslims constantly use phrases such as these: "There is no god but Allah"; "Allah is very great"; "Glory be to Allah"; "Praise be to Allah"; "If Allah wills"; "In the name of Allah, the merciful and compassionate." These daily expressions indicate how the Islamic understanding of Allah affects life in the world. Allah is the creator, sovereign ruler, defender and protector, merciful and almighty. He directs human beings, and humanity, in turn, surrenders to his will by obeying his rules as expressed in Sharia law.

Muslims do not spend time talking about the nature of Allah but rather about what Allah wants them to do. As a result, Islam places considerable emphasis on right and pious behaviors (orthopraxy), not right teachings about Allah's being (orthodoxy). The name of Allah is the first word whispered in the ear of a newborn baby, and it is the word recited at funeral processions. Thus, from birth to death, and in all that lies between them, Allah is incorporated into Muslim life.[105]

---

105 See Miller, *Muslim Friends*, 36; Roland Miller, *Muslims and the Gospel: Bridging the Gap* (Minneapolis: Lutheran University Press, 2005), 21–23.

QUESTIONS FOR DISCUSSION
CHAPTER 7

SEE ANSWER KEY ON PAGE 291.

QUESTION 1

What is the implication of Allah's unity on ordinary Muslims?

QUESTION 2

What parallels can we find in the Bible?

QUESTION 3

What connection can we make when the Quran says that Allah is "transcendent and merciful" and what the Bible says about God?

QUESTION 4

What does the Quran mean when it states that Allah is the creator and ruler of life, and what is its connection with the Bible?

QUESTION 5

What does the Quran mean when it states that Allah is the protector and defender, and what is its connection with the Bible?

QUESTION 6

How do Muslims use the names of Allah?

QUESTION 7

How do Muslims relate to Allah in their ordinary life?

CHAPTER 8

GOD IN MUSLIM-CHRISTIAN PERSPECTIVES

Is the god of Islam the same as the God of Christianity? Is the First Person of the Trinity, God, the Father of our Lord Jesus Christ, the same as the god of the Muslims? This question is hotly debated among Christians and Muslims.

For the sake of finding a common bridge in witness, I will tell a Muslim that Christians and Muslims believe in the same God, but then I carefully point out that the basic understanding of God in Islam and Christianity is radically different when it comes to the way God relates to humankind and the way humankind relates to God.

In what sense do Christian and Muslims believe in the same God? Both Christians and Muslims identify their God as the one and only Creator of the world. Both claim He is wholly good, all-powerful, and worthy of worship and obedience. Both Christians and Muslims disagree with atheists and agnostics because they believe God exists.

But there are stark differences that show the Christian God is different from the Muslim Allah. In the context of worship, Christians identify God as He is laid out in the creeds; they name God as "Father, Son, and Holy Spirit." The Church praises, prays to, and baptizes in the name of the triune God. These things constitute the identity of God in the Christian Church. Islam totally rejects these teachings. These differences are so wide and deep that it is natural to say, in this context, that Muslims and Christians do not worship the same God. In this chapter, we will look at these radical differences.

God's Name and Attributes

The Bible ascribes some of the same characteristics to God as does the Quran. God is omnipresent (1 Kings 8:27; Psalm 139:7–10), eternal (Habakkuk 1:12; Jeremiah 23:24); omniscient (Psalm 139; Psalm 147:5), and unchanging (Malachi 3:6; James 1:17). God is good (Psalm 145:9) and merciful (Exodus 34:6; Psalm 51:1; Micah 7:18). However, some attributes of Allah in the Quran are difficult to reconcile with Christian teachings. The Quran describes Allah as the "proud one" and "the one who leads astray," which is recorded twenty times in the Quran. He is the "avenger," "the abase," and the "one who harms." In the Quran, Allah "leads astray whomsoever He will" (Q 13:27; 14:4, 27), the "deceiver" or "misleader," and the best schemer (Q 4:143). If we look at the Bible, these attributes are analogous with those of Satan in the Book of Genesis! Allah is responsible for human disunity (Q 5:48), ignorance (Q 6:35), idolatry (Q 6:137), unbelief (Q 10:99), and even the sin of association, which is idolatry (Q 16:35–36).

The Islamic and Christian Foundations

Islamic teachings on the identity of Allah are concerned about what Allah does, not who Allah is. Islam teaches that Allah is free from personality, which is understood to be a quality of limitation and humiliation. Therefore, Allah's names and attributes expose what he does, what his will is, and how he relates to his creatures. Christian theology is radically different, as it is a systematic exposition of God's nature as well as His attributes. Christian theology tries to explain who God is by what God does.

Christians understand God in a paradoxical way, which Martin

Luther often referred to as the "hidden and revealed God." God is hidden because He is invisible, the unknowable God, and He transcends human understanding; however, in Christ, God reveals Himself to be known by humans.

Christianity does not see the cross as an instrument of torture, but rather the place where God brought life out of death. On the cross, human beings see clearly God's experience, His disposition, and the essence of His love. We also see what humanity is. The cross created a new reality within God's fallen creation. It was a new reality for Satan, when he watched God nail the accusations of the Law to the cross and render them illegible by soaking them in Christ's blood. It created a new reality for death when God laid it to eternal rest in Christ's grave. The cross created a new reality for sinners, since we were buried in Christ's tomb and raised to new life through the death and resurrection of the Crucified One.

Islam and Christianity both speak of God as merciful and forgiving; however, they mean different things by this attribute. In Christianity, the forgiveness that humanity receives is both the work of God and a revelation of His divine personality. In Islam, Allah is excluded from any participation in suffering. Christ's torment in Gethsemane (Matthew 26:36–42) and on Golgotha (Matthew 27:33–50) wins forgiveness for humanity through embracing anguish. It is in suffering that God expresses His nature as a loving God and participant within humanity. God, in the person of Christ, is active in the pain of the cross and the unconditional extent of His humanity. It is through His nature as *agape* love that God establishes a covenant of love between Himself and creation.

Christians believe that "God is love" (1 John 4:8). This statement is considered an obstacle and a path to Christian encounters with Muslims. In Christianity, the love of God is not an abstract concept but is instead a relational truth that has been communicated to humanity in Christ and delivered through the work of the Holy Spirit.

In Christianity, this divine love is the motive of revelation and the source of salvation. The Bible does not describe God as distant, remote, or indifferent; He is Immanuel, God with us.

THE DIFFERENCES BETWEEN LOVE AND AGAPE LOVE

Muslims often misunderstand the Christian concept of love due to the various ways the word *love* is used in English. In the Quran, a few verses mention the love of Allah, such as "And He is the Forgiving, the Loving" (Q 85:14; see also 11:90). More verses describe the love of humans for Allah (see Q 2:165; 3:31; 5:54). In Islam, the most important characteristic of Allah is his oneness and uniqueness. This means that love in Islam is understood in terms of the love of humanity for Allah, not the love of Allah for humankind. While the Muslim concept of love is defined by a longing for Allah and a desire to draw closer to him, it is devoid of any union of love between Allah and humankind. This belief is also why the concept of sin as separation from the love of Allah is totally alien to the Muslim mind.

The specific concept of love in Christianity is called *agape* love. *Agape* is a Greek word that refers to a universal, transcendent love—a love that will withstand all things for the sake of another. This is historically how the Christian Church has talked about God's love for humankind, especially as revealed through the person and work of Christ. John describes this love throughout his Gospel and Epistles.

> For God so loved the world, that He gave His only Son, that whoever believes in Him should not perish but have eternal life. (John 3:16)

> Having loved His own who were in the world, He loved them to the end. (John 13:1)

> Whoever loves has been born of God and knows God. Anyone

who does not love does not know God, because God is love.
(1 John 4:7–8)

Paul gives a beautiful description of this love in 1 Corinthians:

If I speak in the tongues of men and of angels, but have not love, I am a noisy gong or a clanging cymbal. And if I have prophetic powers, and understand all mysteries and all knowledge, and if I have all faith, so as to remove mountains, but have not love, I am nothing. If I give away all I have, and if I deliver up my body to be burned, but have not love, I gain nothing.

Love is patient and kind; love does not envy or boast; it is not arrogant or rude. It does not insist on its own way; it is not irritable or resentful; it does not rejoice at wrongdoing, but rejoices with the truth. Love bears all things, believes all things, hopes all things, endures all things.

Love never ends. As for prophecies, they will pass away; as for tongues, they will cease; as for knowledge, it will pass away. For we know in part and we prophesy in part, but when the perfect comes, the partial will pass away. When I was a child, I spoke like a child, I thought like a child, I reasoned like a child. When I became a man, I gave up childish ways. For now we see in a mirror dimly, but then face to face. Now I know in part; then I shall know fully, even as I have been fully known.

So now faith, hope, and love abide, these three; but the greatest of these is love. (1 Corinthians 13:1–13)

Agape love can be seen through the covenants God made with His people in the Old Testament, and it was articulated in the incarnation, death, and resurrection of Christ in the New Testament. Love is not merely an attribute of God; it is His essence. This loving God cannot be a solitary one; He always seeks communion with His creation in a loving relationship. In this way, the Christian God is fundamentally different from Islam's Allah, who is a distant deity that does not defile himself with creation. Like the Aristotelian god, the Islamic god is an "unmoved Mover," free from need, vulnerability, and passion.

God Reveals Himself as Agape Love

In Christianity, God reveals Himself as *agape* love, meaning that He allows Himself to suffer in the person of Christ. Jesus shares our human experience and participates in our sorrows as the Suffering Servant prophesied by Isaiah. Jesus embraced both the suffering and servant-hood concepts.

In Christianity, the incarnation is the ultimate fulfillment of divine love. In the Book of Genesis, we read about God asking Abraham to sacrifice his son Isaac. On one level, this story shows that the truest test of commitment is found in the willingness to give up that which is most loved. Yet, at a deeper level, the New Testament reveals that "God's love has been poured" (Romans 5:5) on creation, and He "did not spare His own Son but gave Him up for us all" (Romans 8:32). This love breaks into human life and opens the possibility of communion with God. Not only does God call humanity to love Him, but He also enables them with His invitation. He is the one who initiates and maintains it. This encounter engages God and humankind in a graceful embrace, where God, and only God, takes and maintains the initiative. Humanity, in turn, is to fear, love, and trust God. The encounter is like a vortex. Humanity is immersed in the vortex of divine love, driven by God alone. He first loved us with all His heart and soul through Christ, and then He commands us to love Him and our neighbor with all our hearts, minds, and souls (Matthew 22:37).

This intimacy between God and humanity is absent in the Quran. While the Quran contains descriptions of Allah as "the best of those who are merciful" (Q 23:109, 118), this does not suggest any manifestation of emotional involvement or vulnerability toward humanity. The

Allah of Islam cannot show any intimacy or vulnerability to humans. Exhibiting any of these sentiments would be a sign of weakness and not of divine power. Allah reveals his compassion and mercy to people, but he cannot feel anything in his divine essence beyond himself.

DIVINE NATURE EXPRESSED AS AGAPE LOVE

The Quran speaks about Allah as merciful, but it is an expression of his will. Language regarding love is absent in the ninety-nine names of Allah because it is not in his divine essence. In the Quran, Allah is "loving" and "merciful." The Quran and ordinary Muslims prefer to speak about Allah as "merciful," and this attribute appears over two hundred times in the Quran. However, Allah in the Quran only bestows his mercy on those who merit it (Q 4:97–100). Allah can decide to be clement (Q 10:107; 29:21) and grant mercy to whomever he pleases (Q 9:27). Allah is not obliged to love. He dispenses mercy to some and withholds it from others. Allah forgives sin conditionally: only to those who submit to him and obey his will. Therefore, his love cannot be defined as unconditional. He is "Kind unto His servants," but only "If you love God [Allah], follow me, and God will love you and forgive you your sins." Allah does not love those who reject Islam (Q 3:30–32, 45).

In Christianity, the *agape* love reveals the heart of God. It is the very essence of God, who gave Himself on the cross. Paul addressed this point in his Letter to the Ephesians. Paul uses similar language to what the Quran would later employ; however, Paul's message goes far beyond the image of Allah presented by Islam. Paul affirms that God loved us when we did not deserve His love and mercy:

> [We] were by nature children of wrath, like the rest of mankind. But God, being rich in mercy, because of the great love with which He loved us, even when we were dead in our trespasses, made us alive together with Christ—by grace you have been saved—and raised us up with Him and seated us with Him in the heavenly places in Christ Jesus. (Ephesians 2:3–6)

The Love of God for Sinners

This leads us to another point: the love God has for sinners. In Islam, Allah does not love sinners. This statement is repeated twenty-three times in the Quran. He does not love evildoers (Q 3:57) or the deceitful (Q 4:17). In other words, it would be inappropriate to represent Allah as a shepherd who would leave the ninety-nine to rescue one lost sheep (Luke 15:2–7), or as a father who would run to his rebellious son, throw his arms around him, and kiss him (Luke 15:20). It would be inconceivable for a Muslim to declare, "God shows His love for us in that while we were still sinners, Christ died for us" (Romans 5:8).

In summary, Islam preaches that Allah bestowed his mercy on humans by giving them his divine law. Humans, in turn, devotedly serve this divine law; it is not a question of love. The only love at stake is a sort of protective love, a love that when given protects Muslims from the wrath of Allah. A Muslim must merit the forgiveness of sins by his actions, and Allah still reserves the right to punish or save him as he wills. This is why it is so important to share the Good News of Christ's incarnation and sacrifice for us, which reveals that God is unconditional, unremitting love.

The Transcendence of God

Islamic theology also stresses the transcendence of Allah, which is closely related to Allah's unity. Allah's transcendence makes him radically different from all of creation. Allah cannot be touched in any way by humanity, and any compassion that Allah shows is not to be confused with human parallels that would humanize him. Nothing outside of what has been written in the Quran can be said about the god of Islam; even the words of the Quran do not describe him, because his essence is beyond description. Islam considers this distance a gift from Allah to protect humanity from idolatry.

We have seen that Allah is immanent in the life of Muslims. He is present at the heart of human life to maintain it and supply every moment of it. However, even though Allah's immanence is deep in Islam and can foster an extremely rich religious and spiritual life, Allah is still distant, known only by his actions. He reveals himself through the prophets and the Quran; he is not united with his people in a loving relationship. Islam cannot fathom the incarnation, the union of God and humanity in the person of Christ, because it believes in such a distant, remote god.

According to Islam, the mystery of Allah can never be revealed because his transcendence would not allow it. Christianity, by contrast, claims that God is not limited by His transcendence. He is not bound in a prison of indifference and remoteness. God initiates a covenant with humanity and is interested in individual people. He not only creates the world, but He also participates in it.

In the Book of Genesis, God, the architect of the universe, calls Adam and asks him, "Where are you?" (Genesis 3:9). God enters into covenants with His people, first with all humanity after the flood (Genesis 9:8–17), and then with Abraham individually (Genesis 15). This willingness and desire reaches its climax at the crucifixion of Christ, when He died not for Himself but for all humanity. The love of God bridges the gap that separates Creator from creation.

The idea of God's unity and transcendence is connected to God's holiness. In Christianity and Islam, holiness separates God from humanity. In Christianity, humans are rebellious; in Islam, humanity is unholy simply because they are not divine. The Bible emphasizes that apart from Christ, "man shall not see [God] and live" (Exodus 33:20; see also Isaiah 6:5; 1 Timothy 6:16). But in the incarnation, God in Christ has forever resolved the separation between sinful humans and the holy God.

Relating to the Transcendent and Holy God

In Islam, Allah's transcendent holiness makes him inaccessible, and there is no way that humans can ever be united with the divine.

How then does a Muslim relate to this transcendent and holy Allah? The answer is that a Muslim acknowledges Allah through submission. The extent of one's godliness and wisdom are measured according to his or her obedience. Muslims recite the confession of faith, or *Shahada*, "There is no god but Allah," in every call to prayer, as a response to Allah's invitation to submit to his sovereign will.

Christians also respond to God in submission and totally rely on His divine protection, but they do it in response to God's unconditional love for them, out of a desire for fellowship and communion with Him. John expressed it this way: "That which we have seen and heard we proclaim also to you, so that you too may have fellowship with us; and indeed our fellowship is with the Father and with His Son Jesus Christ" (1 John 1:3). In the Book of Revelation, Jesus calls humanity to fellowship with Him: "Behold, I stand at the door and knock. If anyone hears My voice and opens the door, I will come in to him and eat with him, and he with Me" (Revelation 3:20). God in Christ comes to humanity with an invitation and seeks a response.

This emphasis on our communion with God does not exclude His divine power. God is "the Lord of lords" (Psalm 136:3), the only Lord (1 Timothy 6:15). He is majestic in His power (Exodus 15:6) and saves by His power (Jeremiah 27:5). God has power over everything in the universe (Deuteronomy 8:18). The Bible declares that God is Almighty (*El-Shaddai*, Genesis 17:1). This term may be derived from the Hebrew word for "breast" or "bosom." If so, it evokes the image of a mother nursing her child and signifies that the power of God encompasses the ideas of nurture, security, and intimacy (Isaiah 49:14–15; 63:13).

The power seen in Christ is the power of love, which was most evident on the cross (John 3:16). The crucifixion unfolds the intention of God to conquer disobedient human will, sin, suffering, and death. The cross is the power of salvation because only God's love has the power to forgive and overlook the sins of humanity (see 1 Corinthians 1:18). Christianity maintains that the only solution to the problem of evil occurs when God comes among humanity. Only God could provide the holiness that He requires for an intimate relationship with Him.

The power of God in Christ establishes a covenant based on love, not force. Christ has been given "all authority in heaven and on earth" (Matthew 28:18), and He invites humanity to share in His dominion. This dominion was won by Christ, the servant who humbled Himself to the point of dying on the cross, for which He has been highly exalted (Philippians 2:8–10). Christ explains this idea when He calls Himself the Good Shepherd, who "lays down His life for the sheep" (John 10:11). He is the shepherd who leaves the ninety-nine sheep in search of the one, and when He finds it, He rejoices (Luke 15:5–6). Furthermore, in the parable of the prodigal son, Jesus compares God to the father who did not exercise force to restore his rebellious and sinful son but showed love and forgiveness, running up to him and embracing and kissing him (Luke 15:20).

THE FATHERHOOD OF GOD

As Christians, we confess that God is our Father. This belief has been misunderstood and misinterpreted by Islam since its beginning. The Quran clearly states that Allah cannot beget a son and that it is blasphemous to suggest he does (Q 19:35; 6:101; 2:116). For Muslims, addressing Allah as father, referring to Jesus as the son of Allah, or calling other humans the children of Allah is blasphemous.

When explaining to Muslims why God is our Father, it is important to distinguish the Christian understanding of God as Father from pagan religions and Christian heresies, specifically adoptionism. Pagan religions and Christian heresies were both common in Muhammad's lifetime and are referenced in the Quran. Adoptionism began around AD 190, when Theodotus of Byzantium began teaching that Jesus was a normal man whom God adopted into divine sonship because of his unusual virtue and holiness. This adoption was usually assumed to have taken place at Jesus' Baptism. The First Council of Nicaea (AD 325) condemned adoptionism as heresy because it contradicts the doctrine of the Trinity, which identifies Jesus as eternally God. Muslims need to understand that what the Quran rejects in these verses was also rejected by Christianity three centuries before Muhammad was born.

At Jesus' Baptism, God declared from heaven, "This is My beloved Son" (Matthew 17:5). When Christ is called the only Son of God, the Gospel used the Greek word *monogene*, which means "the only begotten of the Father." From its earliest days, the Church has interpreted this term as meaning that Jesus does not having a beginning in time. The term does not mean that God physically procreated and had a son.

When the Bible speaks of the son or children of God, these terms refer to the relationship of humble dependence and obedience to God. To be called a child of God means to be one who obeys God. This is also the language used in the New Testament to describe Christ's unique relationship as the one who is perfectly obedient to the Father.

In Romans 8, Paul speaks about our adoption by God the Father through the Holy Spirit. Since we are adopted into the family of God, we now have the right to call upon God directly as "Abba, Father" (see Romans 8:15). This right of sonship comes through faith, and the relationship of hostility that defined our relationship with God prior to the work of Christ has ended. This type of relationship is what John means when he calls us "children of God, . . . born, not of blood nor of the will of the flesh nor of the will of man, but of God" (John 1:12–13).

Our Christian relationship as children of God our Father has no parallel in Islam. Muslims never address Allah as "Father" or *Abba*, which means "daddy." In Islam, Allah is the Lord and addresses his creation as slaves. In Christianity, God is our Father and we are His children: the Father loves His child, and the child responds to this love with trust and obedience. John emphasizes this relationship in his first Epistle: "See what kind of love the Father has given to us, that we should be called children of God; and so we are" (1 John 3:1). Likewise, Paul shows the radical difference between slaves and children in how we are adopted into God's family through Christ:

> When we were children, [we] were enslaved to the elementary principles of the world. But when the fullness of time had come, God sent forth His Son, born of woman, born under the law, to redeem those who were under the law, so that we might receive adoption as sons. And because you are sons, God has sent the Spirit of His Son into our hearts, crying, "Abba! Father!" So you are no longer a slave, but a son, and if a son, then an heir through God. (Galatians 4:3–7)

Jesus Himself address us as friends, not servants:

> No longer do I call you servants, for the servant does not know what his master is doing; but I have called you friends, for all that I have heard from My Father I have made known to you. (John 15:15)

QUESTIONS FOR DISCUSSION
CHAPTER 8

SEE ANSWER KEY ON PAGE 291.

QUESTION 1

In what ways do Christians and Muslims speak differently about the names and attributes of God?

QUESTION 2

What is *agape* love? How does this term help us understand who God is?

QUESTION 3

In what ways do Muslims and Christians understand God's transcendence differently?

QUESTION 4

How would you explain that God is our Father to a Muslim friend?

CHAPTER 9

The Triune God in the Quran and in the Gospel

As Christians, we worship one triune God; the three persons of the Trinity—the Father, Son, and Holy Spirit—are not three gods, but one God. Islam, however, views the Christian trinitarian God as a form of polytheism. In fact, it falls under the category of association—believing that there are multiple gods alongside God—which is a form of unbelief and an unforgiveable sin. The Quran clearly condemns the Trinity and those who believe in it:

> O People of the Book! Do not exaggerate in your religion, nor utter anything concerning God [Allah] save the truth. Verily the Messiah, Jesus son of Mary, was only a messenger of God [Allah], and His Word, which He committed to Mary, and a Spirit from Him. So believe in God [Allah] and His messengers, and say not "Three." Refrain! It is better for you. God [Allah] is only one God; Glory be to Him that He should have a child. (Quran 4:171)

Misunderstandings and Poor Explanations

When Muslims hear Christians speaking about the Father, the Son, and the Spirit, they think Christians are talking about three separate gods. The Arabic word for "person," *shakhs*, expresses the idea of "a visible shape." Furthermore, the Quran erroneously refers to the Trinity, or "Triad" (*thalatha*) as consisting of Allah, Jesus, and Mary (Q 5:73, 116).

The Context of the Islamic Rejection

When we examine the verses, we see that the Quran is not talking about the Christian concept of Trinity as it is taught by mainstream Christian teaching. The Quran condemns a heretical form of the Trinity that was popular in Arabia before the introduction of Islam, known as Collyridianism (also spelled *Kollyridianism*). Adherents of this heresy worshiped Mary, the mother of Jesus, as a goddess; their name comes from Arabian women who sacrificed small cakes—in Greek *collyris*—to Mary.

When Islam appeared in the seventh century, Muslims confronted the remaining Collyridianists.[106] A closer look at the verses in the Quran that condemn the doctrine of the Trinity confirms this:

> Then God [Allah] will say: "O Jesus son of Mary! Didst thou say unto mankind, 'Take me and my mother as gods apart from God [Allah]?" (Q 5:116)
>
> The Unique Originator of the heavens and the earth! How should He have a child when he has no consort? (Q 6:101)
>
> Say, "He, God [Allah], is One, God, the Eternally Sufficient unto Himself. He begets not; nor was He begotten. And none is like unto Him. (Q 112:1–4)

It is clear from these verses that the Quran is reacting against the Collyridianists, who taught that Mary was a goddess who became God's

---

106 See C. Jonn Block, *The Qur'an in Christian-Muslim Dialogue*, 186.

wife and had a marital relationship that resulted in a son, Jesus. When we speak to Muslims, we can say that we also condemn this heresy, as the Christian Church has since AD 431.

Talking to Muslims about the Trinity

How can we present the doctrine of the Holy Trinity to Muslims? We need to emphasize that Christians believe that God is one. In the Nicene Creed, we say, "I believe in one God." We confess that God is one in essence, which we know from how the Bible speaks about God. Jesus commanded His disciples to "go therefore and make disciples of all nations, baptizing them in *the name* [not names!] of the Father and of the Son and of the Holy Spirit" (Matthew 28:19, emphasis added).

To use a metaphor that Muslims can understand, we can speak about the one God who subsists in three way of existing. First, the one God, creator of all living things, must have personal, eternal existence in Himself. Second, the one God must Himself speak the Word, because He created humanity with the ability to speak. Third, the one God, who breathed life into every living being, must Himself be alive in the Spirit. In presenting the doctrine of the Trinity in this way, we are using language used by the Quran that is familiar to Muslims. In 4:171, the Quran says, "Jesus son of Mary, was only a messenger of God [Allah], and His Word, which He committed to Mary, and a Spirit from Him." And in 3:45, we read, "When the angels said, 'O Mary, truly God [Allah] gives thee glad tidings of a Word from Him, whose name is the Messiah, Jesus son of Mary.'"

Looking at these verses, we see the three points discussed above: the personal existence of God (God the Father); a God who speaks, a word from Him (God the Son, Jesus), and a God who is alive in His spirit (God the Holy Spirit). We can further share that these verses talk about Jesus, the Word of God, and His Spirit. We can then explain that we will never understand a person without his or her word. The honor of a person is to keep his or her word, and we cannot separate the word from the person. The words reflect the personality and the essence of that individual. The Word of God is God.

Learning from the Church Fathers

Some analogies used by Church Fathers in the Arabic Church will help us to talk about the Trinity.[107]

The Sun: the disk, the light and the heat:

As the sun has its *cause*, which is its disk, and its *effects*, which are its light and its heat with which it reaches the creation under it, likewise we can say about God the Almighty that the principle and cause is one, but the effects are two. God is the cause and the effects are two, His Word and His Spirit. As we cannot say that the sun, with its light and heat, is three suns, likewise we cannot say that God the Father, with His Word and Spirit, are three gods.

The sun, with its heat and light, warms up and enlightens the creatures under it. The two features (heat and light) are never separated from the sun, and everybody benefits from them according to their predisposition, yet the heat and the light are never changed or diminished. Likewise, the mind of our Creator provides growth and life to everyone and enlightens, by the light of His knowledge, all humanity according to their predisposition. In doing this, nothing decreases from God, neither His living power provided for the physical bodies, nor His radiant light that enlightens the minds of humans.

The man: mind, word, and spirit:

As from the mind, word and spirit come, the mind being the cause and the principle of the word and the spirit that are never separate from a man, likewise God has a Word and a Spirit, He is their principle, and from Him they occur. The Word, which is the Son, is featured in the form of generation, and the Spirit is featured in the form of procession. They are eternal and are never separate from Him. Thus, just as we can-

---

107 See Abjar Bahkou, *Defending Christian Faith*, 28–40.

not say that mind, word, and spirit are three minds, or three separate persons, likewise, we cannot say that God the Father, the Word, and the Spirit are three gods.

The passersby and the vineyard:

If we pass by a vineyard, and we see it drilled, fenced, and planted, we realize without a doubt that a person had such an effect on it. Yet we do not know whether this was one person or more than one because what we see could have happened in either of the two ways.

Three lamps in one house and three men chanting one psalm:

It is like three lamps, or three lights, lit in one house, and every one of them is filling the house with its light. It would not be possible for anyone to differentiate the light of the one from the others and say, "I saw three lights in the house." Rather, [the person would say,] "I saw one light." Or, if a man hears three persons chanting one psalm, it would not be possible to say, "I listened to three psalms." He would have to say, "I heard one psalm, chanted by three persons."

Explaining the Names of the Trinity

We have learned that when Muslims hear us speak about the Father and the Son, they think about the biological relationship between fathers and sons and the physical relationships between men and women that result in children. So how do we explain God the Father and God the Son?

God the Father

God's title as Father has four different meanings. It has a metaphorical meaning: He is the source and the Creator of all creatures. Thus, He is called the Father of all creatures. The term also has a legal meaning: through adoption, God has accepted us as His children and given us all the rights of children. It has an essential meaning: as a word bursts from the mouth, the Son emanated from the Father before ages; the Word is from His essence. Lastly, it has a spiritual meaning: we are all reborn in the spiritual birth of faith and Baptism.

God the Son

In many linguistic expressions, the word *son* is often used in situations in which it does not indicate physical generation. We can think of students as sons of knowledge, citizens as sons of the homeland, an Egyptian as a son of the Nile, and an Arabic person as a son of the desert. The Arabic language uses metaphorical language to talk about the word that comes from one's mouth, *Bint al-Shafa*, which literally means "the daughter of the lips." Even the Quran uses the word *son* in a metaphorical sense. The Quran instructs Muslims to give alms to the traveler, in Arabic *al-sabil*, which literally means the "son of the road" (Q 2:214). In the hadith, the poor are referred to as members of Allah's family, literally "my sons."

Conclusion: By the Power of God, Not by the Wisdom of Men

The last point we must consider is that when we explain this mystery to Muslims, we should not rely on the wisdom of the world but on the power of God. These techniques for explaining the Trinity to Muslims, regardless of how much studying you do or how eloquent your speech, mean nothing unless we rely on the power of God. When the Church Fathers talked about the Trinity and Christ's coexistence with the Father from eternity, they stated that our minds cannot fathom these ideas; thus, it "must be honored by silence"! "How was He begotten? I repeat the question in indignation. The Begetting of God must be honored by silence."[108] We need to silence our intellectual human mind and ask the Holy Spirit to speak to our hearts and minds as well as the hearts and minds of our Muslim friends.

When we explain the Trinity, we resort to human language and

---

108   Cappadocian Fathers (fourth century); later this quote was used by Arab Christians to talk about the doctrine of the Trinity.

analogies. Ultimately, however, there is no way to think or speak about the relationship of God the Father and Jesus Christ, His Son, other than saying that the Son was begotten from the Father from eternity. Everything else is speculation, and all metaphors break down.

Additionally, we must "pursue righteousness, faith, love, and peace" (2 Timothy 2:22) before entering into theological discussions; in doing so, we can avoid being quarrelsome, patiently correct our Muslim brothers and sisters, and pray that God may lead them to repentance and knowledge of the truth (see 2 Timothy 2:22–25). From this faith and righteousness, God will give us the power to witness to people who are seeking the truth of God. It is only by the power of God that people are repentant and are led to the knowledge of the truth. The apostle Paul himself said that faith rests not "in the wisdom of men but in the power of God" (1 Corinthians 2:5).

Finally, it is more important to pray that the Holy Spirit would work in your Muslim friends than that your arguments would convince them. When God draws people to faith by the power of His grace working through the Word, those people no longer need evidence or logic. Since the testimony is now in their hearts, they have realized that God lives with them and has changed them. They no longer search for God outside of themselves but in Christ their Savior.

I once saw a program on a Christian television channel about the concept of monotheism in Islam. The presenter was a former Muslim from Morocco, who for the previous four years had been presenting a program in Arabic called *Daring Questions*. A man from France called him and said he was a forty-year-old lifelong Muslim. "If I decide to become Christian right now," he asked, "who can guarantee me that in five or ten years some other religion wouldn't be stronger and convince me to change my mind?" The presenter told him, "No one can guarantee such a thing, because coming to Christ and confessing Him as Lord and Savior is not based on intellectual work but on the light of faith that shines in your heart." This is what Paul explained in his second letter to the Church at Corinth:

> For what we proclaim is not ourselves, but Jesus Christ as Lord, with ourselves as your servants for Jesus' sake. For God, who said, "Let light shine out of darkness," has shone in our hearts to give the light of the knowledge of the glory of God in the face of Jesus Christ. (2 Corinthians 4:5–6)

QUESTIONS FOR DISCUSSION
CHAPTER 9

SEE ANSWER KEY ON PAGE 291.

QUESTION 1
What does Islam misunderstand about the doctrine of the Trinity? How does Christianity also reject those misunderstandings?

QUESTION 2
How could you explain the doctrine of the Trinity to a Muslim?

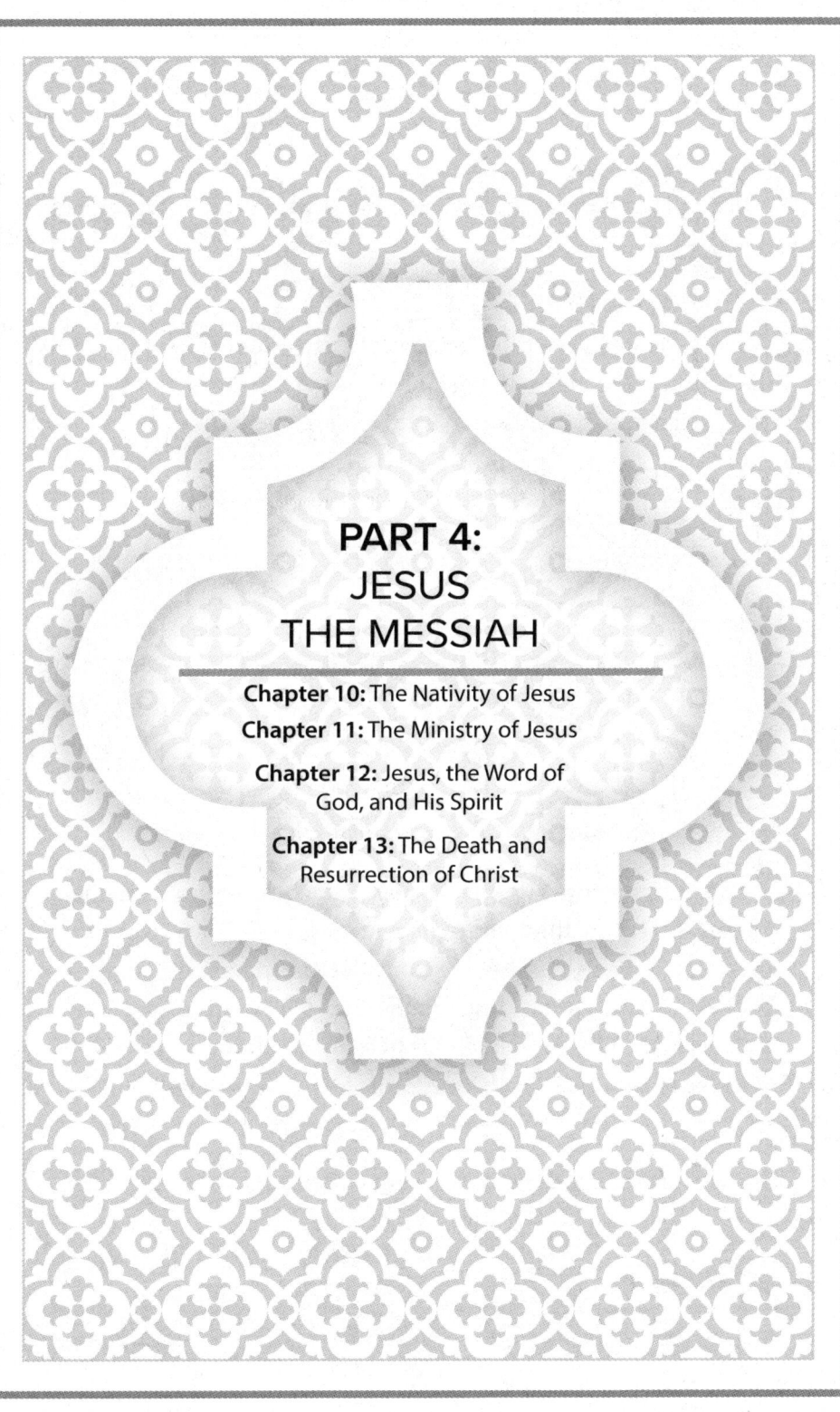

PART 4: JESUS THE MESSIAH

Chapter 10: The Nativity of Jesus

Chapter 11: The Ministry of Jesus

Chapter 12: Jesus, the Word of God, and His Spirit

Chapter 13: The Death and Resurrection of Christ

JESUS THE MESSIAH

Jesus is mentioned by name in 93 verses and 15 surahs in the Quran. The most important ones are 19:16–34; 3:43–49. The Quran uses the following titles to describe Jesus:

- Christ, *Al-Messih* (11 times)
- Prophet, *Nabi* (Q 19:30)
- Messenger, *Rasul* (Q 4:156, 171; 5:78)
- Isa, son of Mary (16 times)
- Son of Mary (17 times)
- Privileged and Nearest to Allah, *Muqarab wa wajih* (Q 3:45)
- Blessed, *Mubarak* (Mariam 19:31)
- The Statement of Truth, *Qaul al-Haq* (Mariam 19:34)

In this section, we will discuss the story of Jesus in the Quran, the titles the Quran gives to Jesus, and how Muslim theologians view Jesus. We'll consider the major differences between the Islamic Jesus and the Christian Jesus, the sources of the Quran's depictions of Jesus, and how we can build a bridge to our Muslim friends to share Christ with them.

CHAPTER 10

The Nativity of Jesus

The story of Jesus' nativity in the Quran begins with the account of Mary. She is the only woman called by her proper name in the Quran. Other women are mentioned but not named: for example, the wives of Noah, Lot, Pharaoh (Q 66:10–12), Imran (Q 3:35), and Zechariah (Q 3:36) as well as the Queen of Sheba (Q 27:22). Most of these women are also unnamed in the Bible. A whole chapter in the Quran is named after Mary. Mary is highly praised; Allah has chosen her, purified her, and placed her above all other women (see Quran 3:42). Among Sufis, which is the mystic branch of Islam, Mary is considered as an example of perfect devotion to Allah. A prominent Muslim mystic order called the *Maryamiyya*, or the Followers of Mary, was established in the twentieth century and seeks to follow Mary's example.[109]

Mary is important in both the Quran and the Bible because she is the mother of Jesus. She has no role to play apart from that, and in both scriptures, Mary humbly accepts the part Allah has assigned to her: consider "prostrate, and bow with those who bow" (Q 3:38–43), and "Behold, I am the servant of the Lord; let it be to me according to Your word" (Luke 1:38).

---

109 For more detailed information about this group, see Mark Sedgwick, *Against the Modern World: Traditionalism and the Secret Intellectual History of the Twentieth Century* (Oxford: Oxford University Press, 2009), 147–60.

This submission and surrender to the will of God is fundamental to both Islam and Christianity, and it is the key to understanding some of its deepest mysteries.[110]

For Muslims, Mary and Jesus are "a sign for the worlds" (Q 21:91; 23:50) because Jesus was born of a virgin. She "was truthful" (Q 5:75). Islamic tradition has valued the purity of Mary. Early Muslim commentators described her as "the virgin, the good, the pure."[111] Later, Islam regarded Mary as sinless and in the company of the prophets. According to tradition, Muhammad said that Jesus and Mary were the only people born without sin.

The Account of Mary

The story of Mary begins in surah 3:35–37. Her mother could not conceive, and she prayed to Allah to give her a child, which she vowed to dedicate to the service of the Lord. Many scholars see a parallel with the story of Samuel in the Old Testament (1 Samuel 1). Mary's mother was surprised when she had a girl, since only males could be dedicated to the temple, so she cried, "My Lord, I have borne a female" (Q 3:36). But then she proclaimed her trust in Allah, who "knows best what she bore, and the male is not like the female" (Q 3:36).

Her mother named her Mary and commended her and her offspring to the protection of the Lord from Satan (Q 3:36). Mary entered into the service of the Lord, who placed her under the care of Zechariah (see Q 3:37).

Zechariah and John

The Quran immediately shifts to the story of Zechariah and John; this story is recorded in surahs 3 and 19. As in the Gospel narrative, Zechariah and his wife were childless and in their old age; Zechariah prayed to Allah to give him a child, and Allah fulfilled his request. The angel of

---
110 See Geoffrey Parrinder, *Jesus in the Qur'an* (London: Faber & Faber, 1965), 61–62.
111 Ibn Ishaq, *Sirat Rasul Allah*, 657.

the Lord came to announce the good news to Zechariah, who did not believe and asked for a sign. The angel replied, "Your sign is that you shall not speak to the people for three days" (Q 3:41).

Surah 3 gives a short description of John and his mission. He is "confirming a word from God [Allah], noble and chaste, a prophet, from among the righteous" (Q 3:39). In surah 19, the Quran explains that his name is "John; We have not given this as a name to any before him" (Q 19:7). This parallels the biblical story in Luke 1:61, when Zechariah wrote that his name shall be called John, and the people were confused because no one in his family had that name. Surah 19:12–16 speaks about the character of John:

> O John! Take the Book with strength! And We gave him judgment as a child, and tenderness from Our Presence, and purity; and he was reverent, and dutiful toward his parents. He was not domineering, rebellious. Peace be upon him the day he was born, and the day he dies, and the day he is raised alive.

John is shown to be a prophet in three ways: first, he comes with a book, which commentators say is the Torah, for John's mission was to confirm the word of Allah (see Q 3:39). Allah granted John the wisdom to understand the Torah since his childhood. Second, he is "one of the upright," like Jesus (see Q 3:39; 6:85). Third, he is an abstinent prophet; this description parallels the Gospel: "he must not drink wine or strong drink" (Luke 1:15). The Quran even invokes peace upon his birth, death, and resurrection in terms closely related to Jesus.

The title of *Baptist* given to John in the Gospel and the concept of Baptism does not exist in the Quran. No mention is made of John's death at the hand of Herod. Outside of the Quran, there are various Islamic stories and legends about John. Some claim that John was the first to believe in Jesus, which could be a parallel to the Gospel of John, when John declared that Jesus was the Lamb of God (John 1:29).

In summary, it is clear that the version of John the Baptist in the Quran is influenced by the Christian tradition. According to the Quran, a chain of prophets carries a mission to uphold the revealed word of Allah.[112]

THE SOURCES OF THE QURAN'S NARRATIVE

The Quran contains stories about Mary that are not found in the New Testament. These stories are recorded in the apocryphal Infancy Gospel of James, which is considered one of the oldest Christian apocryphal books.[113] Scholars have established that the Infancy Gospel of James, which is different from the Epistle of James in the New Testament, was written in Greek in the middle of the second century. It was erroneously attributed to James, the brother of Jesus, the leader of the Jerusalem Church. This book is also called the *Protoevangelium,* which means "pre-gospel," because it contains details of the birth and upbringing of Mary and the delivery of Jesus, before the main events of the four Gospels.

Western Christianity was not familiar with this book until the sixteenth century, but the book has been accepted among Eastern Christians since the fifth century, when it was translated from Greek to Syriac. In the Protoevangelium, we learn about Mary's parents, Joachim and Anna, who were childless. Anna promised that "if I beget either male or female, I will bring it as a gift to the Lord my God." This account is similar to the one in the Quran (see Q 3:35). In both texts, it is the mother who names the child, not the father.

When she was three years old, Mary was taken to the temple, where Zechariah was priest. According to the Gospel of James, Mary "was in the temple as if she were a dove that dwelt there, and she received food from the hand of an angel."[114] The Quran relates a similar sentiment in a dialogue between Mary and Zechariah (see Q 3:38). When Mary came of age, Zechariah gathered the widowers of Israel, who drew lots to

---

112 See Mustafa Akyol, *The Islamic Jesus* (New York: St. Martin's Press, 2017), 107.
113 "Infancy Gospel of James," Early Christian Writings, http://www.earlychristianwritings.com/infancy-james.html.
114 "Infancy Gospel of James," Early Christian Writings.

decide who would be the husband of Mary. Joseph, who was on old man, was chosen and took Mary home.

The Annunciation

In the Quran, the story of the annunciation begins with Mary withdrawing to the East. While she was in hiding there, the angel of the Lord appeared to her to announce the birth of Christ:

> When the angels said, "O Mary, truly God [Allah] give thee glad tidings of a Word from Him, whose name is Messiah, Jesus son of Mary, high honored in this world and the Hereafter, and one of those brought nigh [to Allah]. He will speak to people in the cradle and in maturity, and will be among the righteous." She [Mary] said: "My Lord, how shall I have a child while no human being has touched me?" He said, "Thus does God [Allah] create whatsoever He will." When he decrees a thing, He only says to it, "Be!" and it is." (Quran 3:45–47)

The New Testament contains no text parallel to these verses. It is worth noting that the Quran does confirm the virginity of Mary here and elsewhere (Q 21:91; 66:12). However, there are differences between the Bible and the Quran. We read in the Gospel of Luke, "Mary said to the angel, 'How will this be, since I am a virgin?' And the angel answered her, 'The Holy Spirit will come upon you, and the power of the Most High will overshadow you'" (Luke 1:34–35). In the Quran, the angel makes no mention of the Holy Spirit, or "the power of Most High." Allah sent to Mary his spirit, and he assumed the likeness of a perfect man (see Quran 19:17). He then breathed into her "from his spirit" or "his spirit." Many commentaries on the Quran claim Gabriel is the Holy Spirit. Muslim exegesis interprets the verse as Gabriel breathing into Mary's bosom until the spirit reached her womb or that Gabriel blew into the sleeve of Mary and the side of her chemise.[115]

---
115 *The Study Quran*, 768–69.

The Quran says that Allah "strengthened him [Jesus] with the Holy Spirit" (Q 2:87, 253; 5:110). Elsewhere, the Quran speaks of "the Holy Spirit has brought it down [the book] from thy Lord in truth, to make firm those who believe, and as guidance and glad tiding for those who submit" (Q 16:102). What we notice in these verses is that the Quran never says that the Holy Spirit is the angel Gabriel. The idea is found in the commentaries. Some of them give different interpretations: for example, that "the Holy Spirit" is "a name by which Jesus revived the dead or that it refers to the Gospel itself."[116] These interpretations are based on the Islamic rejection of the mystery of the Holy Trinity. The Holy Spirit as the Spirit of God and the Third Person of the Trinity is emphatically rejected in Islam.

Mary in the Wilderness

After the annunciation, the Quran reports that Mary moved to a distant place. She is an unmarried girl who is about to give birth, alone, in pain, thirsty and hungry. The Quran has Mary giving birth in the wilderness, not in Bethlehem. She is afraid to go and face her people, so she cries to the Lord; the Lord comforts her and miraculously provides food for her, as a stream wells up and fresh dates fall off a date palm to feed her in her hunger (see Quran 19:22–26). This story has parallels with the story of Hagar, who was also pregnant in the wilderness. As with Mary, the Lord appears to Hagar to provide for and comfort her (see Genesis 16:7–14). The story originates in the apocryphal Gospel of Pseudo-Matthew, also known as the Infancy Gospel of Matthew, a Latin writing perhaps compiled in the eighth century.[117] In the text, the miracle is performed by the newborn Christ, who commands a palm tree to bend down and a spring to well up for Mary. A similar story appears in another apocryphal book, the Arabic Infancy Gospel. This text locates the miracle under a sycamore tree at Mataria. The sycamore at Mataria was in Heliopolis (present-day Cairo), Egypt, and it is one of the four

---

116   *The Study Quran*, 42.
117   "The Gospel of Pseudo-Matthew," The Gnostic Society Library, http://www.gnosis.org/library/psudo-mat.htm.

sites of the flight to Egypt venerated by Muslims and Christians.[118]

One theory, called the Kathisma Theory, attempts to reconcile the differences between this legend in Christian apocryphal sources and the Quran. This theory was developed by Stephen Shoemaker.[119] In 1992, the Israeli authorities discovered a Byzantine church on the side of the road between Bethlehem and Jerusalem. The church was called *Kathisma of Theotokos*, or *Seat of the God-bearer*, the title given to Mary by the Eastern Church. According to legend, Mary rested on a rock located between Bethlehem and Jerusalem during the flight to Egypt. Gradually, the rock became a place of Christian pilgrims, and a church was built on top of it in the fifth century. The church was built as a model of the Dome of Rock and was used as a Marian shrine. It was once believed to be the site where Jesus was born, but when Bethlehem was established as the birthplace of Jesus, the significance of this location was reinterpreted, and it became a shrine of Mary's resting place.

The floor of the Kathisma church has beautiful mosaics of a large date palm, flanked by two smaller palms, all of which are laden with dates. Shoemaker believes that this is almost certainly a representation of the date palm from which Mary was miraculously fed. Thus, in the Kathisma church, we see elements of the story found in both the Quran and the Gospel of Pseudo-Matthew.

Additionally, it is possible that the Quran places the spot of Jesus' birth in the wilderness rather than in Bethlehem because the Protoevangelium makes the same mistake, reporting that Mary gave birth in a cave on the side of the road somewhere between Jerusalem and Bethlehem—which is the exact location of the Kathisma church. Shoemaker concludes that it is possible that the writer of the Quran has been

---

118   "The Arabic Infancy Gospel of the Savior," Gnostic Society Library, http://gnosis.org/library/infarab.htm.

119   See Stephen J. Shoemaker, "Christmas in the Qur'an: The Qur'anic Account of Jesus' Nativity and Palestinian Local Tradition," *Jerusalem Studies in Arabic and Islam* (January 1, 2003), http://almuslih.com/Library/Shoemaker,%20S%20%20Christmas%20in%20the%20Qur%E2%80%99%C4%81n.pdf. Shoemaker developed his research in Jerusalem while he was a fellow at the W. F. Albright Institute for Archaeological Research, with the National Endowment for the Humanities research in Jerusalem with a fellowship during the years 1999–2000. His research was presented at the 2002 Pacific Northwest Regional Meeting of the American Academy of Religion, Eugene, Oregon, and the 2002 Annual Meeting of the AAR, Toronto.

influenced by the popular Palestinian traditions surrounding the Kathisma church.

Mary Returns to Her People

After Mary gave birth, she returned to town and faced her people. In the New Testament, God protected Mary from being punished by sending the angel Gabriel to instruct Joseph in a dream to honor his betrothal to Mary. Gabriel tells Joseph not to fear:

> That which is conceived in her is from the Holy Spirit. She will bear a son, and you shall call His name Jesus, for He will save His people from their sins. (Matthew 1:20–21)

Joseph and his connection with Mary and Jesus are absent from the Quran. The Quran's narrative presents Mary as a single mother who trusts Allah to guide and protect her in these challenging circumstances. In the Quran, the Lord commanded Mary not to speak to anyone when asked about the child (see Q 19:26). When asked, she would simply point to the child in the cradle, and Jesus spoke on her behalf and announced his mission:

> Then [Mary] pointed to him. They said, "How shall we speak to one who is yet a child in the cradle?" He [the child] said, "Truly I am a servant of God [Allah]. He has given me the Book and made me a prophet. He has made me blessed wheresoever I may be, and has enjoined [directed] upon me prayer and almsgiving so long as I live, and [has made me] dutiful toward my mother. And He has not made me domineering, wretched [insolent or arrogant]. Peace upon me the day I was born, the day I die, and the day I am raised alive!" (Q 19:29–33)

The story of Jesus speaking from the cradle was interpreted as a miracle given by Allah to Jesus to defend his mother and preach to

The Nativity of Jesus

unbelieving audiences. Some scholars and commentators have hypothesized that this story is connected to the incident in the New Testament in which Jesus, as a child, disputed with the leaders in the temple (Luke 2:46–49).[120]

The story of Jesus speaking from the cradle is also found in the Arabic Infancy Gospel, an apocryphal Christian book believed to be a seventh-century invention that was popular among Syrian Nestorians. The book is in the same genre as the Protoevangelium of James and the Gospel of Pseudo-Matthew, and it heavily borrowed from them. The book focuses on the childhood of Jesus and the many miracles he performed in his infancy, including Jesus speaking from the cradle, telling his mother that he is the Son of God, the *Logos*, sent for the salvation of the world.[121]

The versions of these infancy miracles are different in the Arabic Infancy Gospel and the Quran. In the Arabic Infancy Gospel, Jesus speaks to his mother, while in the Quran, Jesus speaks to the Jews who questioned the chastity of his mother. In the Arabic Infancy Gospel, Jesus says, "I am the Son of God, the *Logos*," while in the Quran, he says, "I am a servant of God [Allah]. . . . He made me a prophet" (Q 19:30). These differences reflect their respective Christologies.

The Quran's version of the story of Jesus' birth ends in a resounding statement against the Christian belief that Jesus is the son of Allah:

> That is Jesus son of Mary—a *statement of the truth*, which they doubt. It is not for God [Allah] to take a child. Glory be to Him! When he decrees a thing, he only says to it, "Be!" and it is. (Q 19:34–35, emphasis added)

Some Muslim commentators interpret this as a statement from Jesus meant to clear up any confusion about his identity. According to Muslims, the real account of Jesus is found in the Quran. It opposes

---

120 Yusuf Ali, trans. *The Holy Qur'an: Text, Translation, and Commentary*, vol. 1 (New York: Hafner Publishing Company), 775; Parrinder, *Jesus in the Qur'an*, 79.
121 Arabic Infancy Gospel, Early Christian Writings, http://www.earlychristianwritings.com/infancyjames.html.

the Jewish account, which rejected his prophethood, and the Christian account, which made him divine.[122] Thus, while the Quran does acknowledge the miraculous virgin birth of Jesus, it does not go far enough: Muslims fail to recognize the incarnation and divinity of Christ, which results in their rejection of Christ—and their need to hear the true Gospel.

---

122 *The Study Quran*, 773.

QUESTIONS FOR DISCUSSION
CHAPTER 10

SEE ANSWER KEY ON PAGE 291.

QUESTION 1

What are the similarities and differences in the accounts of the birth of Christ between the Quran and the New Testament?

QUESTION 2

How might these differences stand in the way of witness to Muslims? How can we share our faith with a Muslim as we speak of Mary and the birth of Jesus?

CHAPTER 11

THE MINISTRY OF JESUS

The hadith claims that Allah sent twenty-four thousand prophets to humans. The Quran names some of them; the rest are unknown. Allah elevated a few of them in rank, including Jesus and his mother, Mary. "We have favored some above others. Among them are those to whom God [Allah] spoke, and some He raised up in ranks. And We gave Jesus son of Mary clear proofs and strengthened him with the Holy Spirit" (Quran 2:253).The Quran gives Jesus many special titles, including one that has a deep connection with the Bible: *al-Massih*, the Messiah. Jesus is called the Messiah eleven times in ten verses in the Quran (see Q 3:45; 4:157, 171–172; 5:17, 19; 5:72, 75; 9:30–31).

THE MEANING OF *MESSIAH*

The term *Messiah* is a Jewish theological term. The Hebrew word *mashiach* is found in its verb form sixty-nine times in the Old Testament; as a verb, it means "to anoint," usually with oil. In the Septuagint, the Greek translation of the Old Testament, *mashiach* was translated as *christos* (from the verb *chrio*, which also means "to anoint"). *Christ* and *Messiah*, therefore, are interchangeable terms in English. In the Old Testament, people were anointed in order to be set apart for a special purpose, such as being a king, priest, or prophet.

The prophets foresaw a divine person who would come to earth in human form (Psalm 110:1; Isaiah 7:14), and God's promised deliverer was to be known as the Messiah. He would be the one the prophet Daniel declared as the coming prince, the Messiah (Daniel 9:26). He would be much more than a prophet; He would be a divine king whose rule would be eternal (Micah 5:2). Isaiah foretold that the Messiah would be God among humanity (Isaiah 9:6–7), the Servant of the Lord who would bear the infirmities of humanity (Isaiah 52:13–53:12).

THE ISLAMIC INTERPRETATION

Despite its occurrences, the title is never explained in the Quran. Muslim exegetes gave various interpretations to its meanings; some of them are close to the Christian and Jewish ones, while some of them contradict even the Islamic teachings about Jesus. Some have claimed that the term derives from the Arabic verb *mūsīha*, which means "to be wiped off," meaning that Allah has "wiped off" or wiped away the sins of Jesus. This contradicts the saying, believed to be from Muhammad himself, that Jesus and Mary were born sinless, which would preclude a need for God to wipe off any sin from Jesus.

Others claim that it refers generally to Jesus being "anointed" with a special blessing (*mūsīha bī al-Baraka*).[123] Still others say that the term derives from the Arabic verb *massa*, which means "to touch." Proponents of this theory say that Jesus' touch purified others from fault, or that he blessed others with his touch.[124] However, this explanation draws on a linguistic mistake, as this word has no etymological connection with the title of *Messiah*. Instead, this interpretation could be drawing from the Quran's accounts of Jesus healing the sick, blind, leprous, and raising the dead (see Q 3:49; 5:110). Jesus healed people and brought the dead back to life by touching them.

This last explanation has similarities with the Gospel, when Jesus preached in the synagogue in Nazareth:

---

123 Geoffrey Parrinder, *Jesus in the Qur'an*, 18.
124 Geoffrey Parrinder, *Jesus in the Qur'an*, 19.

"The Spirit of the Lord is upon Me, because He has anointed Me to proclaim good news to the poor. He has sent Me to proclaim liberty to the captives and recovering of sight to the blind, to set at liberty those who are oppressed, to proclaim the year of the Lord's favor." And He rolled up the scroll and gave it back to the attendant and sat down. And the eyes of all in the synagogue were fixed on Him. And He began to say to them, "Today this Scripture has been fulfilled in your hearing." (Luke 4:16–21)

Likewise, when the disciples of John the Baptist asked Jesus if He was "the one who is to come," (see Luke 7:18–23), Jesus replied:

Go and tell John what you have seen and heard: the blind receive their sight, the lame walk, lepers are cleansed, and the deaf hear, the dead are raised up, the poor have good news preached to them. And blessed is the one who is not offended by Me. (vv. 22–23)

THE MESSIAH'S MISSION

In the Quran, the Messiah came to accomplish a mission. First, he brought the message of Allah to the children of Israel in order to reform Judaism. Jesus said to the Jews:

[I come] confirming that which was before me, the Torah, and to make lawful unto you part of that which was forbidden unto you. And I have come to you with a sign for your Lord. So reverence God [Allah] and obey me. Truly God [Allah] is my Lord and your Lord; so worship Him. This is a straight path. (Q 3:50–51)

The words "my Lord and your Lord," which are quoted four times in three hadiths in the Quran (Q 3:51; 5:72, 117), parallel Jesus' words, "My God and your God" (John 20:17); however, commentators see this statement as a confirmation of Jesus' servanthood.

Second, Jesus the Messiah came to clarify religious disputes among the Jews and reveal his true identity to Christians, who also disputed among themselves about him; he came to bring wisdom to clarify their differences (see Q 19:37; 43:63). Third, Allah gave Jesus clear signs to confirm him as his prophet and messenger (Q 2:253). These signs began with Jesus speaking from the cradle, and we will examine the others in the rest of this chapter.

THE MIRACLES OF JESUS IN THE QURAN

The Quran reports three main miracles, or types of miracles, performed by Christ. In surah 5, Allah speaks on judgment day and addresses Jesus:

> Then God [Allah] will say, "O Jesus son of Mary! Remember My Blessing upon thee, and upon thy mother . . . and how thou wouldst create out of clay the shape of a bird, by My Leave; and thou wouldst breathe into it, and it would become a bird, by My Leave; and thou wouldst heal the blind and the leper, by My Leave; and thou wouldst bring forth the dead, by My Leave. (Q 5:110)

Like the Bible, the Quran reports that Jesus gave sight to the blind. Muslim commentators explain that *blind* means "those who were born blind."[125] This is a clear parallel to the story of Jesus healing a man born blind (John 9). Additionally, Muslims also recognize that Jesus raised the dead. Muslim theologians record that Jesus raised a boy by the name Sam bin Nuh, the son of a widow in the process of burying him, and a man named 'Adhar, which is the Arabic rendition of Lazarus.[126] These parallel the biblical accounts of Christ raising the son of a widow (Luke 7:11–17) and Lazarus (John 11:1–44).

The Quran also says that Jesus created birds out of clay by breathing life into them. The Arabic words used in these passages, for the words

---

125 *The Study Quran*, note on Q 3:49, p. 145.
126 See Neal Robinson, *Christ in Islam and Christianity* (New York: State University of New York Press, 1991), 147; Fakhruddin al-Razi, *Al-Tafsir al-Kabir* [*The Large Commentary*] (Beirut: Dar Al-Fikr, 1970), 2:452.

create (*khalaqa*), *clay* (*teen*), and *breathing* (*nafakha*), are the same words that (otherwise exclusively) describe Allah's creative process. Obviously, this introduces a problem to the Quran's rejection of Jesus' divinity. Commentators have countered by claiming that Allah could have given Jesus special powers or that Allah created life at the same moment Jesus breathed onto the clay or that since Jesus was generated from Gabriel's breath, his own breath could create life.[127]

THE SOURCES OF THE QURAN'S STORY

The first two miracles are connected with the actual ministry of Jesus in the New Testament, but the Quran references the third miracle—creating birds from clay—with little detail. This supposed event is not mentioned in the New Testament. Instead, its full account is found in the unreliable apocryphal text of the Infancy Gospel of Thomas, believed to be written in the second century. The text narrates the infancy miracles of Jesus, including a story of the child Jesus making birds from clay.[128] This and other miracles found in apocryphal literature were written to fill the gap of Jesus' childhood, which the four canonical Gospels mostly skip over. The Church rejected them as canonical books because most of them are regarded as legends, and there is little evidence for their stories.[129]

Another reason for rejecting the apocryphal literature is because these stories do not show Jesus performing miracles to help others. They are merely demonstrations of power, sometimes causing harm to others. For example, in the Infancy Gospel of Thomas, we read that five-year-old Jesus bullied other boys with his supernatural powers. Jesus crippled and killed two other children, and when their parents complained to Joseph, Jesus blinded them. Later, when his teacher remarked that because of his marvelous powers, he must be an angel or God, Jesus laughed and healed all the people he cursed. The story

---

[127] Fakhruddin al-Razi, *Al-Tafsir al-Kabir*, 2:451–52; 3:468–69.
[128] "Infancy Gospel of Thomas," Early Christian Writings, http://www.earlychristianwritings.com/infancythomas.html.
[129] See Geoffrey Parrinder, *Jesus in the Qur'an*, 65.

continues with Jesus using his miraculous abilities to curse some people, cure others, carry water inside his clothes, and even fix furniture. Jesus relents from harming others whenever people exclaim that he must be an angel or God.

JESUS CALLS A TABLE FROM HEAVEN

Another curious miracle recorded in the Quran states that Jesus brought down a table from heaven:

> When the apostles said [to Jesus], "O Jesus son of Mary! Is thy Lord able to send down to us from Heaven a table spread with food?" He said, "Reverence God ["Guard (yourselves) against God"[130]], if you are believers." They said: "We desire to eat from it, so that our hearts may be at peace, and we may know that thou hast spoken truthfully unto us, and we may be among the witnesses thereto." Jesus, son of Mary said, "O God [Allah], our Lord! Send down unto us a table from Heaven spread with food, to be a feast for us—for the first of us and the last of us—and a sign from Thee, and provide for us, for thou are the best of providers." God [Allah] said, "I shall indeed send it down unto you. But whosoever among you disbelieves thereafter, I shall surely punish him with a punishment wherewith I have not punished any other in all the worlds." (Q 5:112–115)

The title of this story is *Ma'ida*, meaning "table," a word borrowed from the Amharic *ma'edde*, meaning "table, dishes, or banquet." (Amharic is the language spoken in Ethiopia.) It is possible that story is somewhat inspired by the feeding of the five thousand (Matthew 14:13–21), the Bread of Life discourse (John 6:22–59), or Psalm 78:18–19.[131] Others have argued that the word *ma'ida* was used to indi-

---

[130] A. J. Droge translation of the Quran, in Gordon D. Nickel, *The Quran with Christian Commentary*, p. 155.

[131] Reynolds, *The Qur'an and the Bible*, notes on Q 5:12, p. 217.

cate the Eucharist in Ethiopian Christianity before the advent of Islam, and that this story is evoking eucharistic imagery.[132]

THE MIRACLES OF JESUS IN ISLAMIC TEACHINGS

According to the Quran, only Allah can heal the sick, raise the dead, and create from clay (see Q 15:26–29; 26:8; 32:7–9; 38:71). The Quran denies the divinity of Christ, insisting that Allah gave Jesus special permission to perform these miracles. Therefore, before each miracle, the Quran includes the phrase, "By My [Allah's] Leave." Muslims believe that Allah gave Jesus the power to perform miracles as a confirmation of his prophethood and, confusingly, as a reproach to Christians, who tampered with the real story to make him divine.

In the biography of Muhammad, we read about a Christian delegate who came to dispute with Muhammad. The delegate told Muhammad that Jesus was divine because he performed miracles that only Allah can perform. Muhammad responded that the miracles were proof of Jesus' prophethood, not divinity, and a rebuke to Christians, who made him divine. Here Muhammad quotes what Jesus said in the Quran: "I have come to you with a sign from your Lord. So reverence God [Allah] and obey me. Truly God [Allah] is my Lord and your Lord; so, worship Him. This is a straight path" (Q 3:51). Muhammad argued that even Jesus was denying what they said about him and proving that Allah is his Lord.[133]

Other Muslim theologians have criticized Christians for arguing that Jesus' life-giving actions proved his divine status. On the contrary, Allah appointed Jesus to perform them just as he chose Moses to perform miracles (Q 26:10–68). Others argue that Allah enabled prophets to perform miracles suited to the circumstances of their time. As Allah sent Moses to outwit the Egyptian magicians who were so highly regarded in that culture, so also he sent Jesus to people who highly

---

132 See Samir Khalil Samir, "The Theological Christian Influence on the Qur'an: A Reflection," in Gabriel Said Reynolds, ed., *The Qur'an in Its Historical Context* (London and New York: Routledge, 2008), 141–62.
133 Ibn Ishaq, *Sirat Rasul Allah*, 271–76.

regarded science to demonstrate that Allah had the power to give life to the dead.[134]

To summarize the Islamic perspective, we can say that Islam considers the miracles of Jesus as evidence of the work of Allah on behalf of his people in the time of Jesus. Just like Moses,[135] Jesus was granted divine power to show that Allah has the power to give, restore, and improve life, while the miracle of calling down a table taught his disciples to trust Allah, the provider.

THE MIRACLES OF JESUS IN CHRISTIAN TEACHING

Jesus heals the blind and the leprous throughout the four Gospels, which provide more detail than the Quran. Mark 8:22–26 records people bringing a blind man to Jesus for healing. Jesus spat into the man's eyes, placed His hands on him, and asked if he could see anything. When the man replied that he could see people who looked like trees, Jesus placed His hand on the man's eyes, and then the man could see clearly. In Mark 10:46–52, a blind man called out in the crowd for Jesus to have mercy on him. When Jesus asked him what he wanted, the blind man said he wanted to see. Jesus told him that he would see because of his faith. This blind man received his sight not by touch, but by word of command. Mark 1:40–45 recounts a leper kneeling before Jesus and declaring that Jesus had the power to heal him if He wished to. Jesus put His hand on the man, said that He wanted to heal him, and pronounced his healing. Jesus told him to show himself to the priest and to take a gift to the temple so that he could resume his former life, but He asked him not to talk about it to other people.

Luke 17:11–19 tells the story of ten lepers asking for healing. Jesus told them to go and show themselves to the priest; on their way, they were healed. Only one came back to thank Jesus. Luke 7:11–17 reports the story of Jesus raising the widow's son, and John 11:1–44 recounts

---
134   Ibn Kathir, *Tafsir al-Qur'an*, 2:41.
135   See the story of Moses in the Quran (Q 26:10–68).

Jesus raising Lazarus from his tomb, four days after being buried.

The Gospels contain many more stories of Jesus healing people: those with evil spirits (Mark 1:21–28), the lame (Mark 2:1–12), and the deaf and mute (Mark 7:31–37). In addition to bodily healing, Jesus performed miracles by providing food and drink (Mark 6:30–44; John 2:1–11) and altering the normal pattern of nature (Mark 5:35–41; 6:45–52).

Sometimes Jesus told those He healed that they were healed because of their faith; for others, healing was granted by the command of Jesus, most obviously when Jesus raised the dead and when Jesus commanded the paralytic to pick up his bed and walk (John 5:1–17). Jesus had multiple intentions in healing people. For example, in Mark 2:1–12, Jesus forgave the sins of the paralyzed man, angering the Pharisees because only God can forgive sins. Jesus asked them whether it was easier to forgive sins or to heal. Then He said to the paralyzed man, "Rise, pick up your bed, and go home" (v. 11), and the man did. Jesus said this to demonstrate that He had authority to forgive sins.

It is therefore evident that Jesus' healing is linked to His divine authority; He heals not only the body but the spirit too. When Jesus forgave the sins of the paralyzed man, He was claiming to be God, a claim which He further confirmed by granting the man bodily healing. This connection between the miracles and divinity of Christ is likewise clear in the Gospel of John. When Jesus said, "I and the Father are one" (John 10:30), the Jewish people picked up stones to stone Him, because they understood this to be a claim of divinity (vv. 30–38). The Early Church always made the connection between the miracles and divine status of Jesus. On Pentecost, Peter declared, "Jesus of Nazareth, a man attested to you by God with mighty works and wonders and signs that God did through Him in your midst, as you yourselves know" (Acts 2:22), and he went on to argue that God had appointed Jesus "both Lord and Christ" (Acts 2:36). This is also why the disciples always healed in the name of Jesus (Acts 3:1–10; 9:34).

Concluding Comments

Islamic interpretation of the title *Messiah* can be summarized in two points. First, Jesus was anointed by blessing; his touch healed the sick and raised the dead. Second, Jesus the Messiah was a prophet with a mission to introduce reforms to the Jews and clarify the disputes among Christians. Jesus gave a final and definitive answer: he was the messenger and the prophet of Allah, but he was not Allah. In the Quran, Jesus condemned Christians for making him divine. Furthermore, the Messiah denounced the Jews for rejecting his prophethood. Jesus' signs and wonders served merely to confirm him as prophet.

The Bible presents the Messiah in a radically different way. Jesus asked His disciples, "Who do you say that I am?" Peter answered, "You are the Christ, the Son of the living God." Jesus responded, "Blessed are you, Simon Bar-Jonah! For flesh and blood has not revealed this to you, but My Father who is in heaven" (Matthew 16:15–17). When Peter called Him the Messiah, Jesus warned His disciples not to tell anyone that He was the Messiah (v. 20). Immediately after this statement, Jesus began teaching "that He must go to Jerusalem and suffer many things from the elders and chief priests and scribes, and be killed, and on the third day be raised" (v. 21). Here Jesus, the Messiah, connects His messianic mission to the cross. This mission is what distinguishes the Messiah of the Gospel from the Messiah of the Quran.

The New Testament indicates that Jesus' messianic mission did not match the expectations of the Jews, who were expecting an almighty king to free them from Romans oppression. On the contrary, Jesus the Messiah came to lay down His life for the world. Jesus told His disciples not to tell anyone He was the Messiah because He did not want people to think He was a military leader preparing to wage war against Rome; rather, Jesus wanted to redefine and reveal what *Messiah* meant.[136]

Jesus' new image of the Messiah is vividly seen in the events of the Last Supper. Jesus prepared His followers for what lay ahead:

---

[136] See Larry Hurtado, *Lord Jesus Christ: Devotion to Jesus in Earliest Christianity* (Grand Rapids, MI: Eerdmans, 2003), 289.

> He took bread, and when He had given thanks, He broke it and gave it to them, saying, "This is My body, which is given for you. Do this in remembrance of Me." And likewise the cup after they had eaten, saying, "This cup that is poured out for you is the new covenant in My blood." (Luke 22:19–20)

In those two elements, He attributed to Himself the role of the Redeemer Messiah, the Lamb of God who takes away the sins of the world.

The final messianic event was Jesus' death, burial, and resurrection, without which all other events would be meaningless. When Jesus cried on the cross, "My God, My God, why have You forsaken Me?" (Mark 15:34), He was echoing the beginning verse of Psalm 22. However, this psalm culminates in the exaltation and praise of God; in this context, the words Jesus uttered from the cross are words not of defeat but of hope in a God who keeps His promises:

> I will tell of Your name to my brothers; in the midst of the congregation I will praise You: You who fear the Lord, praise Him! All you offspring of Jacob, glorify Him, and stand in awe of Him, all you offspring of Israel! For He has not despised or abhorred the afflictions of the afflicted, and He has not hidden His face from him, but has heard, when he cried to Him. (Psalm 22:22–24)

For Christians, the mission and role of the Messiah is central to the revelation of God as participant in His covenant with humanity. Beginning in Genesis (Genesis 3:15), the Bible establishes that blood needed to be shed to cover the sin and nakedness of humankind. The biblical idea of a covenant sealed by a sacrifice is clearly connected to the mission of Christ in the mind of the Early Church (2 Corinthians 5:21). The Bible points to "the Lamb of God" (John 1:29) who served as God's Passover provision from the angel of death (see Exodus 12).

In Christianity, the Messiah reestablishes this right relationship with God by dying for us and our sins (Romans 5:8–11; Hebrews 10:12). At His birth, heaven announced that He was a "Savior" and "Christ the Lord" (Luke 2:11). Andrew told his brother, "We have found the Messiah" (John 1:41), and Martha professed, "Yes, Lord; I believe that You are the Christ, the Son of God, who is coming into the world" (John 11:27).

QUESTIONS FOR DISCUSSION
CHAPTER 11

SEE ANSWER KEY ON PAGE 291.

QUESTION 1

What are the Islamic interpretations of the Messiah? How does the Islamic interpretation prevent true and saving faith in Jesus as God's Son, the promised Messiah?

QUESTION 2

What three miracles (or types of miracles) does Jesus perform in the Quran? What is significant about the vocabulary used here? How might that help you build a bridge to a Muslim friend?

QUESTION 3

How do Christians interpret Jesus' miracles? How do Muslims?

CHAPTER 12

Jesus, the Word of God, and His Spirit

※

The Quran refers to Jesus as "the Word of God [Allah]." This title reminds Christians of the first verse in the Gospel of John: "In the beginning was the Word, and the Word was with God, and the Word was God" (John 1:1). This title is used in the Quran in three places: he is called "a Word from God [Allah]" who will be confirmed by John (Quran 3:39); the angel tells Mary that "God [Allah] gives thee glad tidings of a Word from Him, whose name is the Messiah, Jesus son of Mary" (Q 3:45); and the Quran commands Christians to reject the Trinity and embrace the "true" meaning of *Messiah*: "Verily the Messiah, Jesus son of Mary, was only a messenger of God [Allah], and His Word, which He committed to Mary, and a Spirit from Him" (Q 4:171).

The Quran uses this phrase in two forms: "Word *from* God [Allah]" and "Word *of* God [Allah]." Interestingly, *kalimah*, "word" in Arabic, is feminine, but when the Quran speaks of Jesus as "the Word of [Allah]," the word is masculine, exactly as in the Arabic translation of the Gospel of John. Although Jesus is the only prophet in the Quran with this title, the Christian interpretation of Jesus as the Word of God is totally rejected by Muslims.

Evaluating Islamic Interpretations

The idea of the creative word, the divine *Logos* that was with God in the beginning of time creating all things, does not exist within Islam. In the Quran, heaven and earth are created by Allah's word; however, the word is related to Allah's work of creation: cows, mountains, and trees can all be called the word of Allah. If this is true, then not only Jesus should be called the Word of Allah, but also everything that is created in heaven and earth, even unclean animals, Satan, and hell. Additionally, this title appears alongside other titles that contradict a biblical understanding of Christ. Jesus is called not only the Word of God (Allah) but also his messenger and his Spirit. Again, this supports an interpretation that Jesus is merely a prophet and not Allah. Muslim commentators and interpreters agree, or believe that the Word of Allah is beyond human comprehension.[137]

Within Islam, the Word of Allah can also mean a word similar to the word used in the creation of Adam. Muslim scholars claim that the creation of Jesus is like that of Adam, who was also created by the command of Allah; both Jesus and Adam were spoken into existence, rather than conceived (see Q 3:59).

However, with a closer look, there are some significant differences in the way the Quran treats Adam and Jesus. In the Quran, Allah created Adam and then breathed into him from his Spirit, just like in the account of Genesis. The Quran itself does not say that Jesus was created from the dust of the earth. Jesus is "His Word, which He committed Mary, and a Spirit from Him" (Q 4:171). "And as for she who preserved her chastity, We breathed into her of Our Spirit, and made her and her son a sign for the worlds" (Q 21:91). Jesus is "His Word," not "a Word from God [Allah]." His word expresses himself. Additionally, the Quran never uses "the Word of God [Allah]," "His Spirit," or "His Messenger" in reference to Adam.

---

[137] See Mahmoud Ayoub, *The Qur'an and Its Interpreters*, The House of Imran, vol. 2. (Albany: State University of New York Press, 1984), 131–51.

THE CONTEXT OF THIS PARALLEL

However, this supposed parallel between Adam and Jesus in the Quran reminds us of the real, biblical parallel between Christ and Adam: "For as in Adam all die, so also in Christ shall all be made alive" (1 Corinthians 15:22). Sin and death came into the world through Adam, but through Christ, the Second Adam, life and freedom from sin returned to the world (see Romans 5:12–21). This parallel is also frequent in patristic literature, especially in the Syriac liturgical traditions, where we find parallels between Adam and Jesus. In the ancient Syrian traditions, God created Adam on Friday, the sixth day of the week according to the Jewish numbering; likewise, the Early Church held that Adam sinned and was expelled from the Garden on a Friday. On the same day, Jesus, the new Adam, died on the cross and returned the old Adam back to the garden. While it is true that there is no historical evidence that Adam was created and sinned on a Friday, the point the Church Fathers were trying to make is that creation is intimately connected with salvation and re-creation: Christ is redeeming every element of fallen creation, down to the very day.

SIMILARITY BETWEEN JESUS AND MOSES

Another Islamic interpretation sees Jesus as the Word of Allah because he was given a revealed scripture, like Moses. In this perspective, Jesus as the Word of Allah means three things: his coming was foretold by the word of the prophets; he is the Word that corrected the word of Allah that the Jews and Christians corrupted; and he is the good news that the angel proclaimed to Mary. However, the Quran describes Moses as "the one who spoke to [Allah]," not the word of Allah or his Spirit. Furthermore, Jesus and Moses were not the only ones given a revealed scripture; Abraham, David, and John also received a revealed scripture. Thus, we can ask Muslims: Why was only Jesus given this title? All of them were faithful to their followers, yet no one else was called the Word and the Spirit of Allah.

While the Quran does, in a sense, acknowledge that "In the beginning was the Word, and the Word was with God," it rejects the rest of the verse—the most important part, the part that proclaims the divinity and incarnation of Christ: "and the Word was God" (John 1:1). "The Word became flesh and dwelt among us" (John 1:14). The Quran resoundingly rejects the divinity of Christ, calling it blasphemy (Q 5:17) and denying that Christ ever claimed to be God (Allah) (see Q 5:116), which is simply incorrect.

Logos in Greek Philosophy

When Christians speak about the Word or the *Logos*[138], they do not mean the same thing as Greek philosophers, who also used this term. It is important when speaking to Muslims to make clear that John's prologue to the Gospel is not "borrowing" from Greek philosophy. In the writings of Plato and other philosophies, the *Logos* is not a personal God but rather an impersonal mind and absolute, abstract idea; it is utterly distant from the world, which, according to Plato and Platonist philosophy, is corrupt on account of its materiality. This impersonal, distant god does not care for his creations, nor does he demand anything from them. This idea is at odds with the image of God provided in the Bible—a God who loves His creation, called it very good (Genesis 1:31), and loved it to the point of dying on the cross to redeem it (John 3:16). Based on this brief explanation, we can say that while it is true that John used a term familiar to his Greek-speaking audience, he used it outside of its classical use.

The Logos in the Old Testament

In the Old Testament, The Word of God describes God's dwelling and presence among His people in three important forms[139]. First, the Word of God creates the world, as expressed through the repeated phrase

---

138 See Mahmoud Ayoub, *The Qur'an and Its Interpreters*, The House of Imran, vol. 2. (Albany: State University of New York Press, 1984), 131–51.

139 See Mahmoud Ayoub, *The Qur'an and Its Interpreters*, The House of Imran, vol. 2. (Albany: State University of New York Press, 1984), 131–51.

"God said" (see Genesis 1:3–26). The Word of God also forms, sanctifies, and guides His people. It heals and saves them from all kinds of evil and liberates them from slavery (see Psalm 107:20; Exodus 19:4–6). Finally, the Word of God unites with His people, for example, when the Lord told Ezekiel to eat the scroll, or when He put His Word into Jeremiah's mouth (see Ezekiel 3:1–4; Jeremiah 1:9–10).

THE LOGOS IN THE GOSPEL OF JOHN

These three aspects of the Word of God are fulfilled in the New Testament in the person of Christ[140]. John, in his prologue to his Gospel, connects back to Genesis by repeating the phrase, "In the beginning." John uses this term to mean eternity before the creation of the world, to describe the *Logos*, Jesus, as eternally dwelling with the Father in the Trinity. He goes on to explain that "all things were made through Him, and without Him was not any thing made that was made" (John 1:3; see John 17:5 and Ephesians 1:4). John shifts from speaking of the transcendent, eternal God to explaining the union of divine and human natures in the person of Christ. Jesus is the eternal Word of God who, in the incarnation and in a specific time and space, took on flesh and dwelt among us (see Hebrews 1:1–3; Philippians 2:6–7).

THE LOGOS AS A PERSONAL GOD

Another important aspect of the *Logos* in the Gospel of John is that the Word of God is not an abstract or distant God who does not participate in His creation, as in the Greek and Islamic concepts of God. The *Logos* in Christian teachings is a personal God whose essence is love. He is the God who out of His *agape* love takes the initiative and communicates with His people; He pours out His love in their hearts and enters into a personal relationship with them (see John 3:16; Ephesians 2:4–10). This personal reality is clear in John 1:17, in which John contrasts the word brought by Moses and the Word personified in Jesus: "For the law

---

140   See Mahmoud Ayoub, *The Qur'an and Its Interpreters*, The House of Imran, vol. 2. (Albany: State University of New York Press, 1984), 131–51.

was given through Moses; grace and truth came through Jesus Christ." Looking at these verses, we find a clear answer to the Islamic teaching that equates Jesus and Moses. John argues that Jesus brings something different than Moses, because while God spoke to Moses in giving the Torah, in Jesus He speaks to us personally. Jesus reveals God to us in a way that Moses could not.

John 1:14 explains how the Word of God is a personal reality who gets involved in the re-creation of the world by becoming one of us. The Greek word for "become," *egeneto*, means "becoming different from what was before." In other words, God was in the habit of speaking as the Word, but now God the Word became a human being. This reality, however, was not obvious to everyone who encountered Him. The paradox of Jesus is that this reality was hidden from those who were in a state of rebellion against God. Only when their hearts were softened and their desire for God awakened could their eyes be opened to see the light of God shining on them through Jesus.

JESUS, THE SPIRIT OF GOD

Many verses in the Quran talk about spirit, or *Ruh*, including phrases such as "holy spirit" (*Ruh Al-Qudus*), "our spirit" (*Ruhana*), and "a spirit from him" (*ruhan menhu*). Muslim theologians interpret these verses in a variety of ways. Sometimes these verses are taken as referring to the archangel Gabriel; for example, as the holy spirit who appeared to Mary (see Q19:17). Other times, they are interpreted to mean the spirit by which Allah supports, sustains, and enlightens the minds of his prophets. The Quran asserts that Jesus was created supernaturally, and Allah bestowed on him a holy spirit to protect him from the devil and to complete his mission on earth (Q 2:253; 58:22). Allah also bestowed this spirit on Adam (Q 15:29) as well as on the chosen angels (Q 70:4; 78:38; 97:4). However, when the Quran speaks about Jesus, the Quran uses additional terms such as "Our Spirit" (Q 21:91) and "a Spirit from Him" (Q 4:171).

BUILDING BRIDGES WITH MUSLIMS

The Christian understanding of the Word of God is fundamental to our understanding of the divinity of Christ and of the Trinity, and it is something we ought to share with our Muslim friends. Arab Christian writers who have studied Islam have given us many practical ideas on how to explain the terms *word* and *spirit* to Muslims.

An anonymous Christian writer, probably writing in the eighth century, authored a piece called *Treatise on the Triune Nature of God*. Addressed to Muslims in Arabic, it interprets these titles for Jesus as upholding Christian convictions: "We do not distinguish God from His Word and His Spirit. We do not worship another God alongside from His Word and His Spirit."[141] The author pits the Quran against itself, citing its claims that Jesus is called "His Word" and "a Spirit from Him" (see Q 4:171) and that Christians commit idolatry by worshiping a triune God (Q 5:72–73). He uses terms from the Quran to explain the Trinity to Muslims. First, he denies that Christians worship three gods, as the Quran says they do, but says rather "that God and His Word and His spirit is one God and one Creator."[142] He uses additional quotes from the Quran (4:171; 16:102) to challenge his Muslim readers to accept that God, His Word, and His Spirit are one God and one Lord.[143]

The ninth-century Christian theologian Ammar al-Basri (d. AD 860) also helpfully explains the Trinity to Muslims by answering nine questions on the Trinity posed by Muslims. The first question reads, "Since the creator is one, how can one be three and three one?" Ammar takes a different approach in explaining the term "Word and Spirit of God." He uses the Islamic theological debates about Allah's names and attributes, which were examined in chapter 7. Ammar answers that there are three essential properties in one eternal essence that are not differentiated or separated. Life and speech can be attributed to Him because the creator lives and speaks. The principal

---

[141] Margaret D. Gibson, ed. and trans., *A Treatise on the Triune Nature of God* (Cambridge: Cambridge University Press, 1898), 75.

[142] Gibson, *Treatise on the Triune Nature of God*, 76.

[143] Gibson, *Treatise on the Triune Nature of God*, 77–78.

essence has the attributes of His life and His speech; His speech is the source of His wisdom, and His life is the source of His Spirit.

If the opponent suggests that God's attributes, such as *hearing, seeing, almighty, merciful, generous,* and *kind,* mean that Christians cannot limit God to "threeness," then they must distinguish between God's names and His attributes. The names refer to God's actions, but the attributes refer to properties essential to Him. The only essential properties in God are life and speech. Therefore, life and speech are properties in the structure of the essence and in the quality of His essence and nature.[144]

THE WAY, THE TRUTH, AND THE LIFE

Muslim theologians have struggled with the titles of "Word" and "Spirit" that the Quran gives to Jesus. Some argue that they mean that Jesus is the giver of life and the cause to give life to the creation. Others say these titles mean Jesus brings mercy to the world, or that Jesus resurrects the dead and gives life to hearts.[145] To build a bridge between Muslims and the Gospel, we have to connect these interpretations with what Jesus said about Himself:

> I am the way, and the truth, and the life. No one comes to the Father except through Me. (John 14:6)

> I am the resurrection and the life. Whoever believes in Me, though he die, yet shall he live, and everyone who lives and believes in Me shall never die. Do you believe this? (John 11:25–26)

---

[144] For a study of Ammar al-Basri dialogue with Muslims, see Thomas W. Ricks, *Early Arabic Christian Contributions to Trinitarian Theology* (Minneapolis: Fortress Press, 2013), 139–70. See also Mark Beaumont, "Ammār al-Basrī on the Incarnation," in David Thomas, ed., *Christians at the Heart of Islamic Rule: Church Life and Scholarship in 'Abbasid Iraq* (Boston and Leiden: Brill, 2003), 55–62; Mark Beaumont, *Christology in Dialogue with Muslims: A Critical Analysis of Christian Presentations of Christ for Muslims from the Ninth and Twentieth Centuries* (Eugene, OR: Wipf & Stock, 2005), 67–89.

[145] Munir Khawam, *Al-Massih Fi al-Fikir Al-Islami al-Hadith Wa Fi al-Massihyya (Jesus in Contemporary Islamic Thought and in Christianity)* (Beirut: Khalifa Publishing House, 1983), 224.

Truly, truly, I say to you, an hour is coming, and is now here, when the dead will hear the voice of the Son of God, and those who hear will live. (John 5:25)

Jesus again said to them, "Truly, truly, I say to you, I am the door of the sheep. All who came before Me are thieves and robbers, but the sheep did not listen to them. I am the door. If anyone enters by Me, he will be saved and will go in and out and find pasture. The thief comes only to steal and kill and destroy. I came that they may have life and have it abundantly." (John 10:7–10)

My sheep hear My voice, and I know them, and they follow Me. I give them eternal life, and they will never perish, and no one will snatch them out of My hand. (John 10:27–28)

QUESTIONS FOR DISCUSSION
CHAPTER 12

SEE ANSWER KEY ON PAGE 291.

QUESTION 1
How do Muslims interpret the title "Word of God [Allah]," which was given to Jesus?

QUESTION 2
What is the meaning of the title "the Word of God" in the Bible? How does John use the term *Logos* to reveal the divinity of Christ?

QUESTION 3
How do we build bridges with Muslims when talking about the titles of Jesus?

CHAPTER 13

THE DEATH AND RESURRECTION OF CHRIST

The Quran denies the death and resurrection of Christ; instead, Muslims believe Jesus went directly to be with Allah. This idea is stated in the Quran:

> And for their saying, "We slew the Messiah, Jesus son of Mary, the messenger of God [Allah]"—though they did not slay [kill] him; nor did they crucify him, but it appeared so unto them [it only seemed, or appeared, that way]. Those who differ concerning him are in doubt thereof. They have no knowledge of it, but follow only conjecture; they slew him not for certain. But God [Allah] raised him up unto Himself, and God [Allah] is Mighty, Wise. (Quran 4:157–158)

ISLAMIC INTERPRETATIONS

Muslims commentators disagree about how to handle this statement of the Quran[146]. The central problem is the statement about Jesus only appearing to be dead. Some claim that Christ remained dead for some

---
146 See Mahmoud Ayoub, *The Qur'an and Its Interpreters*, The House of Imran, vol. 2. (Albany: State University of New York Press, 1984), 131–51.

three to seven hours before being raised to heaven by Allah. Others argue that Jesus was indeed crucified, but he did not die on the cross; rather, he secretly survived his execution. Some went so far as to believe that after surviving the cross, Jesus moved to Kashmir, an area in the northern Indian subcontinent, where he ultimately died a natural death. There is still a highly revered Muslim shrine called "the tomb of Jesus" in Kashmir.[147]

Another group of Muslim theologians concluded that Jesus did not die, but someone who looked like him was crucified in his place. This interpretation is called the substitution theory. A third interpretation is based on the swoon theory.[148]

Muslims claim these theories are supported by the New Testament's apparent inconsistencies in the resurrection narrative. The Gospels differ slightly in their descriptions of what the women saw at the tomb: Mark depicts a youth dressed in white, Matthew tells of an angel who rolled back the stone; Luke describes two men who appeared next to the women; John says two angels were sitting where Jesus had been laid. This apparent disagreement among the Gospels reflects the confusion in each of their reports. Muslims conclude that the Quran's version of the story—that Jesus only seemed dead—is more logical than the version told in the Gospels.

Evaluating Islamic Interpretation

Muslim substitution theory, however, is plagued by confusion. Muslim scholars cannot agree on who was substituted for Jesus and have suggested John, Peter, Judas, or even Satan. A prominent medieval Muslim commentator, al-Razi, concludes that "Only God [Allah] knows the

---

[147] For more details about this theory, see the book written by the founder of this sect: Hadhrat Mirza Ghulam Ahmad, *Jesus in India: Jesus' Deliverance from the Cross and Journey to India* (London: Islam International Publications, 2003).

[148] The swoon theory states that Jesus did not really die on the cross. He was crucified and came very close to death and fell into a swoon or faint. The theory claims he was taken down from the cross and laid in the tomb barely alive. After three days, he revived from the coolness of the tomb and managed to roll the stone away. He came out of the tomb and appeared to the disciples, making them think he had risen from the dead.

truth of this matter." Elsewhere, he rejects the theory outright, saying Allah was capable of simply receiving Jesus into heaven, and it would be pointless to condemn an innocent man to death in that case.[149]

Islam's claims against the death and resurrection of Christ are conflicting and unsubstantiated, whereas the narratives of the Passion, death, and resurrection of Christ in the four Gospels are one, supported by witnesses and evidence.

To address the apparent confusion in the Gospel resurrection narratives, we need to examine them based on the rules of hermeneutics (the method for understanding and interpreting texts). We need to interpret unclear statements in light of clear ones, and not the other way around. The Muslim approach of ignoring the clear statements about Jesus' death and instead pointing to unclear hints that he did not actually die is an illegitimate method of investigating a text. Jesus speaks clearly about His death and resurrection. Even if there is some confusion among the narratives, that is not enough evidence to deny the death of Jesus on the cross.

Additionally, the Quran contradicts itself and affirms Jesus' death and resurrection in some places. In the story of the nativity, Jesus spoke from the cradle, prophesying:

> Peace be upon me [Jesus] the day *I was born,* the *day I die,* and the *day I am raised alive!*" That is Jesus son of Mary—a statement of the truth, which they doubt. (Q 19:33–34, emphasis added)

In another surah, Allah speaks to Jesus on the day of judgment:

> O Jesus, *I shall take thee* [in death] and *raise thee unto Me,* and purify thee of those who disbelieved, and place those who followed thee above those who disbelieved, *until the Day of Resurrection.* (Q 3:55, emphasis added)

---

149   Al-Razi, *al-Tafsir al-Kabir,* 3:110.

To reconcile these verses with the remarks denying Christ's death elsewhere, commentators have interpreted these verses to mean the second coming.[150] However, when we examine these verses, we clearly see that there is no future tense in the grammatical construction of this passage that would suggest a post-millennial death. The Quran's plain meaning seems to be that Jesus' physical death occurred at the end of his life on earth.

Additionally, the Quran indicates that Christ could raise the dead. If he was so powerful, why would Allah have to pull a trick? Since Allah was fully able to raise Christ from the grave, just like al-Razi explained, it was unnecessary to kill an innocent substitute in his place. Furthermore, why wouldn't this alleged substitute make any effort to defend himself to declare that he was not the Christ? Similarly, Christ's disciples wrote that they had seen him suffer the death of a criminal at the hands of the Roman soldiers. Of all people, these disciples would have preferred that he finish his life in a manner more suitable for a prophet; therefore, this theory gives no account for the inception of the Christian Church.

Evidence about the Death of Christ on the Cross

The earliest Christian creedal statement can be found in the First Letter to the Corinthians. The letter affirms that Jesus died on the cross, was buried, and was raised on the third day:

> For I delivered to you as of first importance what I also received: that Christ died for our sins in accordance with the Scriptures, that He was buried, that He was raised on the third day in accordance with the Scriptures. (1 Corinthians 15:3–4)

Another one is found in the Letter to the Philippians:

---

150 *The Study Quran* 3:55, 146; 19:33–34, 772–73.

And being found in human form, He humbled Himself by becoming obedient to the point of death, even death on a cross. (Philippians 2:8).

Biblical historians affirm that these doctrinal statements were formulated within five years of Jesus' crucifixion, meaning they were written even before the Gospels; they were proclaimed by the first Christians who lived with and listened directly to Jesus. These historical testimonies are very important because they tell us that Christians were passing down to one another the core doctrine of their faith, and that the death of Jesus was among their first concerns. Furthermore, it affirms how central this teaching was to the early Christians.[151]

These records are more convincing when we read that the leaders of the Jews were trying to explain why Jesus' tomb was empty (Matthew 28:12–15). They did not deny Jesus' crucifixion or death, but instead they claimed that His disciples had stolen His body. So even though they had a perfect opportunity, the Jews never denied Jesus' death on the cross.

THE FOOLISHNESS OF THE CROSS

The cross was one of the most brutal, intricate, and effective methods of execution that humanity has ever devised. The torment of the cross was so extreme that a word was invented to describe it: *excruciating*, from the Latin word (*excruciare*) to describe torment "from the cross." Romans used the penalty of crucifixion to send a message and make a statement to anyone who opposed them. Crucifixion was not only a means for execution but also specifically intended for extreme brutality and humiliation. There were no standard procedures for crucifixion. Executioners were often given license to apply reckless cruelty against their victims. Before the crucifixion, the victim was flogged (as in the case of Jesus), which was itself a horrendous torture. The whip was designed to rip the skin and muscle. The victim was whipped to the bone, their blood would flow like a stream, and their intestines were at times exposed by

---

151 See Nabeel Qureshi, *No God but One* (Grand Rapids, MI: Zondervan, 2016), 164.

flogging.[152] Josephus describes some of the cruelties and humiliations of crucifixion itself. Victims were fixed to the cross in awkward poses, nailed through their ribs, forced to watch the violation of their wives or the slaughter of their whole families, and executed with their sons hung around their necks.[153] That is why the expression, "Get crucified!" was used as a rank obscenity among the lower classes in ancient Rome.

Given the ruthless shame of crucifixion, it would be shocking to hear that Christians centered their message around the cross or that a religious movement started with the absurd proclamation that the founder was crucified. Indeed, people have always ridiculed Christians for this proclamation. Based on these attacks on the cross, Paul assured the Corinthian Church that the message of the cross is still the Good News: "For the word of the cross is folly to those who are perishing, but to us who are being saved it is the power of God" (1 Corinthians 1:18).

The logical question that we must ask is this: Why would Christians focus their preaching on the message of the cross? Why not preach an alternative message, such as the one advocated by Islam, that Jesus survived the cross and that God has taken him to heaven? The answer is found in the same letter to the Corinthians:

> Where is the one who is wise? Where is the scribe? Where is the debater of this age? Has not God made foolish the wisdom of the world? For since, in the wisdom of God, the world did not know God through wisdom, it pleased God through the folly of what we preach to save those who believe. For Jews demand signs and Greeks seek wisdom, but we preach Christ crucified, a stumbling block to Jews and folly to Gentiles, but to those who are called, both Jews and Greeks, Christ the power of God and the wisdom of God. For the foolishness of God is wiser than men, and the weakness of God is stronger than men. (1 Corinthians 1:20–25)

---

152 See Martin Hengel, *Crucifixion in the Ancient World and the Folly of the Message of the Cross* (Philadelphia: Fortress Press, 1977), 9–12.
153 Josephus, *Antiquities of the Jews,* 12:5.4, https://penelope.uchicago.edu/josephus/ant-12.html.

The Sources of the Quran's Story

From the first century, Christianity faced heretical groups that denied the physical death and resurrection of Jesus. These teachings can be seen in the apocryphal gospels. One of these groups holds to the heresy of docetism, from the Greek *dokeo*, "to seem." The sect appeared in the late first and early second century and was condemned at the Council of Nicaea in AD 325. These groups and their writings remained active, however, especially in the Arabian Desert.[154]

Docetism claims that the crucifixion was just an image, a phantom, not the real Jesus, or perhaps a substitute. An apocryphal gospel called the Acts of John recounts a conversation between Jesus and John in a cave outside of Jerusalem. Jesus tells John that the people in Jerusalem assume that he was crucified, but he wasn't.[155] Another apocryphal book was written by the Gnostic Judeo-Christian Basilides. Basilides taught that Jesus must not have had a material body because the material world is evil, and therefore Jesus could not have been crucified.[156]

The New Testament rejected these heresies, especially in the Gospel of John and his two letters. John writes:

> The Word became flesh and dwelt among us, and we have seen His glory, glory as of the only Son from the Father, full of grace and truth. (John 1:14)

> That which was from the beginning, which we have heard, which we have seen with our eyes, which we looked upon and have touched with our hands, concerning the word of life—the life was made manifest, and we have seen it, and testify to it and proclaim to you the eternal life, which was with the Father and was made manifest to us. (1 John 1:1–2)

> By this you know the Spirit of God: every spirit that confesses that

---

154 See Lawson, *The Crucifixion and the Qur'an*, 1–26.
155 "The Acts of John," Early Christian Writings, http://www.earlychristianwritings.com/actsjohn.html.
156 "Basilides," Early Christian Writings, http://www.earlychristianwritings.com/basilides.html.

Jesus Christ has come in the flesh is from God, and every spirit that does not confess Jesus is not from God. This is the spirit of the antichrist, which you heard was coming and now is in the world already. (1 John 4:2–3)

For many deceivers have gone out into the world, those who do not confess the coming of Jesus Christ in the flesh. Such a one is the deceiver and the antichrist. (2 John 7)

The Resurrection of Christ

Muslims are normally less concerned with the supernatural implications of the resurrection than with the physical death of Jesus, because most Muslims believe in Jesus' ascension, which appears in the Quran (Q 4:158). On account of this, Muslims do not see the resurrection as an issue, usually assuming it to be an outcome of the Christian misunderstanding that Jesus died on the cross.

The resurrection of Jesus can be shared with Muslims as a vivid example of God's life-giving power. In the Book of Acts, Peter declared, "God raised Him up, loosing the pangs of death, because it was not possible for Him to be held by it" (Acts 2:24). Jesus died to save humanity, and He is seated in glory to sustain humanity by the Holy Spirit. Anyone who declares the power of His resurrection is saved by faith (Romans 10:9). Without the resurrection, Christianity is a false, useless delusion, and Christians "are of all people most to be pitied" (1 Corinthians 15:19). Christians have hope because through His death Christ killed death, and by His resurrection He destroyed the power of the grave: "'Death is swallowed up in victory.' 'O death, where is your victory? O death, where is your sting?'" (1 Corinthians 15:54–55). This message energized the Early Church to declare, "This Jesus God raised up, and of that we all are witnesses" (Acts 2:32). Jesus' resurrection was the foundation for comprehending His divinity, as when Thomas sees and touches the risen Lord (John 20:28).

In Christianity, Jesus ascends to be seated at the right hand of God, "far above all rule and authority and power and dominion" (Ephesians 1:21); all who believe in Jesus have the hope of being seated with Him in heaven: "If then you have been raised with Christ, seek the things that are above, where Christ is, seated at the right hand of God" (Colossians 3:1). In Islam, Jesus was raised to heaven only to avoid the brutal intent of his enemies. Christians can, in turn, ask Muslims: if the only purpose of Jesus being raised was to rescue him from his enemies, could he not have returned after his enemies had died?

Christianity talks about the crucifixion, death, resurrection, and ascension as one divine mystery. Christians cannot talk about any of these events in isolation. This truth is confirmed by Jesus: "[I am] the living one. I died, and behold I am alive forevermore, and I have the keys of Death and Hades" (Revelation 1:18). Anyone who believes in Him, by faith and through Baptism, is united with Christ and participates in these divine events (see Romans 6:3–13). This connection is completely rejected by Islam. According to Islam, Jesus was simply lifted to heaven like Enoch, who "walked with God, and he was not, for God took him" (Genesis 5:24).

THE SECOND COMING OF CHRIST

In the Islamic perspective, Christ is currently alive in paradise, waiting to come back to earth to finish his ministry that he began before Muhammad. According to the Quran, Jesus will return at the end of time to do two things: to judge humankind and to subdue the Antichrist, called *al-dajjal*, which means "the swindler" or "the imposter" (see Q 43:61). Islam also claims that Jesus will rebuke Christians and affirm the truth of Islam by leading a struggle against infidels and polytheists. He will finally be able to marry, reign as a king, live for forty years, and then die a natural death, when he will be buried in Medina next to Muhammad in a tomb prepared for him long ago. Then he will rise at the resurrection. Jesus is portrayed as a human being and a vengeful warrior.

Jesus' second coming has no salvationary significance in Islam. As Allah's emissary, Jesus will come as a judge to represent Allah, correct wrong, and determine whether individuals will go to hell or paradise.[157]

Examining Islamic ideas about the end of the world, Christians could ask Muslims why this important eschatological role was given to Jesus if he is, as they claim, a mere human and prophet. The Bible answers that Jesus is the judge on the Last Day because He is the Son of God (John 12:46–48). Christians can also discuss with Muslims the exceptional claim that Islam makes about Jesus: Why would Islam describe Jesus as a person with a corporeal body, who dwells uncorrupted in paradise for two thousand years and then returns to earth? Does his body not know the effect of time? Jesus Himself answers this question: "I am from above. You are of this world; I am not of this world" (John 8:23); "No one has ascended into heaven except He who descended from heaven, the Son of Man" (John 3:13).

Concluding Thoughts

Christ's resurrection speaks of God's desire for a covenantal relationship with humanity. Jesus not only ascended into heaven, as Islam acknowledges, but in the resurrection, He also returned to His disciples. The risen Lord Jesus delights in comforting the faithful:

> Why are you troubled, and why do doubts arise in your hearts? See My hands and My feet, that it is I Myself. Touch Me, and see. For a spirit does not have flesh and bones as you see that I have. (Luke 24:38–39)

Christians ought to invite Muslims to come and see (see Matthew 28:6) that Jesus has overcome death. This can be done only by reiterating the biblical account, using Islamic terminology, and giving the vivid example of lives transformed by the reality of the risen Christ:

---

157 For further study in Islamic eschatology, see Samuel Shahid, *The Last Trumpet: A Comparative Study in Christian-Islamic Eschatology* (Maitland, FL: Xulon Press, 2005); Marcia Hermansen, "Eschatology," in *The Cambridge Companion to Classical Islamic Theology*, ed. Tim Winter (Cambridge: Cambridge University Press, 2008), 308–24.

The life was made manifest, and we have seen it, and testify to it and proclaim to you the eternal life, which was with the Father and was made manifest to us—that which we have seen and heard we proclaim also to you, so that you too may have fellowship with us; and indeed our fellowship is with the Father and with His Son Jesus Christ. (1 John 1:2–3)

QUESTIONS FOR DISCUSSION
CHAPTER 13

SEE ANSWER KEY ON PAGE 291.

QUESTION 1

How does Islam reject Christ's death and resurrection? What are the results of this rejection?

QUESTION 2

Where does the Quran's version of the crucifixion likely come from? How can we use this when explaining the importance of the resurrection to our Muslim friends?

QUESTION 3

What does Islam teach about the second coming of Christ?

CONCLUDING NOTES ABOUT THE STORY OF JESUS

When we compare the story of Jesus in the Quran and in the New Testament, we notice the Quran does not tell us anything about Jesus' temptation in the wilderness after His Baptism, His preaching in Galilee, His cleansing of the temple, His agony when praying in Gethsemane, His trial, His death on the cross, and His joy of the resurrection. There is no narrative description of His ministry. Approximately ninety verses in the Quran speak about Jesus, with no fewer than sixty-four treating the nativity, leaving twenty-six or so verses to present the rest of Jesus' ministry. In the New Testament, even the infancy narratives focus on Jesus as the Son of God who comes to save us from our sins. The Quran completely ignores these themes, which are the theological foundations of the Christian message.

It has been suggested that important events are not recorded in the Quran because the Quran is not a literary narrative describing the life of the prophets, like the Bible. Instead, it is a scripture that provides guidance (*huad*) and a reminder (*tadhakur*) to humankind, with greater emphasis on spiritual edification than providing a full account of facts.[158] When it comes to Jesus' story, the Quran's main concern is not to give a full account of his life but instead to put it in the right theological perspective. That is why there is nothing about his Passion, and why the Quran only treats his birth and his identity as a prophet. The Quran does not consider the Passion of Jesus as an event with major theological significance. Jesus is a prophet with a message from Allah, just like Abraham, Moses, and Muhammad, and his mission is not to die on the cross but to be a sign and a warning for his people.[159]

However, in the Bible, the Passion of Christ, and His crucifixion, death, resurrection, and ascension are central to the Gospel. Paul reminds the Church of Corinth: "If Christ has not been raised, then our preaching is in vain and your faith is in vain" (1 Corinthians 15:14).

---

158 Mustafa Akyol, *The Islamic Jesus*, 133.
159 Akyol, *The Islamic Jesus*, 152.

The Bible is about God, but it is about the God who loved us and revealed His love to us in the person of Jesus Christ. It is about the Word becoming flesh and dwelling among us (John 1:14), who gives life to all those who believe in Him (John 20:30–31).

The Quran always sets Jesus parallel to Muhammad. The false Jesus of the Quran is antagonistic: the perspective of the Quran is always aligned to Muhammad's context.[160] The only way for Islam to reconcile the fundamental differences between the life of Muhammad and the life of Christ is to remake Jesus in the image of Muhammad. Muslim commentators explain that the strife and violence seen in early Islam were necessary for the religion to survive.[161] This is in stark contrast to Christ, who rejected secular power and instead took the way of the cross.

Some similarities can be found between Jesus in Jerusalem and Muhammad in Mecca. Both faced opposition and religious rejection. But that is where the similarity ends. Jesus did not conquer Jerusalem; He suffered outside its walls as the cross became His throne. Muhammad's victory was conquering and subduing most of Arabia; Jesus' victory was in His resurrection from the dead.

---

160 For more information about the historical and social background of Jesus in the Quran, see Kenneth Cragg, *Jesus and the Muslim: An Exploration* (Oxford: Oneworld, 1999), 18–38.
161 Cragg, *The Call of the Minaret*, 268.

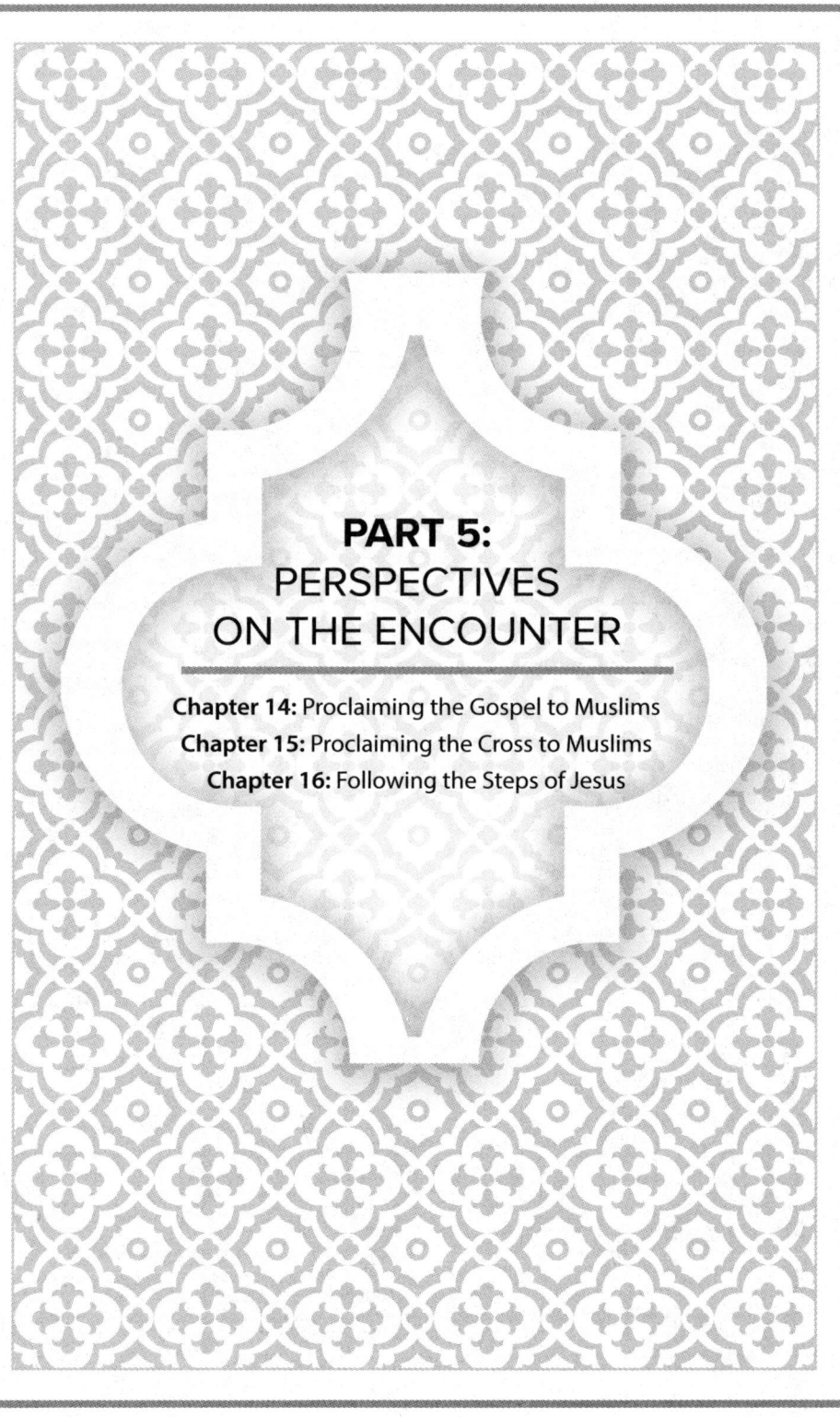

PART 5:
PERSPECTIVES ON THE ENCOUNTER

Chapter 14: Proclaiming the Gospel to Muslims
Chapter 15: Proclaiming the Cross to Muslims
Chapter 16: Following the Steps of Jesus

CHAPTER 14

Proclaiming the Gospel to Muslims

How do we share the Good News with Muslims? The Gospel is about God, who revealed Himself in the person of Jesus Christ. We have dedicated seven chapters to talking about God and Jesus, and in these last three chapters, we will present practical suggestions on how to present a contextualized Gospel proclamation in the Islamic context.

A Look at the Western Presentation of the Gospel

Many books have been written about reaching out to Muslims and many have offered countless practical and theological ideas. However, most of them depart from Western theological frameworks. They speak about salvation in terms of *debt*, *debtor*, and the *indebted*. Humans are indebted sinners who have incurred infinite debt from God. Humans cannot pay the debt of sin, so Jesus paid it by His sacrifice and freed humanity from the debt and punishment of eternal damnation. Others speak of an angry God who needs a satisfactory sacrifice to remove His anger. Jesus died on the cross and satisfied God's anger. The idea of sin is presented as a punishment that brings the judgment of death on us. The forensic view of salvation says that God is a judge, and we stand guilty before Him because of our sins.

There is nothing inherently wrong with any of these ways of

speaking about salvation. That being said, this language is not well suited to Muslim-majority cultures. In other words, if we hope to reach people within an Islamic cultural worldview, we need to present a contextualized message without compromising the Gospel.

The Muslim Worldview and Western Culture

The Muslim worldview is heavily influenced by honor and shame culture; Muslims are more concerned with a person's identity as it relates to the community than as an individual. Honor is more important than being guilty or innocent. The following story illustrates this point.

Jayson Georges was talking with a taxi driver from Central Asia about God. An opportunity arose to share the Gospel, so he said something like this: "Your sins make you guilty before God, but Jesus died so your sins could be forgiven, and you could escape punishment." The driver's eyebrows bunched up in confusion as if he was speaking a different language! At that moment, Jayson realized that his explanation of the Gospel did not resonate in the heart or mind of the driver. This was because the driver hardly sensed personal guilt for any wrongdoing he might have done, so he was not seeking personal forgiveness. Additionally, since the courts in Central Asia are notoriously corrupt, he was very skeptical when he heard legal language (in terms of *guilt*, *restitution*, or *judge*) to explain how God saves people.

Westerners are by nature individualistic. In the West, we tend to view our actions through the lens of law and logic. We experience guilt when we violate an internal, external, moral, or legal law. We experience this guilt internally without requiring another person to ascribe it to us. In such cases, the violations of the law typically affect only those who violate the law. As a result, when someone from a Western culture knows that he or she is guilty of a violation, he or she seeks to be justified via repentance or restitution. If this repentance or restitution is achieved and recognized by the giver or the keeper of the law, then the Westerner has been forgiven; he or she experiences the feeling, both individualistic and internal, of being innocent. This Western cultural view does not require any cooperating group to assign guilt or innocence.

Islamic culture, which is part of Eastern culture, is much more focused on shame and honor within the group, in contrast to individualistic Western guilt-innocence culture. These honor-shame cultures have social interrelationships that are necessary in life. Thus, when an individual has been put to shame, there is very little this person can do by himself or herself to remove the shame. In Eastern culture, *we* is much more important than *me*. One's identity is tied directly to the group. The closest analogy that we might draw in the West is found in sports. The best basketball teams might have one or two players who are more talented than the rest of the team. However, if this team hopes to succeed, each person must take on the new identity assigned to him or her by the team and live it out while he or she is part of the team.

The person who belongs to the group and follows the protocols is saving or building up face (or honor). Arabic and Islamic popular culture uses two expressions when someone brings shame to the group: he is "making the face of the group dark" (*Sawwada al-Wajh*) or he is "lowering or putting down the head of the group" (*Watta al-Ra's*). When someone brings honor to the group, he is "making the face of the group shine" (*Bayyada al-Wajh*) or he is "raising up, or elevating, the head of the group" (*Raf'ah al-Ra's*).

How do we begin to build a bridge with our Muslim friends if we think so differently about such basic things? We must remember that our most basic relationship is the one that we have with God. Both the Bible and the Quran express the foundational principle that God is our Creator. We can compare the story of creation in the Quran (Q 2:29–39; 7:11–26; 15:26–40; 20:15–24) to the creation and fall of humanity in the Bible (Genesis 1:26–31, 3:1–24). We have already summarized it and pointed out the fundamental differences between the Christian and the Islamic story in chapters 5 and 6. However, our goal is not to argue about the differences but to encourage Muslims to open the Bible and read the story with us. Thus, it is important for us also to have the Quran in our hand and open it with respect and read from it.

THE TRANSCENDENT AND MYSTERIOUS GOD

When building bridges, Christians should be sensitive to the religious and spiritual atmosphere of Muslims. The way Islam perceives the transcendence of Allah is a call to Christians not only to respect and admire the transcendence and majesty of God but also to deepen and purify their own faith and religious life. Christians are called to remember that the religious traditions of the Old Testament are no less sensitive to the mystery of God, who is the holy and transcendent God. Jesus, in His total union with the Father, lived out this respect for God's transcendence very deeply, and on this basis He set Himself against the narrow dogmas and rituals of the Pharisees. In this perspective, the mystery of the incarnation, the divinity of Jesus, and the Trinity should be understood from the point of God's transcendence, and it should encourage Christians to an even greater awareness of God, who transcends all human thought and understanding.

Eastern Church Fathers advise us to come close to the divine mysteries with a spiritual attitude of awe, silencing our intellect while proclaiming and confessing the mystery by faith. The Fathers expressed their faith in the transcendence of God in their liturgical chants. One of the well-known chants in the Eastern Liturgical tradition starts with the refrain, "With awe and marveling we proclaim; how wondrous is Your name, O Jesus." Then the long chants continue to narrate the saving work of Jesus and the mystery of His continued transcendent union with the Trinity, even in His immanent presence among us:

> He descended into the Virgin's womb, and He never left the Father's embrace. He came to us as Emmanuel while He resides in the highest. The one who creates embryos in

womb, He became embryo and [as a babe] was wrapped in a swaddling cloth. The hidden one was revealed and the rich one became poor. We proclaim His greatness; He is indescribable because He is a mystery. The one who sits above the Cherubim, He emptied Himself from the glory; the consuming fire came close to us with a human body. As a human, He became hungry and thirsty, and as God, He satiated the hunger and quenched the thirst and comforted [the distressed]. As the Son of Man He slept, and as God He rebuked the wind. As a human He walked among humans, and as a transcendent one He walked above the waters. As a human He cried on the tomb, and as God He called the dead to come out of the tomb. The one who is served by the angels and all the heavenly hosts, He became a servant for the salvation of human sinners. They put on Him a crown of thorns, while He is the one who enthrones the kings. In order to lift the heads of the servants, He became a servant, and like a servant [He] was beaten on the head. He humbled Himself in order to lift up the humbled. In order to release the captives, He voluntarily accepted the chains and shackles. The hands that shaped Adam and healed all the sick were nailed to the cross, and the wonderful face was deformed. The one who established earth for [humankind] to walk on, the one who created the creation, was lifted to the cross. He died by His own will, was buried by His own choice, was resurrected by His own power, and was ascended into heaven by His own might. He is with us and will come again in glory to redeem the purchased, that we may glorify Him forever.[162]

Muslims and Christians can both acknowledge God is sovereign. The Quran describes Allah as totally other, ineffable,

---

[162] This liturgical text was collected and translated into Arabic from various ancient Eastern chants, especially the Ethiopian one, by Rev. Marcus Dawod. It was composed and sung by Maher Fayz. The writer has translated it into English.

incomprehensible, invisible, and inconceivable. Islam and Christianity agree on this point. In Christianity, God is a mystery: "No one has ever seen God" (John 1:18); "Man shall not see Me and live" (Exodus 33:20). The Eastern Church Fathers insisted that a God who is comprehensible is not God, meaning that if we claim to understand God through our reason, God will be nothing more than an idol we have fashioned in our own image. Such a God is definitely not the true and living God of the Bible. Islam and Christianity are in agreement about this point.

The Bible, however, does not stop at the first point but continues to explain how we relate to the God who transcends our understanding. This God of mystery is uniquely close to us, not merely like an atmosphere or a nameless force, but in a personal way. God, who is beyond our understanding, revealed Himself as a person in Jesus Christ:

> Long ago, at many times and in many ways, God spoke to our fathers by the prophets, but in these last days He has spoken to us by His Son, whom He appointed the heir of all things, through whom also He created the world. (Hebrews 1:1–2)

There is a relationship of love between us and the transcendent God. We know God through the loving relationship that He initiated, and we are known to the world by reflecting His sacrificial love on the cross. John explains it in this way:

> Beloved, let us love one another, for love is from God, and whoever loves has been born of God and knows God. Anyone who does not love does not know God, because God is love. In this the love of God was made manifest among us, that God sent His only Son into the world, so that we might live through Him. In this is love, not that we have loved God but that He loved us and sent His Son to be the propitiation for our sins. Beloved, if God so loved us, we also ought to love one another. No one has ever seen God; if we love one another, God abides in us and His love is perfected in us. (1 John 4:7–12)

This idea is radically different from Islam.

Relating to the Transcendent and Mysterious God

As we establish points of agreement and differences between Islam and Christianity, we need to move our conversation to a deeper level by asking how we can come close to God, if He is a mysterious and transcendent God. The Christian answer can be summarized in two practical points: First, acknowledge that God is, and always will remain, a mystery beyond our understanding. Unless we start with a feeling of awe and astonishment, we shall make little progress. Second, we stand before God not as passive creatures but as active listeners and speakers. This is what we do when we gather with other believers for worship or in our individual private prayer: we listen and speak through reading Scripture and praying.

Consider the example of Moses and his three encounters with God. In Exodus 3:2, he sees God in the burning bush; in Exodus 13:21, he sees God in the pillar of cloud and fire that accompanies the people of Israel through the desert; finally, in Exodus 20:21, God speaks to Moses in the thick darkness at the summit of Mount Sinai. In these encounters, Moses both listened and spoke to God.[163]

We need to read Scripture and pray, and we need to lead our Muslim friends to do likewise to discern the call of God: "He who has an ear, let him hear what the Spirit says" (Revelation 2:7). This could be like the journey of Moses with God. Sometimes it is like a vision of light at the burning bush: God speaks to many Muslims through visions and dreams. At other times, the journey is longer and could go through the clouds of fire or through thick darkness. Any situation, no matter how hard or challenging, is an opportunity to witness. In all this, we should keep in mind that discernment is a gift of the Holy Spirit.

---

163 For more on this topic, see Kallistos Ware, *The Orthodox Way* (Crestwood, NY: St. Vladimir's Seminary Press, 1979).

Our final confidence in presenting the Gospel story is based on the fact that the disciples and evangelists themselves came to full faith from their experiences with Jesus. Reading the post-resurrection narratives, we see that the disciples struggled with the same ideas with which Muslims struggle: the divinity of Christ.

THE NEED FOR REPENTANCE

In approaching the mystery of God, we need to repent. The Greek word for repentance is *metanoia*, meaning "change of mind." The longer we stand in the presence of God, the more our minds are renewed. The presence of God in our lives strips us of all our habitual ways of thinking. The Holy Spirit converts not only our intellect but also our inner being:

> Do not be conformed to this world, but be transformed by the renewal of your mind, that by testing you may discern what is the will of God, what is good and acceptable and perfect. (Romans 12:2)

In the context of Muslim-Christian encounters, we can say that conversion is the action of the Spirit of God in men and women who are listening, speaking, and discerning the mystery of God. These spiritual journeys are precious indications of the way by which the Spirit guides people to God. They also reveal which bridges between Islam and Christianity are open and which are closed.

Broadly speaking, a person may go through two progressive levels of conversion, each with specific characteristics. First, there is conversion to God. This means surrendering one's life and person to God because He is our Lord, Master, Creator, and Savior. It is an attitude of adoration, humble thankfulness, repentance, acceptance of God's will for our lives, prayer, and love. It is the basic conversion required for salvation. It is the only attitude that makes further progress possible, since it allows humans to become open to God's voice and to His action. From this starting point, a person can begin to discover God's true identity: who is God, and how can He relate to us? We already explained that Islam and Christianity differ radically on this topic. It is very important to invite all people to discover who God is, what His plan is for our lives, and the way we respond in obedience. This was the conversion preached by the Old Testament prophets and Jesus, calling Israel away from ritualism to a deeper interior religion.

The second conversion is conversion to Jesus, to proclaim and confess Jesus as Lord and Savior. This conversion takes three forms. In the first form, the person is converted to God before coming to know Jesus. In the second form, the person is converted to Jesus directly. In the third form, the Spirit moves in unpredictable ways. In most cases, the Spirit will lead a person first to be converted to God before drawing this person to a conversion to Jesus. The probability of this is increased in Islam, since the focus of attention is primarily on Allah and secondarily on his prophets. But the Spirit of God moves in unpredictable ways, and there is no way to know how He will lead any individual.

USING THE QURAN AS BRIDGE

As a model of evangelism, we saw that Jesus used the Hebrew Scriptures and familiar themes when teaching the disciples. We can use a similar method when we meet with Muslims by using the Quran as a bridge. When Paul visited the temple of the Jewish community in Thessalonica, he met with fellow Jews on their own turf, the synagogue, and "on three Sabbath days he reasoned with them from the Scriptures, explaining and proving that it was necessary for the Christ to suffer and to rise from the dead" (Acts 17:2–3). Paul used the Torah as a bridge to talk about Jesus.

Paul also worked among them from the inside of their religious and national lives. In fact, he made such an impact that many of them came to believe the Good News: not only Jews but also a great many of the foreigners who were living there too (Acts 17:4). Too often, we come across as the all-knowing Westerners, insisting on displacing the cultural norms of people in the Middle East with our own cultural traditions. We come across as saying, "You are Muslims; we are Western Christians. You must come to us and follow our ways. If you do not adapt to our culture, you cannot become members of God's people." We might not come right out and say it in those actual words, but our methods and lifestyle imply it.

Paul used language and cultural expressions that were familiar to his audience. While in the synagogue in Thessalonica, Paul began by talking about the Messiah and what the Old Testament said about His predicted suffering, death, and resurrection. After that, he introduced Jesus of Nazareth as the fulfillment of these prophecies. As a result, some Jews and many God-fearing non-Jews accepted Jesus as the Messiah (Acts 17:4). Using Paul's method, we can begin our conversation with Muslims by talking about what the Quran says about Jesus, which will open the door for curiosity about the full identity of Jesus Christ. But first, we must meet them in their comfort zone, the Quran, before we try to expose them to the truth in the Bible.

What are the benefits of using the Quran? First, Muslims will be more amenable to listening to what you have to say about the Bible when they see that (in some places) the Quran says the same or similar things. It would be insensitive if we were to completely disregard the Quran, and it will be difficult, if not impossible, to discuss spiritual things with Muslims if we ignore their primary spiritual guidebook. Second, beginning the conversation with the Quran establishes common ground with the traditions of our Muslim friends. We see an example of this cultural bridge in the account of the apostle Paul arriving in Athens to present the Good News of salvation to the philosophers and the idol-worshiping people of that culturally rich city (see Acts 17:16–34).

HIS MESSAGE AND HIS WITNESSES

When we listen, speak, repent, and discern, we learn that we are not managers or owners of the message. In order to receive guidance from God in our approach to non-Christians, we need to rely on the promise of Christ: "You will receive power when the Holy Spirit has come upon you, and you will be My witnesses in Jerusalem and in all Judea and Samaria, and to the end of the earth" (Acts 1:8).

QUESTIONS FOR DISCUSSION
CHAPTER 14

SEE ANSWER KEY ON PAGE 291.

QUESTION 1

What are the analogies used in the West to present the Gospel?

QUESTION 2

What is the honor-shame paradigm found in Eastern cultures, including Muslim culture?

QUESTION 3

Why is it important to talk to Muslims about the transcendence and mystery of God?

QUESTION 4

What are the two kinds of conversion discussed in this chapter?

QUESTION 5

Why is it important to use the Quran as a bridge to present the Gospel?

CHAPTER 15

PROCLAIMING THE CROSS TO MUSLIMS

☙☙☙

In the 2012 film *The Hobbit: An Unexpected Journey*, the wizard Gandalf invites Bilbo Baggins to join the quest to retake the Lonely Mountain from the dragon Smaug. Bilbo is hesitant and does not want to make this journey; he would rather remain comfortable at home with his books and his rocking chair. Bilbo asked Gandalf what assurance he could give that the journey would be successful. Gandalf could give no assurance except that if Bilbo journeyed with them, he would never be the same.

"You will never be the same!" When we are baptized in Christ, we are not the same people we were before; we are alive in Christ: "If anyone is in Christ, he is a new creation. The old has passed away; behold, the new has come" (2 Corinthians 5:17). As a new creature alive in Christ, we grow daily in the image and likeness of God. This growth happens through carrying the cross and following Christ.

By faith, we are clothed with Christ, and only by grace do we grow to become like Him: "We know that when [Christ] appears we shall be like Him, because we shall see Him as He is" (1 John 3:2). Therefore, unlike Gandalf's response to Bilbo that he has no assurance that the journey will be successful, the Christian does: we have assurance that we will succeed in our journey, through Christ, by the power of the Holy Spirit, because we are a new creation in Christ. As a new creature in Christ, with His confidence and assurance, Christian life is a journey born under the cross, formed, conformed, and transformed in the image of Christ by way of the cross. But before we talk about the cross, we need to talk about sin.

Sin Is Falling Short of God's Glory

Without a doubt, when we define sin, we are affected by our Western exegesis that sees sin from the paradigm of guilt and innocence. We may notice this in a common interpretation of Romans 3:23: "For all have sinned and fall short of the glory of God." Some simply speak of sin as missing the mark or coming up short of perfectly obeying God's Law, which carries the meaning of being guilty. Sin is equated with being guilty for missing the mark.

Falling short of God's glory carries a double meaning. First, people fail to glorify God properly. In other words, sin is equated with imperfectly and incompletely glorifying God. Second, the glorious existence God intended for people is absent. Humanity was deprived of the glory of God at the fall. The glory and honor bestowed on Adam and Eve at creation is now absent in all people. With Christ, humanity is able to regain that glorious existence and can enjoy the glory of the divine.

Sin as Dishonoring and Disobeying God

In this context, the root of human sinfulness and death is dishonoring and disobeying God, and the human problem is one of failing to glorify God as He deserves. John concisely defines sin as lawlessness: "Everyone who makes a practice of sinning also practices lawlessness; sin is lawlessness" (1 John 3:4). This definition helps us see the link between honor and obedience presented in Romans 1. When Adam failed to honor God, he transgressed the Law.[164] The idea of dishonor is directly connected to disobedience. We can read Jesus' command in the same context: "If you love Me, you will keep My commandments"

---
164 See Jayson Georges, Mark Baker, *Ministering in Honor-Shame Cultures* (Downers Grove, IL: InterVarsity Press, 2016), 68.

(John 14:15). In essence, "If you honor Me, obey Me."[165]

SIN AS UNTRUTHFUL DISTORTION OF SOCIAL SYSTEMS

In Paul's letter to the Romans, the sin of humanity is not seen as law-breaking, as such, but rather as opposing God's established code of honor. The results of sin are self-degrading and communally destructive actions that affect others. Paul gives us lists of sinful actions in Romans 1:29–32; Galatians 5:19–21, 26. Another result of sin is the enslavement to the power of sin and, ultimately, death (see Romans 5:21; 6:16–22).[166]

JESUS HONORED GOD

In the Quran, we read Allah's promise to humanity after the fall: "If guidance should come to you from Me, then whosoever follows My Guidance, no fear shall come upon them, nor shall they grieve" (Q 2:38). Later, we see the declaration of Allah to Adam and Satan: "Truly this [Satan] is an enemy unto thee and thy wife" (Q 20:117). We have here two statements: first, the promise of Allah to send guidance, and second, humans and Satan have become enemies of one another. Even though Muslims believe that Islam, as expressed in the Quran, is the light and guidance promised by Allah, we can build a bridge by explaining that in Christianity, God does not send a book—He comes in the person of Jesus.

We can build a bridge by talking about God's proclamation to Satan after the fall: "I will put enmity between you and the woman, and between your offspring and her offspring; He shall bruise your head, and you shall bruise His heel" (Genesis 3:15). We can show that God promised to send humankind someone to deliver them from Satan's power and temptations. Note also that this deliverer was to be from the seed of the woman only, and that no mention is made of the man having

---

165 For more details, see the book by Jackson Wu, *Reading Romans with Eastern Eyes: Honor and Shame in Paul's Message and Mission* (Downers Grove: InterVarsity Press, 2019).
166 See Wu, *Reading Romans with Eastern Eyes*, 110.

anything to do with His conception. We can connect this with the story of the annunciation in the Quran (Q 19:16–21; 3:45–47) and the New Testament (Luke 1:26–36).

The Character of God and the Command of God

We can then return to the character of God. We have already examined how sin is totally against God's nature. The challenging point in building this bridge is the way Islam and Christianity look at God, which we examined in chapters 7 and 8. In the Quran, Allah is portrayed in highly majestic and sovereign terms; however, the word *holy* is attributed to Allah only twice. But when we look at the Bible, we see that in just one verse of Isaiah, the word *holy* is repeated three times: "Holy, holy, holy is the LORD of hosts" (Isaiah 6:3). The Islamic understanding of God's holiness is limited.

Another challenge is that according to Islamic teaching, Allah does not reveal his character; rather, he reveals his will and commands. Therefore, because of the diminished view of how holy God is, it is very hard for Muslims to understand how sinful they are. How did God save us while maintaining His character as a holy, just, and loving God? An analogy taken from the apologetical discourses of Arab Christian writings clarifies the idea of how God related to humanity.

The Analogy of the Disguised King

Theologians as far back as the third-century author Origen have been using this analogy in response to potential objections to the logic of Christian salvation history, taking inspiration from Paul's phrase that Christ took on the form of a servant (Philippians 2:7). Arab Christians have used various versions of this story to explain how God exercised His love at the expense of His power to save humanity. The analogy was used in response to a Muslim critique that the incarnation confesses God to be weak, and that God should have just spoken a word to save

Adam and his descendants, rather than suffer the abasement of death on a cross. To address these attacks, Christian apologists developed the following analogy.

There was a king who had four virtues: justice, power, mercy, and wisdom. A high-ranking servant rebelled against him, and the king expelled him from his kingdom. The rebellious servant, seeking revenge, built an inn and planted a garden in it. Anyone who would travel to the king's palaces must pass by the inn and hear and see all the attractions that the rebellious servant built in it. The inn was built with the evil intention of luring passersby to the palaces of the evil servant.

The king had a trusted and beloved servant. The king loved him and gave him access to all the royal rooms, not forbidding him from any delicacies and enjoyments of the place. The king also warned his beloved servant not to walk toward the inn, and to guard himself from the deceits of the rebellious servant. However, the trusted and beloved servant could not resist the temptation, so he left the royal palace and walked toward the inn. As soon as he entered the inn, he was captured, tortured, and thrown into prison.

The king knew that the rebellious servant's characteristics were harshness, injustice, wickedness, and deceitfulness. The king faced a dilemma: If he neglected the prisoner, he would compromise his mercy; if he exercised his power, he would be acting unjustly; and if he overlooked and did not free the prisoner, his power would be weakened.

To solve such a dilemma, the king did the unthinkable: he disguised himself by putting on servant's clothing, exited his royal palace, and walked toward the inn, where the rebellious servant had imprisoned and enslaved the royal servant.

Because of his disguise, the rebellious servant did not recognize the king when he walked toward the inn and entered it. The evil servant used all the wicked and deceitful tricks that he used on everybody to attract the disguised king, but the king did not surrender to the rebellious servant's temptation. This made the evil servant suspicious. He did not know what to do, other than use his harshness and forceful will on the king. So he captured and harshly tortured and imprisoned the king unjustly.

After much humiliation, suffering, and torture, the king was sent to prison. When he entered the dungeon and was reunited with his servant, the king finally revealed his real identity. The royal soldiers rushed to help him, astonished at his amazing condescension. When the evil servant recognized the king, he was shocked and confused.

After this confrontation, the evil servant's power was diminished, and his transgression made him feel as if he were perishing because he had unjustly wronged the one who could not be defeated by deception. And the king fulfilled his characteristics of mercy and justice. He exercised justice by unjustly being punished and fulfilled his mercy by freeing his faithful servant from the power of evil.

The author concluded his analogy with a dialogue between the king and the evil servant. The evil servant attempted to defend himself by saying that people chose to go with him. The king rejected this explanation and forced the servant to admit that he tempted them. The king then bound the evil servant in chains forever, destroyed the garden, freed the servants, and returned with them triumphantly to his kingdom.[167]

The Analogy as a Gospel Presentation

A Christian easily recognizes the characters and plot points of this analogy: humankind represented by the servant of the king; the fall of Satan and Satan's subsequent temptation of Adam and Eve in the garden; God's plan for salvation; Jesus' incarnation; Satan's temptation of Christ; the crucifixion; the resurrection; and judgment day. The analogy is presented to illustrate the ingenuity of God's plan of redemption.

---

167 See Abjar Bahkou, *Defending Christian Faith*, 32–35; Barbara Roggema, "Ḥikāyāt amthāl wa asmār . . . King Parables in Melkite Apologetic Literature," in Rifaat Ebied, Herman Teule, eds., *Studies on the Christian Arabic Heritage* (Leuven, Belgium, and Dudley, MA: Peeters, 2004), 113–31.

It explains the saving function of the divine disguise by comparing Christ's liberation of humanity from the dominion of death to a noble king going into the land of his enemy to free his servant.

The analogy highlights the shame that the king must endure in order to save his servant. That is a clear bridge to the shame Jesus suffered on the cross. In the Islamic and Arabic context, it brings a great disgrace and shame on a male when somebody hits him on the head or slaps him on the face. Jesus was dishonored in order to honor God.

The Cross in the Islamic Context

Muslims are not in agreement regarding their interpretation of the cross in Christianity. Some Orthodox Sunni Muslims find the very idea of the cross offensive and may refuse to meet in a room in which a cross is displayed. In some cases, they even have asked to be excused from wearing school badges that incorporate the cross. Therefore, with this kind of Muslim, the cross is not the place to start a conversation. It may take years of friendship and slow introduction to biblical ideas before they will be ready to recognize that Christian beliefs at least make sense on the basis of Christian assumptions.

The situation is different for Muslims living in the West, especially young people, who are born and grow up in Europe or America and are exposed to biblical literature. This group of Muslims might be curious to learn more, since they have heard the story of the cross and resurrection and are ready for more explanations. Another factor is the postmodern climate that enables young people to accept the possibility that someone else's faith is valid, even if it is in categorical opposition to their own. In this climate, a simple explanation can make sense, provided that the groundwork has already been laid by explaining sin and the incarnation.

THE CHALLENGES OF THE STORY

Christians believe that on the cross, Christ chose to pay the penalty of human sin and chose to bear an assault and not fight back. For Muslims, neither of these choices makes sense. No human can bear the consequence of sin against another human being, let alone against God. Muslims also struggle to grasp how one person could be a sufficient sacrifice for everyone else's sins. For many, though, it is a moot point, as the Quran explicitly denies the historicity of the crucifixion. Islam denies the crucifixion in three ways: Islam says that it never occurred, that Allah would never allow his prophet to be humiliated in such a shameful way, and that we do not need to be saved from our sins and can save ourselves.

The only way we can explain these challenges to Muslims is by proclaiming Scripture holistically and Christologically. By reading Scripture holistically, we see that the narrative of the Bible flows as a continuous, deeply connected story from Genesis all the way through Revelation. The Old Testament is not detached from the New; rather, the themes presented in the Old Testament find their fulfillment in the New Testament's narrative structure. The entire story is characterized by continuity and fulfillment. The biblical narrative reaches its culmination and its thematic climax with the incarnation, crucifixion, and resurrection of the Son of God.

We should also read Scripture Christologically: we read Scripture through the prism of Christ's incarnation, crucifixion, resurrection, and ascension. The Church Father Irenaeus compares Jesus Christ to the hidden treasure in the field of Scripture. It is the Gospel story that shows us who Jesus is. It is only at the end of the story and at the foot of the cross that the centurion said, "Truly this was the Son of God!" (Matthew 27:54; see also Mark 15:39).

This method helps show our Muslim friends the connections between the Bible and the Quran, which we understand in Scripture by reading them in light of Christ.

THE CROSS AS RESTRAINED POWER, NOT WEAKNESS

The story of the king shows that the incarnation is not weakness on God's part, but rather restraint of His power in order to bestow His mercy upon humankind and defeat Satan. If God had used His power at the expense of His mercy, He would have contradicted His characteristic of mercy, whereas using His mercy at the expense of His power was just, wise, and ultimately effective.

Recent scholars have argued that the Quran and the Bible both present God as acting out of both vengeance and mercy.[168] What these writers miss is that God has reconciled and fulfilled these two attributes on the cross. The Quran leaves us with the dilemma of two contradicting personalities in Allah, and the mercy of Allah is at best unpredictable. The Bible solves this dilemma and assures us that on the cross, God exercised full justice and mercy.

THE CROSS CREATES A NEW AND HONORED IDENTITY

The foundation of this parable is community. The servant loses his community, and the king, out of love, restores him back to fellowship in his kingdom, not using his power and might but suffering on his behalf. People of Eastern cultures need to see the community of God in action as we present the Gospel to them. When we join a community, we become living members, and when we dishonor and disobey the community, we are dead in our sin, living outside of God's family. Shame is a relational issue, and the solution must be relational. The king liberates the servant from prison and from disgrace and exclusion. He grants him a new identity: the servant receives honor and acceptance from the king, and he is restored to full citizenship in the royal kingdom.

In the second letter to the Corinthians, Paul declares, "If anyone is in Christ, he is a new creation" (2 Corinthians 5:17). As we have seen,

---

168   See Reynolds, *Allah: God in the Qur'an*, 7.

most Muslims come from cultures that function collectively. They know that if you are a member of a family, you are implicated in all that happens to that family—good or bad. Paul is telling us that if we are members of Christ, we are implicated in what happened to Him; people who are in Christ died with Him also (Romans 6:3; 2 Corinthians 5:14).

Paul gives this powerful declaration to his readers:

> For you did not receive the spirit of slavery to fall back into fear, but you have received the Spirit of adoption as sons, by whom we cry, "Abba! Father!" The Spirit Himself bears witness with our spirit that we are children of God, and if children, then heirs—heirs of God and fellow heirs with Christ, provided we suffer with Him in order that we may also be glorified with Him. (Romans 8:15–17)

The message of the cross in shame-honor cultures speaks about a new identity and reconciliation. In chapter 8, we saw how the cross creates a new reality for sinners. This new reality is connected to the term *justification*. To be justified is to be made right with God or to be brought into right covenantal standing. In this perspective, to be justified is to be placed in a proper relationship with God and to be a full participant in the community of God's people. To be justified is not only to be declared innocent but also to belong within God's community.[169]

The most relevant parable for explaining this concept in shame-honor cultures is the parable of the prodigal son (Luke 15:11–32).[170] The central figure in the parable is the father who reaches out in love to both sons: the son lost in a foreign land and the other son lost at home. By inviting his sons to come together and eat at one table again as a family, the father pursues restoration and harmony. The father willingly suffered shame to communicate love and forgiveness in order to restore relationships with each son personally and together with the family.

---

169 See Mark D. Baker, *Religious No More: Building Communities of Grace and Freedom* (Downers Grove, IL: InterVarsity Press, 1999), 97–103.

170 Jayson Georges and Mark D. Baker retell an expanded version of the parable from the perspective of honor and shame culture. See Jayson Georges and Mark D. Baker, *Ministering in Honor-Shame Cultures*, 102–5.

LIVING THE CROSS AMONG MUSLIMS

Lefing Lee, a Christian professor of biology, told a story about something that happened to him during a lecture given by the world-renowned South African Muslim apologist Ahmed Deedat, who is well-known for his aggressive and mocking attacks on Christianity. Professor Lee asked Deedat, "I am a Christian, and I see my faith as practical one. I don't understand why you are attacking and ridiculing my faith?" To answer his question, Deedat asked him to come on stage. When Lee stepped up, Deedat got close to him and slapped him in the face. "The slap was so strong that I could not feel my face," Lee said. While Lee was trying to understand what had happened, Deedat said to him, "Now turn your other cheek to me." At that moment, Lee prayed, "Lord, I really need You at this time; give me the strength to turn the other cheek." Lee turned the other cheek. But Deedat said to him, "Take off your shirt and give it to me." Lee took off his shirt and gave it to him. But Deedat did not stop there; he asked him to take off his trousers also. Lee apologized to the crowd and took off his trousers. Lee was in his underwear in front of his colleagues and students. He remembered walking back to his office humiliated and almost naked. He went to his office, closed the door, and began to cry, thanking God for giving him the strength to endure such humiliation. Moments later, Lee heard a knock on the door of his office. When he opened the door, he saw a large crowd of students and professors in front of his office, apologizing to him about what happened. Lee relates, "About 98 percent of them were Muslims."

This story is one of the most inspiring ways of living the cross among Muslims. We might not be asked to take off our shirts and trousers and walk naked; we might not be slapped on the face. But in living the cross among Muslims, we will be humiliated, mocked, and ridiculed, and we are called to love those who persecute us and pray for them.

Muslims often ask why Christians wear crosses as jewelry and put them on their churches. In response, Arab Christians have expanded on the analogy of the disguised and the suffering king:

> It is like a servant who fell into harsh captivity and nearly perished. He was bound in iron chains and confined in the most oppressive prison. To save his valued servant, the king redeemed him by offering himself in his servant's place. The king endured the sufferings the servant would have undergone and secured the servant's freedom. The master wore the servant's filthy prison clothing and carried the heavy chains of captivity on his feet and hands. By doing this, he saved the servant from brutal treatment and destruction. After being thus liberated, the servant demonstrated his gratitude for his master's favor and mercy by walking around wearing the chains and filthy clothing of his captivity. Whenever asked, he proclaimed his master's favor and goodness toward him.[171]

This analogy explains the Christian perspective on the cross. On the cross, the love of Christ encountered a world full of sin. Despite this, "In Christ God was reconciling the world to Himself" (2 Corinthians 5:19).

The love of God encourages believers to live out the moral implications of God as a self-emptying God, who loves us and gave Himself for our salvation. Jesus calls us to imitate His own submission and participate with Him by taking up the cross daily. That is what the servant did in the parable. The king transformed the servant's life from selfish behavior to a new person, who walks around carrying the filthy clothes and the chains as a proclamation of his freedom.

Bearing the cross means being a faithful witness to people despite rejection. The message of the cross inspires believers to respond to critics with patience and love. Paul calls Christians to crucify their selfish and sinful nature (Romans 6:6; Galatians 5:24) because God has crucified the world to us (Galatians 6:14).

---

171   Author's translation of Arabic texts, unpublished.

QUESTIONS FOR DISCUSSION
CHAPTER 15

SEE ANSWER KEY ON PAGE 291.

QUESTION 1
In this chapter, the author stated that before we talk about the cross, we need to talk about sin. How do we explain sin to Muslims?

QUESTION 2
Read the analogy of the disguised king. How might this analogy help you explain the cross to Muslims?

QUESTION 3
What is the Muslim attitude to the cross?

QUESTION 4
How can Christians live the cross among Muslims?

CHAPTER 16

Following the Steps of Jesus

Jesus has given us a training seminar in cross-cultural ministry that can also be applied to Muslims. It is recorded in His encounter with the Samaritan woman in John 4:1–30. Jesus evangelizes to this outcast woman, who came to faith and was then used by God to bring many in her village to salvation (John 4:39).

The primary purpose of this story is to reveal Christ and proclaim Him as the Messiah: "These [things] are written so that you may believe that Jesus is the Christ, the Son of God, and that by believing you may have life in His name" (John 20:31). In this account, we see Jesus' humanity quite clearly. He sits to rest by a well, weary and thirsty. But He also reveals His divinity as He expresses His knowledge of the history of a woman whom He has never met before.

In the story, we see His humanity and His weariness, and at the same time we see His deity and His omniscience. This is the goal of our theological and religious encounters with Muslims. As witnessing believers, we cannot compromise our faith in Jesus, as it is revealed in the Gospel; thus, the need to build the whole conversation on the primary goal of revealing Christ, who is the Messiah, the Son of Man (His humanity) and the Son of God (His divinity).

Jesus taught us five practical steps: He took the initiative, identified her spiritual need, offered her God's mercy and salvation, confronted her sin, and showed her the true way of worship. Let us examine these five steps.

1. Jesus Took the Initiative

When a Samaritan woman came to draw water, Jesus said to her, "Give Me a drink" (John 4:7).

The very first thing we learn about this woman is that she was a Samaritan. The Jews did not associate with Samaritans. John explains, "For Jews have no dealings with Samaritans" (v. 9). This separation meant they did not even use the same utensils. When Jews would scorn someone terribly, they would call that person a Samaritan. In fact, in John 8:48 the Jews said to Jesus, "Are we not right in saying that You are a Samaritan and have a demon?" They were insulting Jesus by telling Him, "You're a demon-possessed Samaritan." There was deep hate and bitterness between the Jews and the Samaritans. However, the Gospels and the Book of Acts provide many instances of Samaritans embracing the message of Jesus. This teaches us one of the fundamentals of evangelism: it is easier to love a person on the other side of the world who lives in a drastically different culture than it is to love our close neighbor whose ethnicity, dialect, traditions, values, and customs are different from our own.

The second thing we learn about her is that she was a woman. The fact that Jesus, as a Jewish rabbi, spoke to a woman in public was a breach of religious etiquette. Despite all the traditional and religious obstacles that stood between them, Jesus broke in, took the initiative, and started the conversation.

The third thing we learn is that she was an outcast and immoral woman; she had been married many times and was currently living in an adulterous relationship. She was an uneducated and careless woman who didn't know the true religion God had revealed through His prophets. She was not seeking Jesus as Nicodemus had. In John 3, Nicodemus came to Jesus by night. He sought out Jesus because he knew Jesus was from God. This woman knew nothing about Jesus and had heard nothing either. She was religiously indifferent. She was from a corrupt culture and society, and yet even from that society she was an outcast. She was the very opposite of Nicodemus, who was a moral, religious, learned, upstanding theologian from the social elite. Yet as categorically opposite as this woman was from Nicodemus, Jesus chose to declare His own identity to her.

John is conveying two important points. First, in this encounter Jesus directly revealed His identity not to a prominent religious leader but rather to this outcast and sinful woman. Second, Jesus' conversation makes it clear to His disciples and to us that Jesus came to save people from every tongue and tribe and nation. This teaches us something important about cross-cultural ministry: if we share the Gospel throughout the world, we will have to speak with people who are ignorant and indifferent to spiritual matters. The people we speak with will be different from us, and they will not be clear about who God really is and who Jesus is. This is the case with many encounters with Muslims: they have mixed ideas about Jesus and the Gospel. Our mission is to cross to their side, take the initiative, and talk to them.

Jesus crosses the cultural, religious, and social barriers by dismissing the woman's indifference, ignorance, and immorality. We often tend to get self-righteous and resentful when we look at our immoral world; for example, it is very easy for us to resent those who are sexually immoral because they corrupt our society and culture. It is very easy for us to resent Islam and Muslims, attacking their scriptures, founder, and practices. However, we need to remember that this is the mission field. These people are not the enemy; rather, they are our mission field, and it is our responsibility in this world to go to them.

For the last fifteen years, I have been involved in the field of Muslim evangelism, and I have taught at various churches on this subject. The common and classic question I am always asked is this: How can we reach out to our Muslim neighbors, co-workers, and students? I have shelves full of books that I call "the gimmicks and programs to reach out to Muslims." However, after fifteen years of studying Islam academically and working in the field of Muslim-Christian relations, I have concluded that none of them will work unless we take the initiative and become a good neighbor to them, figuring out what their needs are and where they are in their spiritual journey.

In 2014, a deacon in my church met a Muslim student from Russia. For security reasons, I will not reveal their names and identities. This Muslim girl had no papers and no job; she was a hard-working girl, and she wanted to make a living in this country. The deacon never tried to convert her; all he did was take the initiative and become a neighbor to her, showing her the love of Christ and helping her stand on her feet. He found her a job, he drove her to work and to school almost every day, and he even gave her a room to stay in for free until she was able to afford rent.

What the deacon did caused him a lot of trouble. At that time, he was engaged and getting ready to be married to his fiancée, who had waited for over ten years for him to get his American citizenship and get her to America. Reaching out and helping a beautiful Russian single girl created a lot of troubles for him—not only from his friends but also from his own immediate family. Rumors began to spread, and he almost broke off his engagement. Taking the initiative and reaching out to others is always risky. But we must always trust God and follow in the steps of Jesus.

2. Jesus Identified Her Spiritual Need

When we follow the story, we see that it wasn't enough just for Jesus to get the conversation started; He immediately guided their discussion from His physical need to her spiritual needs. He had the opportunity because the Samaritan woman was still knocked off balance from His shocking request for a drink.

Jesus' request for a drink not only caught the woman off guard, it also created a point of contact between them. Since everyone has experienced physical thirst and the need for water, Jesus simply used those basic human experiences to start a discussion about her spiritual need.

> Jesus answered her, "If you knew the gift of God, and who it is that is saying to you, 'Give Me a drink,' you would have asked Him, and He would have given you living water." (John 4:10)

Jesus uses the familiar topic of physical thirst to make her sensitive to her deep spiritual need. He uses water as the point of contact for their interaction and a proper illustration of her spiritual needs. Water is precious and essential for life. In the land of Samaria in Jesus' day, it was not easy to find. But Christ had not come there to satisfy her physical thirst. He had come to satisfy her deep spiritual need, and He used the analogy of water to make it clear to her how strong that need was.

This strategy is a great guide for our personal evangelism. We seek and find a common interest or point of reference and begin a conversation, always watching for how we can direct that conversation toward eternal things. Regardless of the topic or the location, even the most casual conversations can fulfill an eternal purpose. It is wise for us to keep watching for opportunities to share God's truth in our everyday discussions, just as Jesus did with this Samaritan woman.

3. Jesus Offered Her God's Mercy and Salvation

We need to keep one thing in mind when sharing the Gospel: its central purpose is not to make us content, give our lives purpose, or make our lives feel complete. It is not a way for us to unlock God's plan for our happiness or fulfillment. These may well flow from God's grace, creating saving faith in us, but none of these are really the primary focus of the Gospel. Christ didn't die to make us emotionally stable. He suffered and died to rescue sinners from being eternally separated from His Father. The Gospel makes atonement available through God's great mercy and grace, and through the atonement Jesus secured, we can enjoy eternity with Him.

This was the offer Christ made to the Samaritan woman by the well:

> If you knew the gift of God, and who it is that is saying to you, "Give Me a drink," you would have asked Him, and He would have given you living water. (v. 10)

With these words, He exposed her spiritual need, and then He encouraged her to ask Him for the living water only He could provide. Her response was skeptical, revealing that she did not quite fully understand what He was saying. She said to Him:

> Sir, You have nothing to draw water with, and the well is deep. Where do You get that living water? Are You greater than our father Jacob? He gave us the well and drank from it himself, as did his sons and his livestock. (vv. 11–12)

Christ was not discouraged by her answer. He replied:

> Everyone who drinks of this water will be thirsty again, but whoever drinks of the water that I will give him will never be thirsty again. The water that I will give him will become in him a spring of water welling up to eternal life. (vv. 13–14)

Here the illustration of water turns the discussion from physical to spiritual need. Jesus was teaching her that something was more important than satisfying her temporary thirst. He had far more important things in mind. He wanted her to enjoy an endless supply of joy, peace, and contentment, eternal satisfaction that far surpassed anything she could imagine. This blessing was permanent, consistent, and everlasting, and He was here to offer it to her. All she needed to do was to ask.

Why did He describe it as living water? Jesus' analogy of water and a well had connections with some Old Testament foundations. Jeremiah 2:13 discussed how Israel, in its disobedience, had foolishly forsaken God, "the fountain of living waters." Instead, they dug out for themselves broken cisterns unable to hold any water. Jeremiah 17:13 warned that all those who forsake the Lord will be put to shame. Those on earth who turn away have forsaken "the fountain of living water." In Psalm 36:9, we read that God is "the fountain of life." Isaiah 12:3 proclaims, "With joy you will draw water from the wells of salvation." Isaiah 55:1 invites, "Everyone who thirsts, come to the waters." Water is life, and we draw our life from God.

Unique to the Gospel of Jesus Christ is the offer of grace we can never earn and the undeserved mercy of God. Islam and every other religion describes what we must do to earn forgiveness and God's favor. But salvation is not something that is achievable for us, and the Gospel is not a do-it-yourself plan. We cannot buy or earn a right relationship with God through our good behavior, ceremonies, and rituals. Nothing we do can merit the eternal blessings that Christ offers freely by His grace. Instead, everyone must be born again. This is also something we do not cause, as Jesus made clear to Nicodemus one chapter earlier.

> Truly, truly, I say to you, unless one is born again he cannot see the kingdom of God. (John 3:3)

> Truly, truly I say to you, unless one is born of water and the Spirit, he cannot enter the kingdom of God. That which is born of the flesh is flesh, and that which is born of the Spirit is spirit. (John 3:5–6)

The Bible teaches us that there is nothing we need to do but simply ask for God's free mercy:

> If you confess with your mouth that Jesus is Lord and believe in your heart that God raised Him from the dead, you will be saved. For with the heart one believes and is justified, and with the mouth one confesses and is saved. . . . Everyone who calls on the name of the Lord will be saved. (Romans 10:9–10, 13)

Like the tax collector who stood at a distance and would not even look up to heaven, "but beat his breast, saying, 'God, be merciful to me, a sinner!'" (Luke 18:13), we can only cry out in repentant faith, trusting His gracious promise to supply what we need so desperately.

God desires to give us the gift of life, like running water. Jesus talks about the gift of God in chapters 6 and 7 of John's Gospel:

> I am the bread of life; whoever comes to Me shall not hunger, and whoever believes in Me shall never thirst. (John 6:35)

> On the last day of the feast, the great day, Jesus stood up and cried out, "If anyone thirsts, let him come to Me and drink. Whoever believes in Me, as the Scripture has said, 'Out of his heart will flow rivers of living water.'" (John 7:37–38)

That is what Jesus offered her in the "living water" (John 4:10) that "will become in [you] a spring of water welling up to eternal life" (v. 14).

4. Jesus Confronted Her Sin

Some Christians share the Gospel by focusing on God's love and all the blessings that flow from faith. But this weak evangelistic method causes many problems, including leading people to a false conversion. If we only talk about God's gifts when we evangelize, everybody will sign up.

But wanting to enjoy the benefits of believing in Christ without sincere repentance is very different from truly turning to Him for salvation, realizing our brokenness, sin, and God's rightful judgment. Having a false assurance of God's grace is a deadly spiritual danger, and being confident in a false and shallow belief can actually harden a person against the truth of God's Word. We have a responsibility to preach the full Word of God—both Law and Gospel—thoroughly and accurately to lost men and women, that God may steer them away from empty professions of faith and shallow biblical understanding.

Often, the best way to break through false faith is by confronting sin. Until a person is able to understand and appreciate the depth and weight of his or her sin, he or she will not truly realize his or her need for a Savior. In fact, people are able to truly repent and believe only when they learn to see their sinful disobedience the way God sees it.

That is what the Samaritan woman at the well learned in John 4. By the time we reach verse 15, it looks as if she were ready to receive the living water Jesus offered her, with all its benefits. But Christ knew her heart and the sin she harbored there. With a simple command, He gently but directly exposed her sin:

> Jesus said to her, "Go, call your husband, and come here." The woman answered Him, "I have no husband." Jesus said to her, "You are right in saying, 'I have no husband'; for you have had five husbands, and the one you now have is not your husband. What you have said is true." (John 4:16–18)

5. Jesus Showed Her the True Way of Worship

In the world, there are really only two kinds of people: those who worship God acceptably, and those who do not. For those who do not have faith in Christ, those who stand apart from God's work in their sinful life, it is impossible for their worship to be acceptable. True worship is intricately connected to faith and salvation. Seeking to avoid exposing her hidden sin, the woman tried to steer the conversation to the topic of worship.

> The woman said to Him, "Sir, I perceive that You are a prophet. Our fathers worshiped on this mountain, but You say that in Jerusalem is the place where people ought to worship." (John 4:19–20)

The Samaritan woman wanted to know which religious system was correct. She wanted to know whether the Samaritan or the Jewish system of works would give her absolution. The Samaritan faith was a

Judeo-pagan hybrid. She thought the Jewish system was entirely based on the Law and the Prophets. Which temple should she visit in order to be fully reconciled with God? Where does she need to go, and what does she need to do to find forgiveness and peace? Millions of people are still asking these questions.

Christ gave her a monumental answer. Out of all four Gospels, it was the most clear and definitive teaching on the theology of worship. He started with a denunciation of external forms of worship.

> Woman, believe Me, the hour is coming when neither on this mountain nor in Jerusalem will you worship the Father. You worship what you do not know; we worship what we know, for salvation is from the Jews. But the hour is coming, and is now here, when the true worshipers will worship the Father in spirit and truth, for the Father is seeking such people to worship Him. God is spirit, and those who worship Him must worship in spirit and truth. (John 4:21–24)

Jesus clearly explained that it is not the place of worship that matters. What she was looking for did not depend on a ceremony or ritual. Instead, true worship was about loving God and honoring, obeying, and serving Him from the heart.

Through this simple conversation, Christ brought in a new era of worship—one that wasn't bound to external rites and symbols. True worship rises up out of the love of God and the knowledge of Scripture. Not bound to a temple building, it can happen anywhere and everywhere.

It's important to remember this point when we share the Gospel with nonbelievers. Salvation doesn't require us to pray a special prayer, walk down an aisle, or perform any other ritual. We simply bow to the Lord in repentance and faith, submitting to His Word, and worshiping Him in spirit and truth. Anything short of that is empty religion.

Back to the story about the deacon in my church and the Russian

Muslim girl. When he would her drive to work, he would always listen to sermons and worship songs in the car, and she had no other choice but to listen. The young girl had an encounter with the Gospel of Christ, and she started to ask questions. A few weeks passed by. One day, I got an urgent call from the deacon, saying, "Father, she wants to be baptized." I responded that she first needs to go through instruction, because we always want to make sure that it is not just an emotional experience. For six months, I instructed her in the faith through the catechism. At 4:00 p.m. on Sunday, November 9, 2013, we baptized her. At her Baptism, she shared her story:

> I was born and raised in a Muslim family with respect for Muslim faith and traditions. I wasn't allowed to speak about God, only about Allah. In addition to that, I wasn't allowed to enter the church, because Islam considers that a sin, which I used to hear constantly from my parents and grandparents. The stories about Jesus were brought to us as myths and legends, and thus not true. As time passed by, I started to realize that I am on a wrong way. Something happened that affected me deeply. . . .
>
> [The deacon] has introduced me to Jesus Christ. Before that, I had been lost, confused, missing something in my life. He talked a lot to me about Jesus and how full of grace and mercy Jesus is. He has also shown me many biblical documentary movies about Jesus and stories of miracles performed by Jesus. I started realizing how loving Jesus is and how much He cares about me. He has always been with me at my bad and good times. Rev. Bahkou took time to deeply instruct me in the faith. He studied the Bible with me and taught me the most important definitions of the Christian vocabularies of faith. . . .
>
> I know something powerful happened today at my Baptism, and there will be a definite change in my walk and

relationship with Jesus. I am starting life fresh in this house of God, with you as a witness. My heart brought me and led me to Christ. I am so grateful for His grace and mercy. We all struggle every day, but it's a good struggle with faith in our hearts. Today, I have become a child of Christ, and I will keep studying more about the faith and keep improving my relationship with Jesus. My faith means peace and hope in my soul. I will grow spiritually, and I am ready to live for Jesus in my example for others.

What the deacon did with the girl was similar to what Jesus did with the Samaritan woman. Let us analyze her testimony. First, the deacon took a risky initiative when he began to help her. Second, the simple conversations between them led to spiritual conversations, which led to eternal truth about the Good News of the Gospel confronting her inner being. Third, he continued the conversation and proclaimed to her the real story of Jesus Christ, who so loves us and gave His life for us. Then, she became a child of God.

The Missionary Task of the Church

The last command Jesus left for His Church before He returned to heaven is the Great Commission. The Gospels and the Book of Acts record it. Matthew reports:

> And Jesus came and said to them, "All authority in heaven and on earth has been given to Me. Go therefore and make disciples of all nations, baptizing them in the name of the Father and of the Son and of the Holy Spirit, teaching them to observe all that I have commanded you. And behold, I am with you always, to the end of the age." (Matthew 28:18–20)

The Great Commission contains one primary imperative and central command, to "make disciples," and three dependent participles: "go," "baptizing," and "teaching." The imperative explains the central aim of the Great Commission, while the participles describe aspects of the process.

As believers, when we consider the Great Commission, we must consider five important facts. First, we must engage in an intensive and extensive proclamation of the Gospel among the nations. Second, we must lead people to experience the grace of God, made available through the death and resurrection of Jesus Christ, offering forgiveness of sins in His name to all who will believe the Gospel. Third, we must build new believers into new congregations of God through the practice of Baptism. Fourth, we must teach them the value and greatness of the gifts of the Holy Spirit, leading them in a walk of obedience and dependence upon the Holy Spirit. Fifth, we must mold them into true Christian disciples by instructing them to be like their Lord and Master.

Applying the Great Commission

The Great Commission calls us as a community and as individuals to take the Gospel to all nations. But how can we do that effectively? We can consider three important points:

1. It is a privilege to be witnesses of Jesus.

A witness, in the technical sense, is someone who has seen the risen Jesus and knows about His Gospel. Through Baptism, you and I became part of God's mission. When we were baptized, we were put to death. We died! God wanted our sinful nature to be put to death so that He could live in us, or even better, we could live in Him. Living out our Baptism includes participating in God's mission. It is a great privilege when we really live in Christ. You and I are new people. No greater or more wonderful thing could have happened to you and me in Christ than a life that will never end. Through Baptism, we are already privileged to be part of God's mission.

2. We do not need to learn many theological terms or formally study apologetics in order to be witnesses.

We simply need to proclaim the Gospel, sharing the story of Jesus and how He works through His Holy Spirit in our lives. When we share God's involvement in our lives, we verbalize Jesus' story and we learn to hear how God works in a variety of ways. God becomes visibly present to others.

    3.   We do not share Jesus by ourselves.

Jesus has provided His Spirit, who dwells in us to help us make sense of His Gospel. Jesus has given us faith. Sometimes you might not feel like your faith is perfect, but it is something given to you by God. Christ has given you new life. Christ was a missionary to you, bringing you the hope and faith you have. He is the one who sees us through the day when we don't know how we will make it. He is the one who keeps us going, even when we feel like giving up. Jesus is our great missionary. And we are already part of God's mission.

QUESTIONS FOR DISCUSSION
CHAPTER 16

SEE ANSWER KEY ON PAGE 291.

QUESTION 1

What are the five steps that Jesus used to reach out to the Samaritan woman?

QUESTION 2

How do you apply the Great Commission?

Conclusion: Encounter and Mission

In this book, we have examined many theological and historical topics at the heart of Christian-Muslim interreligious dialogue. Clearly, many Christian beliefs differ from those held by Muslims. We should not try to dilute or ignore these differences, for they will not simply disappear. It is every bit as important to keep these differences in mind as it is to recognize the beliefs Christians and Muslims hold in common.

What can we learn from the past? What are the perspectives for fruitful encounters? How can Christians and Muslims create an environment that combats and discourages extremism?

Encounter as a Missionary Mandate

Mission and *encounter*: these words should never be divorced from each other because they belong together. Many Christians are suspicious of the idea of dialogue simply because that has sometimes been used as a substitute for mission. Instead, these two concepts must shape each other.

Encounter speaks about a deliberate effort to engage with another person with genuine respect. It involves a willingness to listen and understand, and it involves being ready to learn and to be challenged. It also includes a desire to relate, communicate, and understand one another. Christian-Muslim dialogue focuses on the two systems of belief and what implications these have for individuals and communities, both in this life and the next.

We have seen in this book that Christian-Muslim dialogue goes back to the time of Muhammad. For many centuries, Christians in the West dealt with the Muslim world either by ignoring it or confronting it. Since our world has become a "global village" in which Muslims and Christians live next to one another, ignoring Muslims is no longer an option. It is far better for us to encounter one another with gentleness and respect. Such an outlook is a good way of testing our commitment to speaking the truth to and loving people of other faiths. Dialogue between Christians and Muslims is a serious business. Its primary concern is the truth about God, ourselves, our fellow human beings, and the world we share.

This dialogue requires a healthy fear of God. One of the fundamental convictions that Christians and Muslims share is that "there is no god but God." This agreement provides an opening to dialogue, rather than extremism or dismissal. Political correctness, ignorance, and theological relativism may lead to an agreement between us, but it would only be superficial. On the other hand, we could engage in confrontational debate, but that runs the risk of causing antagonism, which will only hinder the search for truth. Only love showing itself in genuine, peaceful relationships will be able to create the necessary conditions to permit the truth to emerge and mutual understanding to develop.

Some Christians only relate to Muslims through confrontation. For them, polemics are the most legitimate way to approach Islam. This approach is counterproductive. It usually provokes a defensive response, causing Muslims to become more radical in their beliefs. It often leads to an offensive reaction, too, with Muslims attacking Christianity even more vehemently. A polemical engagement with Islam tends to produce more heat than light and is incompatible with "the gospel of peace" (Ephesians 6:15), which is about loving and forgiving to bring about reconciliation. At the same time, Muslims and

Christians should use an apologetic approach in their dialogue, such as the kind we use in this book. Christian-Muslim encounters often take the polemic form because Christianity and Islam make conflicting claims about God's revelation (the coming of Christ for Christians and the coming of Muhammad for Muslims). Additionally, Islam claims to acknowledge Christianity and Judaism as God-given religions, and yet at the same time it rejects the very heart of the Gospel: the divinity of Christ and His crucifixion and resurrection.

Many Christians and Muslims advocate that Islamic and Christian teachings are fundamentally the same but superficially different. My perspective in this book is that Islam and Christianity are superficially the same but fundamentally different. For this reason, we use apologetics in our encounters. Christian apologetics is about giving a defense of the faith to those who ask about the reason of the hope within us (1 Peter 3:15). This defense, however, should be done with gentleness and respect. Even when the debate becomes heated, the Christian apologist must refrain from polemics, personal attacks, and scornful or hostile arguments about Muslims and their religion.

Encounter as a Spiritual Journey

A fourth-century Desert Father in Egypt, Serapion the Sindonite, once traveled to Rome. There he was told of a woman who always lived in one small room, never going out. Curious, Serapion went to visit her and asked, "Why are you sitting here?" She replied, "I am not sitting; I am on a journey."

"I am not sitting; I am on a journey." Applying this to the Muslim-Christian encounter, we can say that dialogue is a journey not limited to verbal engagement. Dialogue is a journey of an open attitude toward others, a disposition that reaches out and welcomes people who are different or even antagonistic. We are active travelers on a journey that is not measured by the hours of the watch or the days of the calendar; rather, it is a journey out of time into eternity. It is a journey through the inward space of the heart, yet it is lived, incarnated and expressed through outward means.

In this journey, we learn that we are "sojourners and exiles" (1 Peter 2:11) or pilgrims dwelling in tents and longing for our eternal home in heaven. Muslims and Christians alike can relate to this metaphor. One of the Five Pillars of Islam is the *hajj*, or pilgrimage. All of us are on a journey to an eternal destination, the celestial city. We have seen in this book that Muslims and Christians draw radically different maps on how to accomplish these objectives, yet both see themselves as pilgrims on a journey.

From the biblical perspective, we make progress as we love the Lord with all our hearts, souls, and might (Deuteronomy 6:5) and as we love our neighbors as ourselves. As pilgrims, born according to God's likeness and image, we are daily formed, conformed, and transformed according to the perfect reality of the image of God. This journey will not be completed in this lifetime (see 1 Corinthians 13:12; 2 Corinthians 3:18). Based on this biblical perspective, faith is a journey of a community of travelers, who together as saints and sinners are living and growing together in the divine gifts God created in them in Baptism. It is a lifelong journey motivated by building a living faith and a living community of believers.

The road map of this journey is Jesus Christ. When Jesus talked to His disciples about His departure from this world, the disciples asked the same question:

> "Lord, we do not know where You are going. How can we know the way?" Jesus said to him, "I am the way, and the truth, and the life. No one comes to the Father except through Me." (John 14:4–6)

One of the most ancient names for Christianity is "the Way" (see Acts 19:23; 24:22). This name draws our attention to the practical character of the faith. Christianity is more than a theory about the universe;

it is a way of life. Understood in this way, Christian-Muslim encounters are a journey at three distinct and interrelated levels. We meet first as human beings, second as monotheistic believers, and third as witnessing believers. We will take Jesus' journey with the disciples of Emmaus, recorded in Luke 24:13–35, as a model for this journey.

First Level: Meeting as Human Beings

That very day two of them were going to a village named Emmaus, about seven miles from Jerusalem, and they were talking with each other about all these things that had happened. While they were talking and discussing together, Jesus Himself drew near and went with them. But their eyes were kept from recognizing Him. And He said to them, "What is this conversation that you are holding with each other as you walk?" And they stood still, looking sad. (Luke 24:13–17)

The first step of the journey begins with Jesus approaching the two disciples (vv. 13–16), taking the initiative and beginning a friendly, casual conversation (v. 17). Jesus did not start with theology; He simply walked with them and joined their journey. Muslims and Christians meet as human beings created according to God's image. We share much in common: our physical and emotional needs, our human and spiritual aspirations, our joys and sorrows, and our hopes and struggles. Here are practical initiatives and suggestions to apply to Muslim-Christian dialogue.

> *Good neighborly relations:* We can invite one another to our houses, initiate informal visits of religious leaders and ordinary believers to one another, and send mutual messages on the occasions of festivals.

> *Service:* Ministry can be informal or professional, including all the activities of *diakonia*: serving others to fulfill the commandment to love one's neighbor as oneself. Ministry should be performed in a spirit of respect and love, without discrimination on religious grounds, so that Christians and Muslims may meet on the level of their common heritage as men and women or as members of the same nation.
>
> *Spiritual emulation and sharing; discussions and conference:* We can share encounters in which believers open their hearts to one another in order to explain how they pray or struggle to remain faithful. Some countries have even organized live-in sessions, where Christians and Muslims spend some days together to share their spiritual experiences. Many colleges around the world organize weekly Bible and Quran reading groups. Conferences are organized at the local, national, and international level, between official and unofficial representatives.

Muslims and Christians believe in creation, human stewardship, divine guidance, sin, forgiveness, and final judgment. We share many moral standards with regard to ethics, such as the sacredness of human life, family values, sexual fidelity, and a commitment to the poor. Even though the way we think of these is not identical, it is a good way to meet and listen to one another and to gain self-understanding, which will lead to a constructive dialogue and discussion.

I taught Arabic language and culture for over ten years at Baylor University in Waco, Texas. My work at Baylor allowed me to interact with many Muslim students, and I gave many seminars about Islam and the Gospel. In these seminars, we would invite a Muslim scholar or cleric to talk about the Muslim perspective on topics such as God and salvation. These talks provided an opportunity for a genuine and often animated interaction between the audience and the speaker. At Baylor, we usually took students in the Arabic and Islamic courses to visit the Islamic centers in Central and North Texas. At Concordia Seminary, I also lead a field trip to different Islamic centers in St. Louis. These trips are a requirement for students who are taking courses in cross-cultural ministry and Islam. These visits give us an opportunity to interact with the leaders of the Islamic centers and to listen to how Muslims talk about their faith and what challenges they are facing. Students are always challenged and enriched by these types of activities.

In 2016, a Muslim student from my Arabic courses sent me a note after graduating from Baylor: "I admit attending Baylor was a religious shock, but somehow you helped me through it. Thank you for trusting me and believing in me."

> *Prayer:* We can offer to pray for one another in case of difficulties, trials, bereavements, sickness, and journey. We can learn to choose words that can be understood and accepted by a mixed audience on some occasions: burial, public ceremonies, school assemblies, and so on.

The first Arabic worship I led at Peace Lutheran Church in Hurst, Texas, was on Palm Sunday of 2011. But on the Friday before Palm Sunday, something providential happened: I had a call to officiate a funeral, though it was not like any normal Christian funeral; the lady who had passed away was Christian, but her husband was Muslim. The funeral service had fifty-five attendees, only five of whom were Christian—the rest of them were Muslim. I had the privilege to share the Gospel with fifty Muslims! I did not compromise my faith in the centrality of Jesus Christ and His message of salvation. I spoke about how our life is connected with the life and death of Christ in faith and Baptism, and how our earthly life is nothing but a transition to the eternal life, when we proclaim and confess Jesus as our Lord and Savior. My relationship with the family continued, and the first donation to our ministry came from this Muslim family. When her son got married, he invited my wife and me to his wedding. To this day, her son donates money for our ministry.

The invitation to conversion: We can converse in a genuine and kind way with our Muslim neighbors. Christ invited people to come and follow Him. A real encounter cannot exclude such invitations if they fit within the spiritual climate of the encounter and are respectful of the personal vocation of each one. Every activity can become a missionary-dialogue event, as long as it is carried out with the aim of making the light of Christ more visible and more easily understood to Muslims.

SECOND LEVEL: MEETING AS MONOTHEISTIC BELIEVERS

Then one of them, named Cleopas, answered Him, "Are You the only visitor to Jerusalem who does not know the things that have happened there in these days?" And He said to them, "What things?" And they said to Him, "Concerning Jesus of Nazareth, a man who was a prophet mighty in deed and word before God and all the people, and how our chief priests and rulers delivered Him up to be condemned to death, and crucified Him. But we had hoped that He was the one to redeem Israel. Yes, and besides all this, it is now the third day since these things happened. Moreover, some women of our company amazed us. They were at the tomb early in the morning, and when they did not find His body, they came back saying that they had even seen a vision of angels, who said that He was alive. Some of those who were with us went to the tomb and found it just as the women had said, but Him they did not see." And He said to them, "O foolish ones, and slow of heart to believe all that the prophets have spoken! Was it not necessary that the Christ should suffer these things and enter into His glory?" And beginning with Moses and all the Prophets, He interpreted to them in all the Scriptures the things concerning Himself. (Luke 24:18–27)

The conversation between Jesus and the two disciples moved to a second level, spiritual and theological. It moved to the most important and decisive point between Islam and Christianity: "Jesus of Nazareth, . . . a prophet mighty in deed and word before God and all the people" (v. 19).

These disciples believed in Jesus as a prophet and a great man, but they did not believe in His resurrection from the dead (vv. 19–24). Muslims have the same idea about Jesus that these disciples had. We need to walk with them and witness to them about Jesus.

Jesus started a spiritual and theological conversation by calling the disciples "foolish ones, and slow of heart to believe all that the prophets have spoken!" (v. 25). Starting a conversation with such a confrontational approach, which might end any kind of encounter, is not recommended! One can, however, start by proclaiming the Scriptures from our own Christian perspective, just as Jesus did: "And beginning with Moses and all the Prophets, He interpreted to them in all the Scriptures the things concerning Himself" (v. 27).

After this interaction on the road to Emmaus, Luke tells us that Jesus continued to instruct His disciples on the reality of the cross and His resurrection. These are the major theological differences between Islam and Christianity. As followers of Christ, we need to learn about Muslims because they believe in Abraham, Moses, David, the Prophets, and Jesus, but interpret them differently. Their eyes are closed to the reality of Jesus Christ, who suffered, died, and rose on the third day. The eyes of Muslims are also closed to the reality and truth of God's forgiveness that comes to us through the crucified and risen Christ.

THIRD LEVEL: MEETING AS WITNESSING BELIEVERS

When He was at table with them, He took the bread and blessed and broke it and gave it to them. And their eyes were opened, and they recognized Him. And He vanished from their sight. They said to each other, "Did not our hearts burn within us while He talked to us on the road, while He opened to us the Scriptures?" (Luke 24:30–32)

Jesus continued to witness to them concerning His death on the cross and the hope of His resurrection, culminating in the breaking of the bread. In the Eucharist, we proclaim the Gospel: "For as often as you eat this bread and drink the cup, you proclaim the Lord's death until He comes" (1 Corinthians 11:26), and we invite people to respond with "Amen" to the promises of Jesus. It is through the proclamation of the Gospel that the eyes of the people are opened. At the end of every Eucharist, after our eyes have seen the salvation that the Lord has prepared in the sight of all nations (Luke 2:29–32), we are sent out to the world to witness about what the Lord has done for us.

We mentioned earlier that the Quran relates the story about Jesus calling down a table, or *ma'ida*, which is one of the names of the Holy Eucharist used by the Ethiopian Church. In the story, the disciples asked Jesus to send a table from heaven. Jesus fulfilled their request, calling down a table from heaven. This table is a feast and a sign for his disciples. After eating, the disciples are at peace because they learned the truth about Jesus and have become his witnesses, but those who did not believe in what Allah sent from heaven will be punished (see Quran 5:112–15). We can build off of this story to make a connection to the Eucharist with Muslims and explain the meaning of the Lord's Supper.

When discussions lead to spiritual and religious matters, we need to be equipped to speak about the story of Jesus and other prophets in the Quran and their connections to the Bible. These stories, with their similarities and differences, attract the attention of Muslims and make them curious to read the story of Jesus in the Bible, which is the most important point in presenting the Gospel to Muslims. In this conversation, we need to remember that we cannot by our strength make Muslims believe in Jesus Christ. We are only proclaimers of the Gospel; thus, learning about the Quran and the Islamic teachings and their connection to the Bible is a proclamation. It is ultimately the Holy Spirit who calls and gathers Muslims to Him. He enlightens and sanctifies the hearts of Muslims. In the first chapter, we discussed how Christianity and Islam are both religions driven by missionary zeal. Muslims and Christians both claim to be God's witnesses on earth; however, they have many mistaken notions and misunderstandings about the faith of the other. Removing misunderstandings and building trust is an integral part of dialogue. As we explain our faith to our Muslim friends, and as we better understand when they explain theirs, we will be much better equipped to bear witness to the hope that is within us (see 1 Peter 3:15).

The goal of our encounters with Muslims is to let them experience the love and forgiveness of Christ by proclaiming the Gospel to them. When Muslims come to Christ, they become disciples of Christ and will share their new faith with others, just like Peter shared the Good News of Christ's resurrection with the other disciples (see Luke 24:33–35).

A Fruitful Outcome of the Encounter

The most important outcome of the Emmaus journey is that the disciples trusted Jesus. They urged Him to come in and dine with them. Christians and Muslims meet to build an environment of trust, friendship, and respect.

> So they drew near to the village to which they were going. He acted as if He were going farther, but they urged Him strongly, saying, "Stay with us, for it is toward evening and the day is now far spent." So He went in to stay with them. (Luke 24:28–30)

Our relationship with Muslims, and with anyone who does not know Christ, must be a relationship based on friendship and trust. Before inviting them to church, we need to earn their trust, enter their house, and eat meals with them. This might take months or years. It all depends on where they are in their spiritual journey.

Encounters and dialogue should build better relationships between the two communities and strengthen their social commitments. However, two important matters need to be considered when Muslims and Christians are in dialogue: conversion and tolerance. While conversion is the hoped-for outcome, it is the Holy Spirit's responsibility. The goal of our encounter and dialogue is to understand one another and to share the Gospel in the way that best resonates with them. But it is important to remember that Christianity and Islam differ significantly with regard to conversion.

When we look at many Islamic countries, we see that there is no genuine dialogue. Conversion from Islam to Christianity is not always allowed. Arab countries are spending millions of dollars to sponsor conferences and interfaith dialogue, but in countries such as Iran and Saudi Arabia, one cannot bring a Bible into the country or conduct a Bible study at home. Here in the West, Muslims are free to build mosques, practice their religion, and call people to Islam. In America, your life will not be threatened if you convert to Islam; on the other hand, in many Islamic countries, and even in the closed Muslims communities in the West, your life and the life of your family is in danger if you even try to read the Bible or learn more about Christianity.

Tolerance is also vital to these discussions. Being tolerant does not mean denying or minimizing the theological differences between Christianity and Islam. Genuine tolerance between Christians and Muslims will only occur when they have accepted the idea that debate and dialogue may lead to conversions either to Christianity or to Islam. True tolerance is accepting the other, not just ignoring the distance between us. It lies in measuring the distance that separates us accurately and recognizing that whoever wants to cross over has the right and freedom to do so.

A Christian Perspective on Muslim-Christian Encounters

In their scriptures, Muslims find a lot about Christianity and Christians. But the reverse is not true. Christians do not find anything about

Islam in the Bible, because Islam is a post-Christian religion. But even so, Jesus gave us a clear and helpful command about how we should relate to people in general: "So whatever you wish that others would do to you, do also to them, for this is the Law and the Prophets" (Matthew 7:12). Start by thinking about how we want Muslims to relate to us and to our faith. Let's highlight some implications the Golden Rule has for Christians who want to engage with Muslims.

First, to love our neighbors as ourselves, we must show respect to Muslims, and that means respecting the very heart of their identity—their prophet, their religion, and their scriptures. This attitude requires us to treat them with kindness and respect, and to avoid trick questions, derogatory comments, and inflammatory language.

Though it is true that some Muslim polemicists and extremists will not comply with the recommendation of the Quran to argue with Jews and Christians "in the best possible way" (Q 29:46), their behavior is no excuse for Christians to repay in kind with hurtful criticisms of Islam. This does not mean we cannot critique Islam. Instead, it means that when we have critical comments to make, we need to put them in the least offensive language possible. Jesus charged His disciples not to be naive and to look critically at self-proclaimed prophets (Matthew 7:15–20); in the same passage, He commands them to take a long, critical look at themselves (Matthew 7:1–5, 21–23).

Additionally, we need to study Islam to understand what motivates Muslims and how we can best befriend them. Christians need to use Islamic materials when they interact with Muslims, but it is extremely important that we do so from a humble attitude. We also need to be willing to acknowledge that the Muslim community is the custodian of its own tradition. We are not the authoritative interpreters of their scriptures; its members are. We need to avoid approaches that tend to Christianize Islam, as well as those that demonize it. Neither of these approaches does justice to Islamic teaching, which should be considered on its own merits.

A Christian perspective on Islam should be simultaneously incarnational and critical. It should concern itself more with Muslim people than with Islam. First and foremost, Muslims are human beings made in God's image and loved by God just as much as we are. Since we are disciples of Jesus Christ, we are under a double obligation: to love our Muslim neighbors as ourselves, and to share the Good News with them. Not only do those two commands go hand in hand, but also the second is best carried out as we practice the first. Dialogue is indeed the privileged way of "speaking the truth in love" (Ephesian 4:15), to Muslims as well as to members of all other religious communities.

We Are His Witnesses

As we engage with Muslims, we need to remember that we are empowered by the Holy Spirit to be His witnesses. This means two important things. First, we are always challenged to pause, listen, speak, and discern the guidance of the Holy Spirit. Jesus is the Master and the Shepherd, and His sheep hear His voice. The source of our guidance is the Bible, which provides many examples of men and women who testify of such guidance. Second, the Word is in need of witnesses. When we talk to Muslims about Jesus, we need to emphasize that He is someone—a person and not an abstract dogma. He is present and alive. He Himself is the Message and the kingdom. Christianity means knowing Him, not just knowing about Him. Our mission is to bear witness to His presence in our lives and to introduce others to the experience of His friendship.

Real Christianity begins when a person starts to discover Jesus as a friend, even though he or she understands little about His divinity; compare the experience of the first disciples, who progressed in intimacy with Jesus without yet realizing He was God. Therefore, rather than discussing dogma, it is better to bear witness to how we know Jesus in a personal way. When we speak about His divinity, we cannot reduce it to pure dogmatic discussions. Postpone the theological discussion and put emphasis on the Gospel passage, in which we catch a glimpse of the prayerful intimacy between Christ and God (see John 17). When we speak about His life, we need to explain His miracles as a manifestation of God's love rather than His power. We can recall His parables, teaching, mission, ministry, and His concern for all humankind, finally culminating in Him sending His disciples to the whole world.

The Role of Religion

At the conclusion of this book, one last question remains: Does religion play an essential role in creating conflicts between people? In my opinion, the answer is yes: religion plays some role, but not the primary one. My perspective is that fanaticism and intolerance, not religion, divides people. We encounter similar cases outside the realm of religion, such as in Nazism, Stalinism, and other anti-religious, secular political systems, which are clear examples of fanaticism and intolerance. Fanaticism is accompanied by superstition and ignorance. Enlightened personalities and educated religious leaders always discern between authentic faith and superstition and fanaticism; the latter lead to bigotry in rituals and religious observances.

A bigoted person follows burdensome views and judgments that make dedication to religion restrictive and tedious. This trend turns people away from religion instead of to religion. When we trace the rise of materialistic ideas and pagan movements, we see that many of them emerged within a milieu of religious ignorance and repulsive sectarian fanaticism. They were wrong reactions against this cruel environment. Religious bigotry enhances atheistic extremism and prepares a suitable atmosphere for it. At this friction point, anxiety, violence, and chaos erupt until a situation similar to that of the mob of the French Revolution develops. The angry people in France shouted, "Hang the last king with the guts of the last clergyman."

In conclusion, we need to keep in mind that no cultural tradition, religious or secular, can ever remain static or exist in isolation. As in the sphere of subatomic physics, interaction is inevitable in that there exists an underlying interrelationship between everything and everyone. This interaction can be positive or negative, enriching or impoverishing, creative or destructive, depending on the attitude of the individual or community concerned.

In the case of the Muslim-Christian encounters outlined above, plenty of tensions between the different actors can be found in the pages of history; however, of much greater and more lasting importance are the manifold spiritual, intellectual, and cultural offspring to which these encounters have given birth over the course of the centuries.

Here at the beginning of the twenty-first century, we are all, in some way or another, descendants of these past cultural encounters; in each generation, it remains a challenge to every individual and to every community to use this inheritance from the past, either in a rigid and destructive way or in a creative and constructive way.

>	Rev. Dr. Abjar Bahkou
>	Concordia Seminary, St. Louis, MO
>	Wednesday, May 20, 2020

Answer Key

QUESTIONS FOR DISCUSSION

CHAPTER 1

QUESTION 1

We define Islam in terms of submission and peace. In their daily lives, Muslims practice absolute submission to the will of Allah, believing that by living this life of submission, they obtain peace with Allah. How would you define Christianity?

ANSWER 1

> Christianity is the belief in Jesus Christ as the only Savior and Redeemer of the world (see John 14:6; Acts 4:12; 1 John 5:11–12). Peace, forgiveness of sins, and reconciliation with God are gifts from Jesus, not because we practice certain rules and regulations. They are given totally free, won through the sacrifice of Christ on our behalf (see 2 Corinthians 5:19; Colossians 1:19–22).

QUESTION 2

The three tenets of Islam—the existence of Allah, the Quran, and Muhammad—are proclaimed in what is called the "Islamic confession of faith" (the *Shahada*). It states, "I bear witness that there is no god but Allah and Muhammad is his prophet." Any person who converts to Islam must publicly recite the *Shahada* three times. If you are asked to summarize the Christian confession of faith in three tenets, what would you say, and how would you share it with your Muslim friend?

ANSWER 2

> If we want to summarize the faith in three tenets, we can talk about God, Jesus, and Scripture. The First Article of the

Apostles' Creed is a good starter ("I believe in God, the Father Almighty, maker of heaven and earth") because Muslims can relate to the First Article of faith and its explanation as it is recorded in Luther's Small Catechism. Jesus reconciles us to God the Father and redeems creation. While Muslims can accept part of the Second Article of the Apostles' Creed ("who was conceived by the Holy Spirit, born of the virgin Mary"), Muslims reject the rest of the Creed's testimony about Christ. However, this does not mean that we do not need to share! Rather, share the Gospel stories, emphasize that Jesus is Lord and God incarnate, and let the Holy Spirit call and enlighten the minds of Muslims. Finally, we can tell Muslims about the Bible and distinguish between our belief that the Bible is divinely inspired and their belief that the Quran was dictated by the angel Gabriel.

QUESTION 3

We talked about two major local and missiological challenges in responding to Islam; however, these challenges are also opportunities. How can we face these challenges?

ANSWER 3

In the Great Commission (Mathew 28:18–20), Jesus Christ commanded His Church to make disciples by going, teaching, and baptizing. Try to meet Muslims in your neighborhood or at work or school. Build relationships with them, learn their stories, and see where they are in their spiritual journey. Take this as an opportunity to share the Gospel story with them!

CHAPTER 2

QUESTION 1

What is Sharia law? What would be the consequences of Sharia law being implemented in your country?

ANSWER 1

> Sharia law is a comprehensive system that deals with religion and civil matters. In Islam, there is no separation of church and state. This means that the government can legislate aspects of religious life, including requiring dress codes for women, banning eating, drinking, and smoking in public during Ramadan, and banning the sale of pork or alcohol.

QUESTION 2

What are the sources of Sharia law?

ANSWER 2

> The sources of Sharia law are the Quran, the life of Muhammad, and the hadith literature.

QUESTION 3

What are the four main juridical schools that interpret Sharia? What are the differences between them?

ANSWER 3

> The Maliki rite gives priority to the hadith and the practice of the first Muslims in Medina. The Hanafi rite is known for allowing a higher degree of juristic flexibility than other schools. The Shafi'i rite teaches that jurisprudence is a collective enterprise that requires the consensus of scholars and the community. The Hanbali rite is the most strictly literalist and is associated with extremist groups such as Wahabis, al-Qaeda, ISIS, and Boko Haram.

QUESTION 4

Which of the four schools that interpret Sharia would work with our current system of government? Which are not compatible?

ANSWER 4

While the Hanafi rite can be more flexible, since the school allows a higher degree of juristic flexibility through the application of personal judgment (*ra'y*) and juristic references (*Istihsan*), all the schools of Islamic jurisprudence follow the same definition of Sharia. Therefore, none of them are compatible with our system of government.

QUESTION 5

What are the three important differences between Islam and Christianity with regard to the Law?

ANSWER 5

First, Islam is legalistic with regard to rituals. For example, prayer and fasting must be accomplished in a certain way, or Allah will not accept them. Christians believe that God hears our prayers regardless of how we pray. Second, Christianity considers the inner, spiritual life of the believer to be very important, whereas Islam is more concerned with right outward living. Third, Christians serve and worship God as a response to His love for us through Christ, while Muslims are obligated to do these things to earn admission into paradise.

QUESTION 6

How should we talk to Muslims about how we view the Law as Christians?

ANSWER 6

First, show your Muslim friend that Christians acknowledge the Law by talking about the Ten Commandments, either from the Bible or the Small Catechism. Second, share the three differences between the Law in Christianity and Islam. Third, explain that the Law, for Christians, is love; it is a spiritual law. Discuss how the Law shows that our efforts to appease God's wrath will always fail, and only the sacrifice of Jesus Christ saves us from sin. Consider sharing Matthew 7:12; Luke 6:32–35; John 15:13; John 3:16; and Ephesians 2:8–9 with them.

CHAPTER 3

QUESTION 1

In Islamic teaching, the Quran is "the word of Allah," "divine guide to humankind," and a "divine miracle." How is this different from what Christianity says about the Bible?

ANSWER 1

The Quran and the proclamations therein are very legalistic: Allah has given this book so that you will read it and do the right things to please him. For Christians, the Bible is the way God has made Himself known to humankind through human history, a loving act of self-disclosure ultimately intended to save us from our sin and reconcile us to Him through Jesus Christ.

QUESTION 2

What is the Quran's perspective on the Bible?

ANSWER 2

The Quran is seen as the final, complete revelation of Allah, the standard by which all other scriptures are judged. Therefore, the Bible is regarded as the word of Allah only insofar as it agrees with the Quran. The Quran contains some parts of the Bible, such as the Psalms and some stories from the Gospel accounts, but it does not always match what the Bible says. Muslims believe that the Christian Bible is falsified, and the stories in the Quran are the true version.

QUESTION 3

What are the critical questions with which the Quran challenges Christians?

ANSWER 3

Why are there four gospels, and not just one?

Why does the Bible not agree with the Quran (unless the Bible is wrong or corrupted)?

Why are the books of the Bible named after the people who transmitted the Word of God, especially since not all of the Gospel writers were witnesses of Christ?

QUESTION 4

How do you respond to these challenges?

ANSWER 4

The writers of the books of the Bible wrote under the inspiration of the Holy Spirit: God led people by His Spirit to write down His Word, but they still maintained their unique ministry and personality (for example, Matthew wrote to a Jewish audience, Paul was a missionary to the Gentiles, and so on).

The Gospel is not primarily a book. The Greek word *euangelion* means "the good news [of salvation]," which is the message of Jesus. This message was delivered orally by Jesus, and then transmitted, also orally, by the disciples, who had lived with Him and were witnesses of His life, death, and resurrection. The text of the Gospels has remained the same since they were compiled in the first century, apart from minor variations.

QUESTION 5

What do we mean when we say that revelation has a historical character?

ANSWER 5

Revelation is a sacred history of God developing and achieving His saving plan through a series of events linked together. That is the reason that the exodus, the Sinai covenant, and other events of Old Testament history still have great significance for us today. Further, revelation took place in and through human history. God revealed Himself in the historical facts and events that make up human life.

QUESTION 6

When did God give us His final revelation?

ANSWER 6

In the risen Christ, God's revelation is present in all its fullness. Since God's whole saving plan has been accomplished, all that remains is that humanity should share in the knowledge and love of Christ, through faith created and sustained by the Spirit through the Word and Sacraments. Only in and through the risen Christ is it possible for humankind to respond to God's advances. This is why Christ instituted the Church and entrusted it with His Word and Sacraments, through which His Spirit comes to dwell in our hearts.

QUESTION 7

How do we read the Bible to Muslims?

ANSWER 7

In the appendix on pages 354–56 of *Luther's Small Catechism with Explanation*, we read five important ways to read the Bible by yourself and how to share its truths with others: "1. The Bible is about forgiveness and life in Jesus. 2. Scripture interprets Scripture. 3. Testament interprets Testament. 4. Words do things. 5. God the Holy Spirit helps us." We can apply these five steps in answering the many questions that Muslims have when they read the Bible.

CHAPTER 4

QUESTION 1

What is the Quran's attitude toward other religions?

ANSWER 1

The Quran states clearly that Islam is superior to all religions. The Quran presents conflicting ideas about how to convert non-Muslims, whether by persuasion and tolerance or by violence and the sword. Muslims are not supposed to be friends with Christians or Jews, and they ought instead to subdue them and exact the *jizya*, the tax on nonbelievers, from them.

QUESTION 2

What was Muhammad's attitude toward Judaism?

ANSWER 2

Muhammad's attitude toward the Jews had three phases: reconciliation, conflict, and schism. Initially, Muhammad tried to reconcile Islam and Judaism and show that Islam would unite the Abrahamic faiths. Conflict arose when the Jews refused to recognize the legitimacy of the Quran. As a result, Muhammad proclaimed eternal and temporal punishment for Jews who refused to convert to Islam.

QUESTION 3

What is the Quran's attitude toward Christianity?

ANSWER 3

As with Judaism, Muhammad's attitude toward Christianity had three phases: reconciliation, conflict, and schism. Muhammad initially praised Christianity and presented Islam as a fulfillment of Christian Scriptures. The Quran then criticized Christianity and claimed that Christians corrupted the true message of Jesus. This eventually led to schism, and the Quran condemned Christianity and called for Christians to be put under submission.

QUESTION 4

Looking at these conflicting attitudes, what are the implications for contemporary Muslim-Christian encounters?

ANSWER 4

The Quran presents two very different approaches to interfaith dialogue. Different Muslims in different periods of time may lean one way or another, and either way, they can find verses in the Quran that back up their views. Some overarching themes, though, include the following: Islam and Muslims are superior; Muslims ought to convert their neighbors; and Muslims understand Christianity better than Christians.

QUESTION 5

What is the status of Judaism and Christianity in Islam?

ANSWER 5

Judaism and Christianity are given temporal protection within Muslim states, so long as they pay the tax on non-Muslims, the *jizya*, as a sign of their humiliation. However, while their scriptures are hypothetically genuine, the Torah and the Bible have been corrupted, and their true message is maintained within the Quran alone. Furthermore, Islam is the true path to salvation.

QUESTION 6

How could you respond to a Muslim's misinterpretation of John 15:23–16:1?

ANSWER 6

Read John 14:16–17, 25–26; 16:7–15 with your Muslim friend. Talk about how when Jesus calls the Holy Spirit "the Spirit of truth" (John 16:13), He is saying that the Holy Spirit is part of the triune God ("I am the way, and the truth" [John 14:6]). You can also compare the character and ministry of the Holy Spirit and Muhammad (see pp. 103–104).

CHAPTER 5

QUESTION 1

What are the main differences between the versions of the story of creation in the Quran and in the Bible?

ANSWER 1

> The Quran outlines a master-servant relationship between Allah and humankind, whereas the Bible illustrates a relationship characterized by self-giving love. The Quran does not highlight the fact that humanity was made in the image of God like the Bible does, nor does the Quran say that death and a fallen, sinful human nature resulted from the fall. Because of this, there are also no themes of redemption and foreshadowing of Christ's sacrifice on the cross in the Quran. These elements are present in Genesis.

QUESTION 2

How might you explain the concept of the image of God to a Muslim?

ANSWER 2

> First, it is important to make clear that the image of God does not refer to what God looks like; God the Father is spirit and has no image, and to imply otherwise would offend Muslims and misrepresent Christian doctrine. Instead, bearing the image of God means having dominion over the rest of creation, having rational thought and a tripartite being (body, mind, and spirit), and being a person capable of self-reflective moral awareness and relationships with both God and other human beings. Second, the image of God can also be understood as Christ (Colossians 1:15–16; Hebrews 1:3).

CHAPTER 6

QUESTION 1
According to Islam, how is a person saved?

ANSWER 1
Salvation is achieved by keeping the Five Pillars of Islam (proclaiming the faith through the *Shahada*, praying five times a day, observing Ramadan, giving alms, and going on a pilgrimage to Mecca, if possible; additionally, *jihad* is sometimes counted as the sixth pillar). However, there is no real assurance for salvation. Some say that reciting the *Shahada* is enough; others say that dying a martyr for Islam assures your salvation; still others say there is no way to know for sure.

QUESTION 2
Explain the idea of salvation by intercession in Islam.

ANSWER 2
Some parts of the Quran indicate that you can be saved by the intercession of others, including angels, other believers, or Muhammad. Some say that Allah only allows the world to continue existing because of the presence of the faith, or, according to the Sufi mystics, the presence of the one perfect man of each age. Others say that Muhammad will intervene, but only to convince Allah to judge all people, not to save anyone.

QUESTION 3
Explain the two formulas for salvation:

Islam: Faith + works + Allah's mercy = salvation

Christianity: Faith + grace = salvation + works

ANSWER 3
In Islam, salvation comes through the faith of the believer, the works of the believer, and Allah's mercy at the point of judgment. In Christianity, works are a result of being saved (sanctification). It is important to tell our Muslim friends that as Christians, we

believe works are important as an outward sign of salvation, as many Muslims think that Christianity grants *carte blanche* for sinning after conversion.

QUESTION 4

Why do Islam and Christianity differ so greatly on the topic of salvation?

ANSWER 4

Islam and Christianity disagree on the doctrine of sin. Muslims do not view sin as a radical problem; therefore, salvation is also not a radical solution. In Islam, humankind can save itself. In Christianity, sin has utterly destroyed our relationship with God and corrupted our whole being. Therefore, salvation is radical: it requires God taking on human flesh and dying in our place in order to restore our relationship with God.

QUESTION 5

How can you build a bridge to explain salvation to Muslims?

ANSWER 5

We can point out that the Quran calls Jesus pure and faultless, characteristics not applied to Muhammad himself. Christians can answer that only Christ's purity indwelling in our hearts can purify us from our sins (see 1 John 1:5–7). Additionally, we can discuss Jesus' role as mediator, which was foretold by Moses and the prophets (see Matthew 27:51; Hebrews 9:1–4; Luke 24:25–27; 1 Timothy 2:4–5).

CHAPTER 7

QUESTION 1

What is the implication of Allah's unity on ordinary Muslims?

ANSWER 1

Muslims confess that Allah is alone (simultaneously denying polytheism and trinitarianism) and that there is no other being like him. Association with other gods (including the triune God of the Bible) is the unforgiveable sin. Further, declarations about the unity of Allah are common in the liturgical and daily lives of Muslims.

QUESTION 2

What parallels can we find in the Bible?

ANSWER 2

The *Shahada* draws from the Quran's confessions about the unity of Allah: "There is no god but God [Allah]" (Q 37:35); "He is God [Allah], [he is] One" (Q 112:1–2). This is similar to the *Shema* in Deuteronomy: "Hear, O Israel: The LORD our God, the LORD is one" (Deuteronomy 6:4). We can also see parallels between the *Shahada*, the *Shema*, and our trinitarian invocation ("In the name of the Father and of the Son and of the Holy Spirit") in how these invocations function in worship and prayer.

QUESTION 3

What connection can we make when the Quran says that Allah is "transcendent and merciful" and what the Bible says about God?

ANSWER 3

The Arabic words for *merciful* and *compassionate* share a common root word with words such as *womb* and *family life*. The Quran says that examples of Allah's mercy can be seen in a mother's love for her child, the eyes Allah has given us with which we see, the food the earth provides to us, and the generosity and kindness we show to others. Some examples of similar passages in the Bible include Isaiah 49:15; 54:10.

QUESTION 4

What does the Quran mean when it states that Allah is the creator and ruler of life, and what is its connection with the Bible?

ANSWER 4

> The Throne Verse in the Quran (Q 2:255) talks about the transcendence and holiness of Allah in ways that are similar to a number of Old Testament passages (Daniel 6:26; Psalm 121:4; 103:19).

QUESTION 5

What does the Quran mean when it states that Allah is the protector and defender, and what is its connection with the Bible?

ANSWER 5

> The Quran talks about Allah as being a warrior god who joins his people in battle (Q 22:38; 2:250, 286; 48:4, 7; and others). All these descriptions are similar to the images and descriptions of the God of Sabaoth, that is, hosts or angel armies, as presented in the Old Testament.

QUESTION 6

How do Muslims use the names of Allah?

ANSWER 6

> Muslims call upon Allah using whatever name is most appropriate for their present need. For example, if a Muslim was seeking forgiveness from Allah for a sin he or she had committed, he or she should call upon Allah by the name *al-Ghaffer*, meaning "the ever-forgiving."

QUESTION 7

How do Muslims relate to Allah in their ordinary life?

ANSWER 7

> Muslims are more concerned with right practice (orthopraxy) than right belief (orthodoxy), and so most Muslims spend little

time contemplating the being of Allah. However, their speech and actions are saturated by a sense that Allah is real and demands submission (for example, saying *Inshallah*, or "If Allah wills," in everyday speech).

CHAPTER 8

QUESTION 1

In what ways do Christians and Muslims speak differently about the names and attributes of God?

ANSWER 1

While the Bible and the Quran use similar language to describe God (*omnipresent, omniscient, eternal, merciful,* and so on), there are some irreconcilable differences. The Quran describes Allah as the "proud one," "the one who leads astray," the "avenger," "the abase," and the "one who harms." While Christians believe we can know God and that God is love, Muslims believe that Allah is ultimately transcendent: he has no personality and can only be described according to his actions.

QUESTION 2

What is *agape* love? How does this term help us understand who God is?

ANSWER 2

God is love, but we use the word *love* in many different ways. *Agape* is a Greek word that refers to unconditional, sacrificial love. This is not the conditional love of Islam; love and forgiveness is granted by Allah only in exchange for right behavior. For the Christian, *agape* love is the very essence of God, that He will suffer all, even death on a cross, to restore communion with us, His lost and straying sheep.

QUESTION 3

In what ways do Muslims and Christians understand God's transcendence differently?

ANSWER 3

In Islam, Allah's transcendent holiness makes him inaccessible. There is no way that humankind can ever be united with the divine. The only possible relationship to this transcendent god is submission; there is no loving fellowship or communion here. In Christianity, while God is certainly transcendent, He is not limited by His transcendence. Instead, the Second Person of the Trinity, Christ Jesus, took on human flesh to bridge the gap between us and the transcendent Godhead, loving us and empowering us to love Him in return.

QUESTION 4

How would you explain that God is our Father to a Muslim friend?

ANSWER 4

First, it is important to explain that Christians do not consider God to be a father in the way that pagan gods are. God is not Zeus; He does not procreate with mortal (or immortal) women to bear offspring. Second, we are not adoptionists; we do not believe that Jesus was a man who was adopted by God and elevated to divinity on account of his good works. Instead, God is our Father and we are His children because these terms explain the relationship of mutual love, God's protection, and our dependence and obedience. When we say that Jesus is the Son of God, we mean that He is of the same substance as the Father and does not have a beginning in time, not that He is God's biological offspring.

CHAPTER 9

QUESTION 1

What does Islam misunderstand about the doctrine of the Trinity? How does Christianity also reject those misunderstandings?

ANSWER 1

The Quran was likely responding to Christian heresies such as adoptionism and Collyridianism, which Christians have also rejected for some 1500 years! Adoptionism taught that Jesus was a man who became God or was adopted because of his good works. Collyridianism teaches that the Trinity consists of God, his wife, Mary, and their son, Jesus.

QUESTION 2

How could you explain the doctrine of the Trinity to a Muslim?

ANSWER 2

It's important to distance the orthodox Christian understanding of the Trinity from the heretical understandings against which the Quran is arguing. We can agree with Muslims that these are wrong. Instead, we can show them that Christians believe that Jesus is eternally begotten from the Father. Finally, it is important to remember that it is not our ingenious metaphors or skillful arguments that will convert someone; conversion is the work of the Holy Spirit.

CHAPTER 10

QUESTION 1

What are the similarities and differences in the accounts of the birth of Christ between the Quran and the New Testament?

ANSWER 1

> The Quran and the Bible have many of the same major plot points: an angel appears to Mary to announce that she will give birth to a son, miraculously, because she is a virgin; she does so, though the community is suspicious of her; she and Jesus (and, in the Bible, Joseph) flee to Egypt. The Quran also introduces a number of story elements that are likely drawn from Christian apocryphal texts, including Mary fleeing to the wilderness, giving birth, and miraculously being fed, as well as Jesus speaking as an infant.

QUESTION 2

How might these differences stand in the way of witness to Muslims? How can we share our faith with a Muslim as we speak of Mary and the birth of Jesus?

ANSWER 2

> Muslims acknowledge that Jesus was born of the Virgin Mary, and they have a lot of respect for Mary. Pointing out the parallels in early Christian texts may be helpful. However, it is also important to recognize that Muslims stop short of accepting the divinity of Christ; Muslims do not believe that Jesus is the Son of God. It's important to share this with our Muslim friends, as their rejection of the incarnation feeds into their rejection of Christ's sacrifice for sin and salvation.

CHAPTER 11

QUESTION 1

What are the Islamic interpretations of the Messiah? How does the Islamic interpretation prevent true and saving faith in Jesus as God's Son, the promised Messiah?

ANSWER 1

Islam fundamentally rejects the divinity of Christ; thus, Muslims are bound to misinterpret the term *Messiah*. Muslims may claim that this title refers either to the special blessing Allah granted to Jesus as a special prophet, or to Jesus' healing and miraculous touch.

QUESTION 2

What three miracles (or types of miracles) does Jesus perform in the Quran? What is significant about the vocabulary used here? How might that help you build a bridge to a Muslim friend?

ANSWER 2

In the Quran, Jesus heals the sick, raises the dead, and makes clay birds come alive by breathing on them. This last miracle is not in the Bible; however, the words used for *create*, *clay*, and *breathing* are all otherwise exclusively used to describe the creative action of Allah. This provides a possible avenue for sharing the Good News of Christ with a Muslim friend, because it opens a conversation to Christ's divinity.

QUESTION 3

How do Christians interpret Jesus' miracles? How do Muslims?

ANSWER 3

Christians see Jesus' miracles as signs of God's love and mercy, as well as the divinity of Christ. Muslims see Jesus' miracles as signs of Allah's power and Jesus' status as a prophet.

CHAPTER 12

QUESTION 1

How do Muslims interpret the title "Word of God [Allah]," which was given to Jesus?

ANSWER 1

> Muslims acknowledge that Jesus is the Word of God (Allah), but they do not use this to mean that he is God, coeternal with the Father, in the way that Christians do. Rather, they understand this title in a number of ways, including as a reference to Jesus' created state or the special blessing he received from God to prove his prophetic validity.

QUESTION 2

What is the meaning of the title "the Word of God" in the Bible? How does John use the term *Logos* to reveal the divinity of Christ?

ANSWER 2

> In the Old Testament, the Word of God is connected to creation and God dwelling with His people. John reiterates these points in the prologue to his Gospel, showing that Jesus Christ is both God and man, the Word spoken at the beginning of time and dwelling in the Trinity before creation, who was made man in the incarnation in order to save us.

QUESTION 3

How do we build bridges with Muslims when talking about the titles of Jesus?

ANSWER 3

> The Quran is inconsistent in how it speaks about Jesus; therefore, we can introduce a discussion of the Trinity by pointing out these contradictions and the essential unity of God in Christianity. Likewise, some commentators say that it means Jesus is merciful or brings healing, which can help us start a conversation about who Jesus really says He is.

CHAPTER 13

QUESTION 1

How does Islam reject Christ's death and resurrection? What are the results of this rejection?

ANSWER 1

Islam claims that the story of the resurrection is inconsistent; therefore, it rejects both the resurrection and the crucifixion, instead believing that Jesus either survived the crucifixion, was assumed directly into heaven, or had a lookalike replace him on the cross. This is a denial of the divinity and work of Christ.

QUESTION 2

Where does the Quran's version of the crucifixion likely come from? How can we use this when explaining the importance of the resurrection to our Muslim friends?

ANSWER 2

The Quran was likely influenced by docetism, a heretical sect popular around Arabia that denied the bodily crucifixion of Christ. The Quran also probably draws on Gnostic gospels, which denied the loving, present nature of God and instead presented a distant God like that of Islam. Knowing this, we can underscore the importance of God's loving presence and desire to be in communion with His creation, even to the point of Jesus dying to reconcile us to Him.

QUESTION 3

What does Islam teach about the second coming of Christ?

ANSWER 3

Islam holds that Jesus will return like a vengeful warrior to fight the Antichrist, rule as a king, die, be resurrected, and judge individuals on the Last Day. Christians can share the Gospel by asking Muslims why Jesus alone receives these special privileges and abilities if he is not God.

CHAPTER 14

QUESTION 1

What are the analogies used in the West to present the Gospel?

ANSWER 1

People from the West typically use analogies relating to debt or the legal system (also called the forensic view of salvation). Additionally, they also speak in terms of personal guilt or feelings of guilt. These aren't bad analogies, but they are not always helpful when speaking to people who do not come from a Western society.

QUESTION 2

What is the honor-shame paradigm found in Eastern cultures, including Muslim culture?

ANSWER 2

Societies based around paradigms of honor and shame are more concerned with their relationship with the community than their individual state. *We* is more important than *me*, and they may not readily grasp Western and individualistic ways of speaking about personal salvation.

QUESTION 3

Why is it important to talk to Muslims about the transcendence and mystery of God?

ANSWER 3

As Westerners, we face a steep cultural barrier when speaking to Muslims. By starting at the basics—God as our Creator and God as an unknowable mystery—we can establish some common ground. These concepts are familiar to Muslims, and we can open a door to the intimate relationship we have with the transcendent God through Christ by first addressing these things.

QUESTION 4

What are the two kinds of conversion discussed in this chapter?

ANSWER 4

We discussed being converted to God and being converted to Jesus. Converting to God consists of being made aware of His transcendence and immanence in our lives, while converting to Jesus consists of confessing Christ as Lord. Usually, the first happens before the second.

QUESTION 5

Why is it important to use the Quran as a bridge to present the Gospel?

ANSWER 5

The New Testament shows the importance of avoiding unnecessary cultural offense—the Gospel is offensive enough on its own. By starting with the Quran, we are more likely to get a sympathetic hearing from Muslims than we would if we led by rejecting their main religious text. Additionally, we can lead them to the Bible by first showing them the passages where the two texts agree.

CHAPTER 15

QUESTION 1

In this chapter, the author stated that before we talk about the cross, we need to talk about sin. How do we explain sin to Muslims?

ANSWER 1

Using language familiar to honor-shame cultures is helpful in speaking about sin to Muslims. Sin means we are not properly honoring God; rather, we are dishonoring Him, and as a result we have been alienated from God.

QUESTION 2

Read the analogy of the disguised king. How might this analogy help you explain the cross to Muslims?

ANSWER 2

The analogy of the disguised king helps explain why God (temporarily) restrained His power in the incarnation and crucifixion of Christ, in order to fulfill His characteristic of being merciful. The king suffers shame in order to restore His servant to honor.

QUESTION 3

What is the Muslim attitude to the cross?

ANSWER 3

Muslims do not believe that the crucifixion of Jesus ever occurred. They also believe that Allah would not allow his prophet to be shamefully killed. Further, because Muslims believe each individual will be held personally responsible for their actions, and that salvation is possible through right action, they do not believe that the cross was necessary.

QUESTION 4

How can Christians live the cross among Muslims?

ANSWER 4

Christians are called to bear the cross among Muslims by suffering humiliation. Muslims may mock or ridicule you or your faith, though hopefully not as intensely as Professor Lee experienced in the story related in the chapter. Still, like Professor Lee, we are called to suffer for the sake of Christ, which is a powerful witness to Muslims.

CHAPTER 16

QUESTION 1

What are the five steps that Jesus used to reach out to the Samaritan woman?

ANSWER 1

>Jesus took the initiative, identified her spiritual need, offered her God's mercy, confronted her sin and salvation, and showed her the true way of worship.

QUESTION 2

How do you apply the Great Commission?

ANSWER 2

>We acknowledge that it is a privilege to be witnesses of Christ. As we live out our new identity in our Baptism, we witness to Christ. We also do not need to learn lots of theological terms or formally study apologetics; the Holy Spirit works through us, regardless of our skill. All we need is a humble faith and loving spirit. Finally, we never share Jesus alone, as we are always accompanied by the Holy Spirit and by the Body of Christ.

Bibliography

Accad, Elias. *Building Bridges: Christianity and Islam*. Colorado Springs: NavPress, 1997.

Accad, Martin. *Sacred Misinterpretation: Reaching across the Christian-Muslim Divide*. Grand Rapids, MI: Wm. B. Eerdmans Publishing, 2019.

"Acts of John." Early Christian Writings. http://www.earlychristianwritings.com/actsjohn.html.

Ahmad, Bashir-ud-Din Mahmud. *The Holy Quran: English Translation and Commentary*, vol. 1. Qadian: Sadr Anjuman Ahmadiyya, 1947.

Ahmad, Hadrat Mirza Ghulam. *Jesus in India: Jesus' Deliverance from the Cross and Journey to India*. London: Islam International Publications, 2003.

Ajijola, Adeleke. *The Essence of Faith in Islam*. Lahore, Pakistan: Islamic Publications, Ltd., 1978.

Akhtar, Shabbir. *A Faith for All Seasons: Islam and the Challenge of the Modern World*. Chicago: Ivan R. Dee, 1991.

Akyol, Mustafa. *The Islamic Jesus*. New York: St. Martin's Press, 2017.

Al-Miskeen, Matta. *Al-Madkhal Li-Sharh Injeel al-Qeddees Yohanna* (Arabic). Cairo: Monastery of Anba Makkar Publishing, 1989.

Al-Razi, Fakhruddin, *Al-Tafsir al-Kabir* (*The Large Commentary*). Beirut: Dar Al-Fikr, 1970.

Al-Tahtawi, Muhammad Izzat. *Christianity and Islam* (Arabic). Egypt: Dar al-Ansar, 1987.

Ali, Ameer. *The Spirit of Islam*. Delhi: Islamic Book Trust, 1981.

Ali, Ayaan Hirsi. *Heretic: Why Islam Needs a Reformation Now*. New York: Harper Collins, 2015.

———. "Why Islam Needs a Reformation," *Wall Street Journal*, March 20, 2015. https://www.wsj.com/articles/a-reformation-for-islam-1426859626.

Ali, Yusuf, trans. *The Holy Quran: Text, Translation, and Commentary*, vol. 1. New York: Hafner Publishing Co., 1946.

Anthony, W. Sean. "Muhammad, Menahem, and the Paraclete: New Light on Ibn Ishaq's (d. 150/767) Arabic Version of John 15:23–16:1." *Bulletin of the School of Oriental and African Studies*, vol. 79, no. 2 (June 2016): 255–78.

"Arabic Infancy Gospel of the Savior." The Gnostic Society Library. http://gnosis.org/library/infarab.htm.

Arberry, Arthur. *Revelation and Reason in Islam*. London: George Allen & Unwin, 1958.

Ayoub, Mahmoud. *The Qur'an and Its Interpreters*. The House of Imran, vol. 2. Albany: State University of

New York Press, 1984.

Ayoub, Mahmoud Mustafa. "The Idea of Redemption in Christianity and Islam." In *Mormons and Muslims: Spiritual Foundations and Modern Manifestations*, edited by Spencer J. Palmer, 157–69. Provo, UT: Religious Studies Center, Brigham Young University, 2002.

Badawi, Muhammad Aboukhir. *Islam in Britain: A Public Lecture 1981*. London: Ta-Ha Publishers, 1981.

Bahkou, Abjar. *Defending Christian Faith: The Fifth Part of the Christian Apology of Gerasimus*. Boston: De Gruyter, 2014.

Baker, Mark D. *Religious No More: Building Communities of Grace and Freedom*. Downers Grove, IL: InterVarsity Press, 1999.

"Basilides." Early Christian Writings. http://www.earlychristianwritings.com/basilides.html.

Beaumont, Mark. "ʿAmmār al-Baṣrī on the Incarnation." In *Christians at the Heart of Islamic Rule: Church Life and Scholarship in ʿAbbasid Iraq*, edited by David Thomas, 55–62. Boston and Leiden: Brill, 2003.

———. *Christology in Dialogue with Muslims: A Critical Analysis of Christian Presentations of Christ for Muslims from the Ninth and Twentieth Centuries*. Eugene, OR: Wipf & Stock, 2005.

———. *Jesus in Muslim-Christian Conversation*. Eugene, OR: Cascade Books, 2018.

Bekele, Anna, and Patrick Sookhdeo, eds. *Meeting the Ideological Challenge of Islamism*. McLean, VA: Isaac Publishing, 2015.

Bell, Richard. *A Commentary on the Qurʾan*, edited by Clifford Edmund Bosworth and M. E. J. Richardson. Manchester: University of Manchester, 1991.

———. *The Origin of Islam in Its Christian Environment*. London: MacMillan, 1926.

Bistros, Salim. *al-Lahoot al-Masihe wa al-Insan al-Muʾasar*, part 2 (Arabic). Beirut: Al-Maktabah al-Bulsyya, 1989.

Block, C. Jonn. *The Qurʾan in Christian-Muslim Dialogue: Historical and Modern Interpretations*. London and New York: Routledge, 2014.

Bof, G. "Uomo." In *Nuovo Dizionario di Teologia*, sixth ed., edited by G. Barbaglio, S. Dianich, 1830. Milan: San Paolo, 1994.

The Book of Common Prayer of the Antiochian Syrian Church, trans. Bede Griffiths. Kerala, India: De Paul Press, 1970.

Bristow, George. "Abraham in the Qurʾan." In *The Quran with Christian Commentary: A Guide to Understanding the Scripture of Islam*, by Gordon D. Nickel, 90–92. Grand Rapids, MI: Zondervan, 2020.

Brown, Daniel. *A New Introduction to Islam*. Hoboken, NJ: Wiley, 2004.

Carroll, Michael. *The Cult of the Virgin Mary: Psychological Origins*. Princeton: Princeton University Press, 1992.

Caspar, Robert. *A Historical Introduction to Islamic Theology: Muhammad and the Classical Period*, Studi Arabo-Islamici del PISAI, no. 11. Rome: Pontificio Istituto di Studi Arabi e d'Islamistica, 1998.

———. *Islamic Theology: Doctrines*, vol. 2, Studi Arabo-Islamici del PISAI, no. 17. Rome: Pontificio Istituto di Studi Arabi e d'Islamistica, 2007.

Cook, David. "Muhammad and Christianity." In *Routledge Handbook on Christian-Muslim Relations*, edited by David Thomas, 57–66. London and New York: Routledge, 2018.

Cragg, Kenneth. *The Call of the Minaret*, third edition. London: Oneworld, 2000.

———. *Jesus and the Muslim: An Exploration*. London: Oneworld, 1999.

Crone, Patricia, and Michael Cook. *Hagarism: The Making of the Islamic World*. Cambridge: Cambridge University Press, 1977.

Crone, Patricia. "Jewish Christianity and the Qur'an (Part One)." *Journal of Near Eastern Studies*, vol. 74, no. 2 (2015): 225–53.

———. "Jewish Christianity and the Qur'an (Part Two)." *Journal of Near Eastern Studies*, vol. 75, no. 1 (2016): 1–21.

Daftary, Farhad. *The Isma'ilis: Their History and Doctrines*. Cambridge: Cambridge University Press, 1990.

———. *A Short History of The Ismailis: Traditions of a Muslim Community*. Edinburgh: Edinburgh University Press, 1998.

"Demographics." Arab American Stories. https://www.arabamericanstories.org/arab-americans/demographics.Doughty, Charles Montagu. *Travelers in Arabia Deserta*, vol. 1. Cambridge: Cambridge University Press, 1888.

Droozah, Muhammad Izzat. *The Modern Commentary* (in Arabic). Aleppo, Syria: Dar Ehiaia' Al-Ulum Al-Arabia, 1962.

Elass, Mateen. "Apocryphal Details in Quranic Stories." In *The Quran with Christian Commentary: A Guide to Understanding the Scripture of Islam*, by Gordon D. Nickel, 299–301. Grand Rapids, MI: Zondervan, 2020.

El-Bizri, Nader. "God: Essence and Attributes." In *The Cambridge Companion to Classical Islamic Theology*, edited by Tim Winter, 121–40. Cambridge: Cambridge University Press, 2008.

Esposito, John, and Dalia Mogahed. *Who Speaks for Islam? What a Billion Muslims Really Think*. New York: Gallup Press, 2007.

Farah, Caesar E. *Islam: Beliefs and Observances*, seventh edition. Hauppage, NY: Barron's Educational Series, 2003.

"The Future of World Religions: Population Growth Projections, 2010–2050." *Pew Research Center* (April 2, 2015). https://www.pewforum.org/2015/04/02/religious-projections-2010-2050/.

Gaudeul, Jean-Marie. *Called from Islam to Christ: Why Muslims Become Christians*. Oxford: Monarch Books, 1999.

———. *Encounters and Clashes: Islam and Christianity in History*, vol. 1. Studi Arabo-Islamici del PISAI, no. 15. Rome: Pontificio Istituto di Studi Arabi e d'Islamistica, 2000.

Geisler, Norman L., and Abdul Saleeb. *Answering Islam: The Crescent in Light of the Cross*. Grand Rapids, MI: Baker Publishing, 1993.

Georges, Jayson, and Mark D. Baker. *Ministering in Honor-Shame Cultures: Biblical Foundations and Practical Essentials*. Downers Grove, IL: InterVarsity Press, 2016.

Gibson, Margaret D., ed. and trans. *A Treatise on the Triune Nature of God*. Cambridge: Cambridge University Press, 1898.

Goldman, David. *How Civilizations Die (And Why Islam Is Dying Too)*. Washington DC: Regnery, 2011.

Goldziher, Ignaz. *Introduction to Islamic Theology and Law*. Princeton: Princeton University Press, 1981.

"The Gospel of Pseudo-Matthew." The Gnostic Society Library. http://www.gnosis.org/library/psudomat.htm.

Griffith, Sydney. *The Bible in Arabic: The Scriptures of the "People of the Book" in the Language of Islam*. Princeton: Princeton University Press, 2013.

———. "The Bible in the Qur'an." In *Routledge Handbook on Christian-Muslim Relations*, edited by David Thomas, 42–48. London and New York: Routledge, 2018.

———. "The Gospel, the Qur'an, and the Presentation of Jesus in al-Yaʿqubi's Taʾrikh." In *Bible and Qurʾan: Essays in Scriptural Intertextuality*, edited by John C. Reeves, 130–46. Boston: Brill, 2003.

Hämeen-Anttila, Jaakko. "The Christian Context of the Qurʾan." In *Routledge Handbook on Christian-Muslim Relations*, edited by David Thomas, 23–32. London and New York: Routledge, 2018.

Hengel, Martin. *Crucifixion in the Ancient World and the Folly of the Message of the Cross*. Philadelphia: Fortress Press, 1977.

Hermansen, Marcia. "Eschatology." In *The Cambridge Companion to Classical Islamic Theology*, edited by Tim Winter, 308–24. Cambridge: Cambridge University Press, 2008.

Hoover, Jon. "Creation in the Quran." In *The Quran with Christian Commentary*, by Gordon D. Nickel, 224–25. Grand Rapids, MI: Zondervan, 2020.

Hurtado, Larry. *Lord Jesus Christ: Devotion to Jesus in Earliest Christianity*. Grand Rapids, MI: Eerdmans, 2003.

Husain, Ed. *The House of Islam: A Global History*. New York: Bloomsbury Publishing, 2018.

Ibn Ishaq. *Sirat Rasul Allah* (Arabic),

edited by Ismael Bin Ummar. Beirut: Dar Al-Ma'rifah, 1960.

Ibn Kathir. *Tafsir al-Qur'an*. Beirut: Dar Al-Fikr, 1970.

"Infancy Gospel of James." Early Christian Writings. http://www.earlychristianwritings.com/infancyjames.html.

"Infancy Gospel of Thomas." Early Christian Writings. http://www.earlychristianwritings.com/infancythomas.html.

Jabbour, Nabeel. *The Crescent through the Eyes of the Cross*. Colorado Springs: NavPress, 2008.

———. *The Rumbling Volcano: Islamic Fundamentalism in Egypt*. Pasadena, CA: Mandate Press, 1993.

Janosik, Daniel J. *John of Damascus: First Apologist to the Muslims*. Eugene, Oregon: Pickwick Publications, 2016.

Jeffery, Arthur. *The Foreign Vocabulary of the Qur'an*. Baroda, India: Oriental Institute, 1938.

Josephus, Flavius. *Antiquities of the Jews*. https://penelope.uchicago.edu/josephus/ant-1.html.

Khawam, Munir. *Al-Massih Fi al-Fikir Al-Islami al-Hadith Wa Fi al-Massihyya (Jesus in Contemporary Islamic Thought and in Christianity)*. Beirut: Khalifa Publishing House, 1983.

Khoury, Adel Theodor. "Abraham: A Blessing for all Nations" (Arabic). *Al-Massarah*, vol. 90, no. 87 (2004): 394–508.

Klausner, Joseph. *Jesus of Nazareth: His Life, Times, and Teaching.* New York: MacMillan, 1946.

Kolb, Robert. *Speaking the Gospel Today: A Theology for Evangelism*. St. Louis: Concordia Publishing House, 1995.

Latourelle, René. *Theology of Revelation*. Staten Island, NY: Alba House, 1966.

Lawson, Todd. *The Crucifixion and the Qur'an: A Study in the History of Muslim Thought*. London: Oneworld, 2009.

Lipka, Michael, and Conrad Hackett. "Why Muslims Are the World's Fastest-Growing Religious Group." *Pew Research Center*, April 6, 2017. https://www.pewresearch.org/fact-tank/2017/04/06/why-muslims-are-the-worlds-fastest-growing-religious-group/.

Lodahl, Michael. *Claiming Abraham: Reading the Bible and the Qur'an Side by Side*. Grand Rapids, MI: Brazos Press, 2010.

———. "Disputing Over Abraham Disputing with God: An Exercise in Intertextual Reasoning." *Christian Scholar's Review*, vol. 34, no. 4 (Summer 2005): 487–504.

Lüling, Günter. *A Challenge to Islam for Reformation: The Rediscovery and Reliable Reconstruction of a Comprehensive Pre-Islamic Christian Hymnal Hidden in the Koran under Earliest Islamic Reinterpretations*. Delhi: Motilal Banarsidass, 2003.

Luomanen, Petri. *Recovering Jewish-Christian Sects and the Gospel*. Leiden: Brill, 2012.

Luther, Martin. *Luther's Small Catechism with Explanation.* St. Louis: Concordia Publishing House, 2017.

Luttikhuizen, Gerard P. "Elchasaites and Their Book." In *A Companion to Second-Century Christian "Heretics,"* edited by Antti Marjanen and Petri Luomanen, 335–64. Leiden: Brill, 2005.

Luxenberg, Christoph. *The Syro-Aramaic Reading of the Koran.* Berlin: Hans Schiler, 2007.

M'ade'dono: The Book of the Church Festivals: According to the Ancient Rite of the Syrian Orthodox Church of Antioch, translated from the original Syriac by Murad Saliba Barsom. New Jersey: The Syrian Orthodox Church of the United States of America and Canada, 1974.

Martindale, Paul. *A Muslim-Christian Dialogue on Salvation: The Role of Works.* Missio Nexus, January 1, 2010. https://missionexus.org/a-muslim-christian-dialogue-on-salvation-the-role-of-works/.

Mazuz, Haggai. "Christians in the Quran: Some Insights Derived from the Classical Exegetic Approach." *Studia Orientalia*, vol. 112, no. 6 (July 2012): 41–53.

McGrath, Alister. *Christian Theology: An Introduction*, third ed. Oxford: Blackwell Publishing, 2001.

Mead, John Clark. *The New World War.* Maitland, FL: Xulon Press, 2002.

Migliore, Daniel. *Faith Seeking Understanding: An Introduction to Christian Theology*, second ed. Grand Rapids, MI: Wm. B. Eerdmans Publishing, 2004.

Miller, Roland. *Muslims and the Gospel: Bridging the Gap.* Minneapolis: Lutheran University Press, 2005.

———. *Muslim Friends: Their Faith and Feeling.* St. Louis: Concordia Publishing House, 1995.

Mir, Mustansir. *Understanding the Islamic Scripture: A Study of Selected Passages from the Qur'an.* London: Pearson Longman, 2008.

Mourad, Suleiman A. "Christians and Christianity in the Sira of Muhammad." In *Christian-Muslims Relations: A Bibliographical History, vol. 1 (600–900)*, edited by David Thomas and Barbara Roggema, 57–73. Boston and Leiden: Brill, 2009.

———. "Mary in the Qur'an: A Reexamination of Her Presentation." In *The Qur'an in Its Historical Context*, edited by Gabriel Said Reynolds, 163–74. London and New York: Routledge, 2008.

Muhammad Ali, Maulvi. *The Holy Qur'an: Containing the Arabic Text with English Translation and Commentary.* Lahore: Ahmadiyya Anjuman-i-Ishaat-i-Islaam, 1920.

Murray, Robert. "The Ephremic Tradition and the Theology of the Environment." *Hugoye: Journal of Syriac Studies*, vol. 2., no. 1 (January 1999): 67–82. https://

hugoye.bethmardutho.org/article/hv2n1murray.

Nasr, Seyyed Hossein. *Ideals and Realities of Islam*. London: George Allen & Unwin, 1975.

———, editor-in-chief. *The Study Quran: A New Translation and Commentary*. New York: HarperOne, 2015.

Nazir-Ali, Michael. *Islam: A Christian Perspective*. Exeter: Paternoster Press, 1983.

Nickel, Gordon D. *The Quran with Christian Commentary: A Guide to Understanding the Scripture of Islam*. Grand Rapids, MI: Zondervan, 2020.

Nöldeke, Theodor. *The History of the Qur'an*. Leiden and Boston: Brill, 2013.

O'Shaughnessy, Thomas J. *The Koranic Concept of the Word of God*. Rome: Pontificio Istituto Biblico, 1948.

Parrinder, Geoffrey. *Jesus in the Qur'an*. London: Oneworld, 2013.

Peters, Francis E. *Judaism, Christianity, and Islam: The Classical Texts and Their Interpretation, vol. 1: From Covenant to Community*. Princeton: Princeton University Press, 1990.

———. *Muhammad and the Origins of Islam*. Albany, NY: State University of New York Press, 1994.

Qureshi, Nabeel. *No God but One: Allah or Jesus?* Grand Rapids, MI: Zondervan, 2016.

Rahman, Fazlur. *Major Themes of the Qur'an*, second edition. Chicago: The University of Chicago Press, 2009.

Reynolds, Gabriel Said. *Allah: God in the Qur'an*. New Haven and London: Yale University Press, 2020.

———, ed. *New Perspectives on the Qur'an: The Qur'an in Its Historical Context 2*. London and New York: Routledge, 2011.

———. "On the Qur'an's *Ma'ida* Passage and the Wanderings of the Israelites." In *The Coming of the Comforter: When, Where, and to Whom? Studies on the Rise of Islam and Various Other Topics in Memory of John Wansbrough*, edited by Carlos A. Segovia and Basil Lourié, 91–103. Piscataway, NJ: Gorgias Press, 2012.

———. *The Qur'an and Its Biblical Subtexts*. London and New York: Routledge, 2010.

———. *The Qur'an and the Bible: Text and Commentary*. New Haven and London: Yale University Press, 2018.

———, ed. *The Qur'an in Its Historical Context*. London and New York: Routledge, 2008.

Ricks, Thomas W. *Early Arabic Christian Contributions to Trinitarian Theology*. Minneapolis: Fortress Press, 2013.

Rida, Muhammad Rashid. *Tafsir al-Manar* (Commentary in Arabic), vol. 6. Cairo: Matba'at Al-Manar, 1928.

Robinson, James M. *Jesus: According to the Earliest Witness*. Philadelphia: Fortress Press, 2007.

Robinson, Neal. *Christ in Islam and

Christianity. New York: State University of New York Press, 1991.

Roggema, Barbara. "Ḥikāyāt amthāl wa asmār . . . King Parables in Melkite Apologetic Literature." In *Studies on the Christian Arabic Heritage*, edited by Rifaat Ebied and Herman Teule, 113–31. Leuven, Belgium, and Dudley, MA: Peeters, 2004.

Sahas, Daniel J. *John of Damascus on Islam: The "Heresy of the Ishmaelites."* Leiden: Brill, 1972.

Sahih Bukhari, English translation. https://www.sahih-bukhari.com.

"Sahih Muslim," compiled by Imam Muslim ibn al-Hajjaj al-Naysaburi. Sunnah.com. https://sunnah.com/muslim.

Samir, Samir Khalil. "The Theological Christian Influence on the Qur'an: A Reflection." In *The Qur'an in Its Historical Context*, edited by Gabriel Said Reynolds, 141–62. London and New York: Routledge, 2008.

Sardar, Ziauddin. *Desperately Seeking Paradise*. London: Granta Books, 2004.

Seale, Morris. *Muslim Theology: A Study of Origins with Reference to the Church Fathers*, vol. 1. London: Luzac & Co., 1964.

Sedgwick, Mark. *Against the Modern World: Traditionalism and the Secret Intellectual History of the Twentieth Century*. Oxford: Oxford University Press, 2009.

Segovia, Carlos A., and Basil Lourié, eds., *The Coming of the Comforter: When, Where, and to Whom? Studies on the Rise of Islam and Various Other Topics in Memory of John Wansbrough*. Piscataway, NJ: Gorgias Press, 2012.

Shahid, Samuel. *The Last Trumpet: A Comparative Study in Christian-Islamic Eschatology*. Maitland, FL: Xulon Press, 2005.

Shehimo: Book of Common Prayer (Syrian). Holland: Bar-Herbeaus Verlag, 1998.

Shoemaker, Stephen J. "Christmas in the Qur'an: The Qur'anic Account of Jesus' Nativity and Palestinian Local Tradition." In *Jerusalem Studies in Arabic and Islam* (January 1, 2003). http://almuslih.com/Library/Shoemaker,%20S%20%20Christmas%20in%20the%20Qur%E2%80%99%C4%81n.pdf.

Smith, William. "Comparative Religion: Whither and Why?" In *The History of Religion: Essays in Methodology*, edited by Mircea Eliade and Joseph Kitagawa, 34–66. Chicago: University of Chicago Press, 1959.

Sookhdeo, Patrick. *Dawa: The Islamic Strategy for Reshaping the Modern World*. McLean, VA: Isaac Publishing, 2014.

———. *Understanding Islamic Theology*. McLean, VA: Isaac Publishing, 2013.

———. *Unmasking Islamic State: Revealing Their Motivation, Theology and End Time Predictions*. McLean, VA: Isaac Publishing,

2015.

Sookhdeo, Rosemary. *Stepping into the Shadows: Why Women Convert to Islam*. McLean, VA: Isaac Publishing, 2005.

Taha, Mahmoud Mohamed. "The Second Message of Islam." In *Liberal Islam: A Sourcebook*, edited by Charles Kurzman, 270–83. Oxford: Oxford University Press, 1998.

Tawdros, Moris. *Al-logos, Mafhoom al-Kalima Fi al-'Ahid al-Jadeed* (Arabic). Aleppo, Syria: Mardin Publishing House, 1995.

Tharoor, Ishan. "Chart: There Will Be Almost as Many Muslims as Christians in the World by 2050." *The Washington Post*, April 2, 2015. https://www.washingtonpost.com/news/worldviews/wp/2015/04/02/chart-there-will-be-almost-as-many-muslims-as-christians-in-the-world-by-2050/.

Tornielli, Andrea. "Pope and the Grand Imam: Historic Declaration of Peace, Freedom, Women's Rights." *Vatican News*, February 4, 2019. https://www.vaticannews.va/en/pope/news/2019-02/pope-francis-uae-grand-imam-declaration-of-peace.html.

Valentine, Simon Ross. *Islam and the Ahmadiyya Jama'at: History, Belief, Practice*. London: Hurst & Co., 2008.

Valkenberg, Pim. "Christianity in the Qur'an." In *Routledge Handbook on Christian-Muslim Relations*, edited by David Thomas, 33–41. London and New York: Routledge, 2018.

———. "The Dynamics of the Qur'anic Account of Christianity." In *Routledge Handbook on Christian-Muslim Relations*, edited by David Thomas, 49–56. London and New York: Routledge, 2018.

Van Gorder, A. Christian. *No God but God: A Path to Muslim-Christian Dialogue on God's Nature*. Maryknoll, NY: Orbis Books, 2003.

Van Reeth, Jan M. F. "Who Is the 'Other' Paraclete?" In *The Coming of the Comforter: When, Where, and to Whom? Studies on the Rise of Islam and Various Other Topics in Memory of John Wansbrough*, edited by Carlos A. Segovia and Basil Lourié, 423–52. Piscataway, NJ: Gorgias Press, 2012.

Volf, Miroslav. *Allah: A Christian Response*. New York: HarperOne, 2011.

Waddy, Charis. *The Muslim Mind*. London: Pearson Longman, 1976.

Waldman, Marilyn R., and Malika Zeghal. "Islamic World." *Encyclopedia Britannica*, August 21, 2019. https://www.britannica.com/topic/Islamic-world.

Wansbrough, John. *Quranic Studies: Sources and Methods of Scriptural Interpretation*. Oxford: Oxford University Press, 1977.

———. *Quranic Studies*, with foreword, translations, and expanded notes by Andrew Rippin. Amherst, NY: Prometheus

Books, 2004.

———. *The Sectarian Milieu: Content and Composition of Islamic Salvation History*. Oxford: Oxford University Press, 1978.

Ware, Kallistos. *The Orthodox Way*. Crestwood, NY: St. Vladimir's Seminary Press, 1979.

Williams, Frank, trans. *The Panarion of Epiphanius of Salamis: Books II and III, De fide*. Leiden: Brill, 2013.

Woodberry, J. Dudley, Russell G. Shubin, and G. Marks. "Why Muslims Follow Jesus: The Results of a Recent Survey of Converts from Islam." *Christianity Today*, vol. 51, no. 10 (October 2007). http://www.christianitytoday.com/ct/2007/october/42.80.html?start=3.

Wu, Jackson. *Reading Romans with Eastern Eyes: Honor and Shame in Paul's Message and Mission*. Downers Grove, IL: InterVarsity Press, 2019.